STATE ARCHIVES
OF ASSYRIA STUDIES

Published by the Neo-Assyrian Text Corpus Project, Helsinki
in association with the
Foundation for Finnish Assyriological Research

Project Director
Simo Parpola

Managing Editor
Robert M. Whiting

VOLUME XXI
Sherry Lou Macgregor

BEYOND HEARTH AND HOME

WOMEN IN THE PUBLIC SPHERE
IN NEO-ASSYRIAN SOCIETY

THE NEO-ASSYRIAN TEXT CORPUS PROJECT

State Archives of Assyria Studies is a series of monographic studies relating to and supplementing the text editions published in the SAA series. Manuscripts are accepted in English, French and German. The responsibility for the contents of the volumes rests entirely with the authors.

Published with the support of the
Foundation for
Finnish Assyriological Research

Set in Times
The Assyrian Royal Seal emblem drawn by Dominique Collon from original
Seventh Century B.C. impressions (BM 84672 and 84677) in the British Museum
Cover: Gold seal of Queen Hamâ (see. p. 76), courtesy Muzahim Mahmud Hussein
Typesetting by Robert M. Whiting
Cover design by Teemu Lipasti

Printed in the USA and distributed by Eisenbrauns
Winona Lake, Indiana 46590, USA
www.eisenbrauns.com

ISBN-13 978-952-10-1337-9 (Volume 21)
ISBN-10 952-10-1337-0 (Volume 21)
ISSN 1235-1032 (SAAS)
ISSN 1798-7431 (PFFAR)

BEYOND HEARTH AND HOME

WOMEN IN THE PUBLIC SPHERE
IN NEO-ASSYRIAN SOCIETY

by

Sherry Lou Macgregor

THE NEO-ASSYRIAN TEXT CORPUS PROJECT

2012

To my stalwart and generous sister

Janis Jule King

ACKNOWLEDGEMENTS

This study began as a PhD dissertation at the University of California, Berkeley, and has since been revised and updated. I would like to thank the five immensely helpful professors who advised and encouraged me throughout the initial research and writing. Guitty Azarpay, from my first day as a graduate student until the completion of my dissertation, was an important source of support and inspiration. Her sensible and astute directives and comments always kept me moving toward the completion of this project and degree. Wolfgang Heimpel, a meticulous and thorough scholar, expected me to be the same. My scholarship and understanding of the texts greatly increased under his guidance. Anne Kilmer graciously shared her expertise of ancient Near Eastern music and musicians and was always available for discussions and to lend me materials. Crawford Greenewalt, a classicist and archaeologist, brought a broader perspective to my studies. His well-formed questions and comments were stimulating and extremely helpful.

I am most deeply indebted to my advisor David Stronach whose guidance and insights were invaluable throughout my years in the graduate program. He has since become a good friend and supportive colleague. His continued interest in this project and generosity in sharing his vast knowledge and library are without parallel. And his Scottish witticisms are a continual delight.

I wish to record my particular gratitude to Pauline Albenda, Irene Winter, Zainab Bahrani, Sarah Melville, Mario Fales, Mary Frances Wogec and Kim Codella for their willingness to answer my questions and for their moral support. They continue to inspire me with their scholarship and example. I wish to acknowledge the drawings of Roger Hall. For technical assistance, I wish to thank Alan Lenzi and Karl Garlid. Without their help I would have been lost forever in a maze of templates and formatting devices.

I am grateful to Professor Simo Parpola for accepting my manuscript for publication in this series. I owe a huge debt to Robert Whiting for his painstaking attention to the editing of this volume. His advice, corrections and references are much appreciated.

My gratitude in a wider sense goes back to my formative years when my English teacher, Gordon Nelson, taught me to write correctly and skillfully. But it was my grandmother, Florence Reyes MacGregor, who set such a stellar example for me (and all her descendants). Her advocacy for schooling and education, in her case achieved against great odds, inspired me to take the same path. Finally, I will always be grateful to my parents, Betty and Jack Bowen, for providing a loving family environment and encouraging each one of their children to do and be their best. By setting high standards for themselves and achieving graduate degrees later in life they set an example for me to emulate.

February 2012   Sherry Lou Macgregor

CONTENTS

ABBREVIATIONS

ABL	R. F. Harper, *Assyrian and Babylonian Letters*. 14 volumes. (London and Chicago 1892-1914)
ADD	C.H.W. Johns, *Assyrian Deeds and Documents*. 4 volumes. Cambridge, 1898, 1901, 1901 and 1923.
AfO	*Archiv für Orientforschung*
AfOB	*AfO* Beiheft
AHw	Wolfram von Soden, *Akkadisches Handwörterbuch*.
AJA	*American Journal of Archaeology*
AOAT	Alter Orient und Altes Testament
AR	J. Kohler and A. Ungnad, *Assyrische Rechtsurkunden in Umschrift und Übersetzung nebst einem Index der Personen-Namen und Rechtserläuterungen*. Leipzig: E. Pfeiffer, 1913.
ARINH	F.M. Fales, ed. *Assyrian Royal Inscriptions: New Horizons in Literary, Ideological, and Historical Analysis*. Orientis Antiqui Collectio 17. Roma: Istituto per l'Oriente, 1981.
ARRIM	*Annual Review of the Royal Inscriptions of Mesopotamia Project*
AnSt	*Anatolian Studies*
BaM	*Baghdader Mitteilungen*
BAR	*Biblical Archaeology Review*
BASOR	*Bulletin of the American Schools of Oriental Research*
BiAr	*Biblical Archaeologist*
BiOr	*Bibliotheca Orientalis*
CAD	*The Assyrian Dictionary of the Oriental Institute of the University of Chicago*. Chicago, 1956-2010.
CAH	*Cambridge Ancient History*. 2nd ed. Cambridge, 1970-
CANE	J. Sasson *et al*., eds. *Civilizations of the Ancient Near East*. New York: Charles Scribner's Sons, 1995.
CMS Bulletin	*The Canadian Society for Mesopotamian Studies Bulletin*
CRRAI	Compte rendue, Rencontre assyriologique internationale
CT	Cuneiform Texts from Babylonian Tablets in the British Museum
CTN	Cuneiform Texts from Nimrud I = Kinnier Wilson 1972, II = Postgate 1973b, III = Dalley and Postgate 1984
EI	*Eretz Israel*
FPOA	J.-M. Durand, ed. *La Femme dans le Proche-Orient Antique*. CRRAI 33. Paris: Éditions Recherche sur les Civilisations, 1987.

GH	*Gender and History*
HTR	*Harvard Theological Review*
IA	*Iranica Antiqua*
IEJ	*Israel Exploration Journal*
JAOS	*Journal of the American Oriental Society*
JBL	*Journal of Biblical Literature*
JCS	*Journal of Cuneiform Studies*
JNES	*Journal of Near Eastern Studies*
JSS	*Journal of Semitic Studies*
KAR	E. Ebeling, *Keilschrifttexte aus Assur religiösen Inhalts*. Leipzig, 1919.
MANE	Monographs on the Ancient Near East
Maqlû	G. Meier, *Die Assyrische Beschwörungssammlung Maqlû*. AfOB 2. Berlin: (privately published, 1937) (reprint, Osnabrück: Biblio-Verlag, 1967).
MMJ	*Metropolitan Museum Journal*
NABU	*Nouvelles Assyriologiques Brèves et Utilitaires*
NG	Liverani, Mario, ed. *Neo-Assyrian Geography*. Quaderni di Geografia Storica, vol. 5 Roma: Universita di Roma "La Sapienza," 1995.
Nimrud Conference 2002	J.E. Curtis, H. McCall, D. Collon and L. al-Gailani Werr, eds. *New Light on Nimrud: Proceedings of the Nimrud Conference 11th-13th March 2002*. London: British Institute for the Study of Iraq in association with The British Museum, 2008.
NWL	J.V. Kinnier Wilson, *The Nimrud Wine Lists* (CTN I, London 1972)
OPSNKF	Occasional Publications of the Samuel Noah Kramer Fund
PANEC	Martti Nissinen, ed. *Prophecy in Its Ancient Near Eastern Context: Mesopotamian, Biblical, and Arabian Perspectives*. Symposium Series 13. Atlanta: Society of Biblical Literature, 2000.
PEQ	*Palestine Exploration Quarterly*
PIHANS	Publications de l'Institut historique-archeologique neerlandais de Stamboul
RA	*Revue d'assyriologie et d'archéologie orientale*
RIMA	The Royal Inscriptions of Mesopotamia. Assyrian Periods 2 = Grayson 1991a, 3 = Grayson 1996
RlA	*Reallexikon der Asyriologie und vorderasiantischen Archäologie*. Leipzig and Berlin, 1928-
SAA	State Archives of Assyria I = Parpola 1987a, II = Parpola and Watanabe 1988, III = Livingstone 1989, IV = Starr 1990, VI = Kwasman and Parpola 1991, VII = Fales and Postgate 1992, VIII = Hunger 1992, IX = Parpola 1997, X = Parpola 1993, XI = Fales and Postgate 1995, XII = Kataja and Whiting 1995, XIII = Cole and Machinist 1998, XIV = Mattila 2002, XVI = Luukko and Van Buylaere 2002, XVIII = Reynolds 2003
SAAB	*State Archives of Assyria Bulletin*
SAALT	State Archives of Assyria Literary Texts

SAAS	State Archives of Assyria Studies
Sex and Gender	S. Parpola and R. M. Whiting, eds. *Sex and Gender in the Ancient Near East*. CRRAI 47. Helsinki: The Neo-Assyrian Text Corpus Project, 2002.
WVDOG	Wissenschaftliche Veröffentlichungen der Deutschen Orient-Gesellschaft
YGJA	*Yale Graduate Journal of Anthropology*
ZA	*Zeitschrift für Assyriologie*

ILLUSTRATIONS

INTRODUCTION

This is a study of women in the temples and palaces of Assyria during the Neo-Assyrian period (883-612 BCE). It draws together the information about temple and palace women from currently available sources, textual and visual, and then evaluates them.

While it has been the impression of many scholars that Assyrian women are hidden and unavailable for study nothing could be further from the truth. In Assyria there was a rich tradition of women functioning in temples. Their offices, responsibilities, cultic and non-cultic activities and, in some cases, their personal names were recorded. In the palaces of Assyria the royal women, their personnel, their living quarters, their economic transactions and their political involvements were chronicled. Official monuments, metal and stone sculptures, burial sites and personal objects have survived for modern examination.

The textual evidence examined in this study includes official royal inscriptions, administrative archives, letters, religious texts and records concerning property, marriage, loans and slaves. The visual evidence includes palace reliefs, stelae, ivory and metal objects and jewellery from tombs and other contexts.

The Issue of Gender

In recent years many disciplines have begun paying attention to the issue of gender. It has become obvious that preconceived notions of gender roles and behavior have clouded our modern understanding of women in the ancient world. Unfortunately what has often happened is that scholarly biases have gradually been transformed into an accepted historical reality.

"Present research on women in past societies tries to redress the imbalance of previous analysis, which drew on the perspectives of men in the definition of societal norms."[1] The present study attempts to minimize distortions due to gender presuppositions with regard to women's roles in temples and palaces with the goal of obtaining a more objective viewpoint.

Two examples of *a priori* assumptions which have done much to complicate a proper usage of the available material are the notions (1) that cultic prostitution took place in Assyrian temples and (2) that royal women of

---

[1] Westenholz 1990: 511.

1

Assyria lived in quarters comparable to later Middle Eastern Ottoman harems. In each case a major problem has been that the facts have only been interpreted through frameworks already imposed upon them. Such preconceptions preclude an impartial view of the various roles that women played in Assyrian temples or of the circumstances in which royal women conducted their lives.

Attention is currently being given to the reconstruction of female roles in numerous ancient Near Eastern cultures, but through the end of the twentieth century very little had been written about the role of women in Assyrian society. Notable exceptions to the general rule included Sarah Melville's insightful book on the involvement of one queen in Sargonid politics[2] and the study of Jennifer Arzt which examined the titles, dedicatory objects, burials and representations of Assyrian royal women.[3] The first decade of the twenty-first century has seen a considerable increase in publications dedicated solely to Neo-Assyrian women. This may possibly be the result of the flurry of interest following the discovery of the queens' tombs at Kalhu and the substantial number of publications from the SAA and RIM projects that have made archival texts and royal inscriptions from the Neo-Assyrian period more easily available. There may also have been the desire to complement publications that focused on women in other areas of Mesopotamia as well as women in the larger ancient Mediterranean world. Recent research, however, on Neo-Assyrian women is for the most part text-oriented and limited to the occurrence of women in textual sources and the inferences that can be derived therein. The goal of this study is to integrate visual, textual and archaeological information to provide a more detailed and coherent picture of women in the Neo-Assyrian world.

Assyria and Assyrians in the Neo-Assyrian Period

Assyria lies in the middle Tigris valley in northern Iraq. Initially it roughly constituted a quadrangle with corners at Assur, Nineveh, Arbail and Arrapha. Throughout the Neo-Assyrian period, which spanned the ninth through the seventh centuries BCE, the territorial holdings of Assyria expanded in every direction, eventually to encompass most of Mesopotamia and parts of western Iran, southern Anatolia, Palestine and Egypt.

As a result of imperial expansion, the Neo-Assyrian state became multi-national and multi-ethnic. The Assyrians practiced deportation and resettlement to control conquered people and to utilize their labor and skills wherever they were needed most. One unintended consequence of these policies was that the core region of Assyria came under considerable foreign influence. More and more people in the empire came to speak and write in Aramaic and both external ideas and exotic artistic styles took root in the homeland.

---

[2] Melville 1999.

[3] Arzt 1993: 45-56.

The women in the Assyrian palaces and temples, therefore, lived in an affluent society which maintained contacts with areas throughout the empire and beyond. They became accustomed to foreign artists, entertainers, objects and materials.

There is also evidence that Assyrian royal women became involved in politics. Naqia certainly did during the reign of her son Esarhaddon. Daughters of kings might be required to cement political alliances by marrying foreign rulers and documents suggest that they reported back to the Assyrian court.

Yet politics within Assyria, particularly during the Sargonid period (721-612 BCE), were fraught with difficulties. Kings were killed by enemies who could include their own sons and fathers sometimes chose younger sons to succeed to the throne. In an attempt to contend with such sources of conflict, females as well as males within the royal family sought advice from oracles and prophets, especially female prophets.

During the period encompassed in this study the names of many of the principal wives (MÍ.É.GAL) of Assyrian kings are known. They can be listed as follows:

Queens	Kings	Dates of Reign
Mullissu-mukannišat-Ninua	Aššurnaṣirpal II	883-859
	Shalmaneser III	858-824
Sammuramat	Šamši-Adad III	823-811
	Adad-nerari III	810-783
Hamâ	Shalmaneser IV	782-773
	Aššur-dan III	772-755
	Aššur-nerari V	754-745
Yabâ	Tiglath-Pileser III	744-727
Banitu	Shalmaneser V	726-722
Atalia	Sargon II	721-705
Tašmetum-šarrat and Naqia	Sennacherib	704-681
Ešarra-hammat	Esarhaddon	680-669
Libbali-šarrat	Aššurbanipal	668-631
[Ana-Taš]metum-taklak	unknown (Esarhaddon?)	

Structure of the Present Study

Following the present introduction, the material in this study has been organized (1) to examine the environments of temple and palace and (2) to distinguish the women who lived and functioned within each type of institution.

Chapter one investigates the officiants and participants in Assyrian temples. The first section of the chapter focuses on four positions held by women in Assyrian temples: the *entu*, *šēlûtu*, *ištarītu* and *qadištu*. Particular attention is paid to who filled these positions, what their circumstances were, what their duties were, which temples they were associated with, the types of rituals and activities they participated in and misconceptions about the roles of these cultic functionaries. The second section of the chapter focuses on female prophets (*raggintu*) and their prophecies. Central to their identification are the royal records from seventh-century Nineveh which contain collections of prophecies addressed to the king and queen. Not only do the collections illustrate the prestige and popularity of female prophets but the personal names of the prophets and their city of provenance are also recorded. Finally the textual sources emphasize the importance of the cult of Ištar of Arbail in prophetic announcements.

Chapter two investigates the musicians who performed in both temples and palaces. It begins with a discussion of the types of musical instruments which were played, i.e., chordophones, aerophones, membranophones and idio-phones, and what is known about the female musicians who played them. Particular attention is paid to the dominance of foreign female musicians and the fact that the musicians performed in groups which were either all female or a combination of female and male musicians.

The next section of chapter two investigates the textual evidence which includes royal inscriptions, lists of personnel from palaces and temples, the Nimrud Wine Lists and ritual texts. The final section is concerned with visual evidence: palace reliefs and ivory objects that functioned as either decorative plaques on furniture or containers called pyxides. A review of the visual scenes explores where the scenes take place, the types of occasion requiring music, the arrangement of the figures, the number of musicians and whether they were Assyrian or non-Assyrian. Both textual and visual sources indicate that female musicians performed in palaces, in temples, as well as in public.

Chapter three examines the large numbers of Assyrian palace women: servants, officials and royalty. Textual sources identify the women by personal names and titles and describe their concerns, activities, legal dealings and wealth. First the households of palace women are examined. Specific information identifies which cities, palaces and even areas within palaces that royal women occupied. Next the land grants, properties, gifts and general wealth are discussed. Finally the focus is on the personnel who serve in the households, the chief administrator (*šakintu*), the scribes, the eunuchs and the military units.

The last section of chaper three is concerned with the royal women themselves. Textual and visual sources provide considerable information on the daughters, sisters, queens and queen mothers. Their activities, marriages, titles, symbols and burials are discussed. The chapter concludes with studies of four Assyrian queens: Sammuramat, Tašmetum-šarrat, Ešarra-hammat and Libbali-šarrat.

Chapter four examines the textual and visual sources concerning an extra-ordinary Assyrian queen: Naqia/Zakutu. Her life spanned the reign of four Assyrian kings: her father-in-law Sargon II, her husband Sennacherib, her son Esarhaddon and her grandson Aššurbanipal. Although much is known about her activities once she entered the royal household nothing is known about the family she was born into, where she came from and even who her children were, with the exception of Esarhaddon. Her use of two names, one

West Semitic and the other Akkadian, is discussed as are the titles she used. Her extensive religious activities, her involvement in Assyrian politics and what little personal information is known about her are analyzed, as are the various theories which have been proposed concerning how she became such an influential and respected queen. A detailed discussion explores the one visual image of her: a bronze relief fragment in which she is viewed following an Assyrian king. A description of the bronze relief and of bronze-working in Assyria, the possible functions of the bronze relief, the inscriptions and images on the relief and finally where its placement might have occurred are examined. The unusual occurrence of a queen mother instituting a loyalty oath for her grandson after the death of her son, the king, offers a final point of interest.

CHAPTER I

TEMPLE WOMEN

Throughout the history of Mesopotamia, women have had a strong visual presence in religious and temple spheres.[1] In this arena they held cultic, administrative and domestic positions. From the Early Dynastic through the Late Babylonian periods both pictorial and textual evidence is known. While this evidence focuses primarily on women's ritual functions, it is generally not specific enough to define these functions precisely nor to indicate the status of the women involved.[2] Lexical lists which give the titles held by these women are also problematic. There are no accompanying job descriptions nor is it certain that over time the tasks were even the same ones.[3]

In the Neo-Assyrian period, textual information regarding women in religious environments appears not only in the lexical lists, but also in administrative lists, letters, legal documents, ritual texts and other literature. Although there are more references to the prophets than any other one category of religious women, all temple women still remain elusive. References to their presence, cultic activities and official duties exist here and there but not enough to make a complete picture. Specific information on the rituals performed by the women officiants is once again sketchy at best. Nevertheless, many titles for women serving in Neo-Assyrian temples are known. In the first section of this chapter the *entu*, *šēlûtu*, *ištarītu* and *qadištu* will be discussed. An investigation of female prophets and their prophecies, with a special emphasis on the prophets of Ištar, will conclude the chapter.

---

[1] Richard Henshaw in his book on cultic personnel states that "More and more evidence points towards women having roles in the cult of the countries of the ANE because of the nature of **polytheism** and when we turn our interest to the Hebrew Bible and **monotheism** ... we discover that women were excluded to a large extent." (Henshaw 1994: 3).

[2] Asher-Greve 1987: 27.

[3] Joan Westenholz (1989a: 251) has observed that "Religious symbols and titles undergo change continually in a complex fashion by which older elements are replaced in time by newer ones or persist but are reinterpreted to fit into a new total system of meanings."

WOMEN CULTIC OFFICIANTS

Entu

The title *entu* can be traced historically as a cultic office for women in various Mesopotamian temples as early as the third millennium BCE.[4] It is nevertheless a position/title that is fraught with confusion and ambiguities largely because very few descriptions of the *entu*'s cultic activities exist.[5] An exception is a set of tablets which describe the installation ceremonies of the *entu* (NIN.DINGIR) of IM, the storm god, at Emar, a 13th-century BCE city in northern Syria on the Euphrates River.[6]

What is known is that many of the women in Mesopotamia who filled the role of *entu* were royal women, the daughters or sisters of kings.[7] They managed extensive estates and supervised the large numbers of people who worked for the temple. While the office of *entu* was clearly one of longevity and prestige in southern Mesopotamia it is unclear whether this office had the same importance and status in Assyria. Only a few references for the *entu* are to be found in texts from the Neo-Assyrian period: lexical lists, a ritual text and a few omens.

The *entu* is mentioned in the Neo-Assyrian lexical list Lú=*ša* (MSL XII). These references occur on Tablet IV where both the Sumerian expressions LUKUR (of Utu) and NIN.DINGIR are used.[8] The *entu* appears in the ritual text *Maqlû*. In an incantation she is mentioned carrying the *terhu*-vessels for libations while the *qadištu*s carried the fir cones (*terinnu*) for annointing.[9] The *entu* is also mentioned in astrological reports of Assyrian kings. In one such report the king is told that if a particular eclipse occurs he will fall ill but recover and, in his stead, his daughter the *entu* will die. In other reports

---

[4] P. Weadock (1975: 127-128) lists at least 15 *entu*s whose names are known. They date from the Early Dynastic III period to the Old Babylonian period and then the Neo-Babylonian period under Nabonidus.

[5] The lack of specific information regarding the duties and responsibilities of temple personnel is consistently noticeable when women's cultic roles are examined and studied.

[6] While the Emar text was fundamentally Syrian, it indirectly reflected Babylonian, Assyrian, Hittite and Ugaritic ritual traditions. In it the installation of the *entu* of Baal took place over a nine day period. The chosen woman processed between her father's house and the temple on various days of the ceremony. She was anointed, shaved, enthroned and given gifts. Eventually, after much feasting and many offerings, she took up residence in the temple (Fleming 1992).

[7] In contrast, the Emar installation text states that the *entu* may be "the daughter of any son of Emar" therefore, at Emar she is not necessarily selected from the royal family (Fleming 1992: 49).

[8] MSL XII, lú=*ša* IV:27 for LUKUR, MSL XII, lú=*ša* IV:6 and MSL XII, lú=*ša* I:194-195; for NIN.DINGIR, MSL XII: 129, 128, 102). The latter example shows that the NIN.DINGIR logogram was used for both *entu* and *ugbabtu*, which has added considerable complexity to the modern understanding of the texts.

[9] *Maqlû* VI 39-40.

it is said that if the moon is surrounded by a halo and Scorpius stands in it: *entu*s will be made pregnant.[10]

Šēlûtu

A woman connected with a temple might have considerable status but the opposite was true as well. There are recorded instances of girls or women being given to the temple by their parents, the king or the queen or as acts of piety by a lay person. Such a girl or woman was generally referred to as a *šēlûtu* or votary. Two seventh-century documents from the administrative wing of the North-West Palace at Kalhu, ND 2309 and ND 2316, mention two such cases.[11] In ND 2309 a father sold his daughter for ten silver sheckels to the *lahhennutu* (female steward) of the *šakintu* (female chief administrator) of the old palace to become a votary of the goddess Mullissu. ND 2316 is an unusual document. The queen dedicated a girl to become a votary of the goddess Mullissu. At the same time the girl was married to a weaver and, most interesting, the document protected her from her husband's creditors. Postgate has remarked that it seems curious that the girl should simultaneously be dedicated to a temple and married to a weaver. He points out that throughout Mesopotamian history temples have traditionally acted as homes for people who had no patriarchal household of their own. In this particular case, if the girl's new husband decided to divorce her, she could fall back on her position as a votary of Mullissu which would provide her with an alternative home.[12]

A somewhat similar circumstance is mentioned in the text IM 76882 from the Šamaš Gate area at Nineveh. An Egyptian sold a slave specifically to become the wife of another Egyptian. If the new husband later decided to divorce his wife, he could not resell her. Instead she would pay him one-third of the purchase price and then she with her sons would become a votary of Ištar of Arbail, at least for as long as the husband was alive. Postgate comments that it is unclear whether this document improves the woman's circumstances as it does not constitute a genuine manumission.[13]

Votaries are mentioned in other contexts as well. One appears listed among the gardeners in the Harran Census.[14] The sons of votaries are mentioned in a letter to the king which complained that a particular priest had taken them over along with a field, a house and people and made them his own, much to the displeasure of the priest reporting.[15]

---

[10] SAA VIII 104, 147, 307, 480. According to Renger the *entu* was not allowed to have children (Renger 1967: 141).

[11] Parker 1954: 30, 39, 40.

[12] Postgate 1979: 98-99.

[13] *Ibid.*

[14] SAA XI 219 r. iv 13. There is possibly a connection to the grove belonging to Ištar of Hu(zirina) that follows (SAA XI 219 r. iv 16).

[15] SAA XIII 126.

Votaries are mentioned in connection with many different temples such as the temples of Ištar of Arbail, Adad of Kurbail and Aššur of Assur so it would seem they were a presence at all, or most, Assyrian temples. Yet the lives and situations of most votaries remain a mystery. Some were given to the temple as gifts, thus seeming to be the equivalent of slaves. Other votaries were able to marry and have children and live in their own homes. The fact that some votaries could keep their children surely indicates that their life experiences and circumstances were of a higher order than that of many temple women. One votary had enough status and credibility to report to the king himself (although the topic of her report is not known).[16] Nevertheless, one of the most explicit definitions of a votary merely says a "person dedicated to a deity"[17] and so the title (or description) continues to remain elusive and indeterminate.

Ištarītu

The *ištarītu* was specifically devoted to the goddess Ištar and could marry and have children. Although no texts have been found which mention her participation in cultic events, the *ištarītu* appears in Neo-Assyrian lexical lists, in a *Maqlû* incantation and in wisdom literature. What turns out to be most curious is the company she keeps.

In two different lexical lists the *ištarītu* is mentioned along with the *qadištu, amalu* and *kulmašītu*,[18] and with the *amalu* and *šugētu*.[19] Although these cultic offices had a long history in Mesopotamia the overall picture is quite blurred. The activities of these temple women appear to have varied considerably. Some officiants were associated with sorcery (the *qadištu* and *kulmašītu*), some with ecstatic actions (the *amalu*), some with musical celebrations (the *kulmašītu* and *qadištu*) and some with possible sexual activities (the *qadištu, šugētu* and *kulmašītu*). In the Neo-Assyrian period these offices generally had a negative image, which is puzzling.

In *Maqlû*,[20] the *ištarītu, qadištu, nadītu* and *kulmašītu* are mentioned along with a number of witches and sorcerers (all female) who are capable of causing great harm.[21] Parpola has suggested that they may have been impersonating the witch and thereby providing a tangible object for exorcistic

---

[16] SAA XIII 148.

[17] *CAD* Š/3, 264b, s.v. *šūlûtu* A.

[18] Henshaw 1994: 203 (MSL IV 17f Tabl. II).

[19] Henshaw 1994: 213 (Diri IV 188ff, CAD A/2 2a).

[20] According to Abusch, who has written extensively on the incantations and rituals in *Maqlû* ("Burning"), the text is most likely a first millennium creation. It is the longest and most important Mesopotamian text directed against witches and witchcraft. It was performed during a single night and the following morning. In the Neo-Assyrian period there is evidence (SAA X 274) that the king himself performed the ritual (Abusch 1989a: 40).

[21] It was said that all night and all day they capture, stalk, dirty, bind and kill deities and/or humans (*Maqlû* III 40-55).

activity.[22] Or these cultic women may have been thought to be potential sorcerers or witches. Witchcraft in Assyria and in Mesopotamia was taken very seriously as it was considered the cause of illness or misfortune. Elaborate rituals such as *Maqlû* were devised to counteract the threat of witchcraft. But the question remains as to why these particular cultic women were thought to be prone to sorcery that could go awry? Who were they and what had they done to cause such suspicions?

A clue can be found in a collection of moral exhortations where the *ištarītu* is mentioned along with the *harimtu* and *kulmašītu*.[23] Prospective husbands were advised not to marry a *harimtu* because her "husbands are legion" nor "a *kulmašītu* whose favors are many." This advice implies that these women were not inclined to monogymy, some were already sexually active and therefore they were not good marriage material. But in the case of the *ištarītu* the reason given was that she was already "dedicated to a god" and therefore her primary commitment would not be to her husband.

The *ištarītu* would thus appear to be an example of a woman who chose to have an occupation and activities outside the structure of the home and the family. Could this then have been the reason the *ištarītu* was included with those women who were viewed with suspicion and alarm?

Anthropologists, sociologists and historians who have sought to understand the phenomena of sorcery and witchcraft over the ages have noted that their existence often indicates lines of stress in a society. For instance, when there are structural and functional changes in the family or changes in the status and role of women or demographic changes, accusations of witchcraft often occur.[24] Women and men in marginal social categories were the most vulnerable to these accusations and women in particular were regarded as having the greater propensity for sorcery and witchcraft. Rivkah Harris has noted that in Mesopotamia: "A rich vocabulary exists for witches and sorceresses who are thought to possess great powers and esoteric knowledge ... (and) ... abound for women who are regarded as powerful, disruptive elements in the social order, enemies of the order and well-being of the community."[25]

Women in Mesopotamian society were at a distinct disadvantage. Their social status was not equal to that of men; their protection under the legal system was markedly inferior to that of men; their position within the structure of the family was insecure and with marriage they presumably entered their husband's family where they were outsiders. Were women who had lives outside of their homes and who acquired certain skills and abilities seen as

---

[22] Parpola 1983: 183.

[23] It is not known exactly when the *Counsels of Wisdom* was compiled but it was popular in Neo-Assyrian times. There were at least three copies in the libraries of Aššurbanipal at Nineveh and at least one copy at Assur. (Lambert 1960: 96-97, 102-103).

[24] Ben-Yehuda 1989: 239.

[25] Harris 1990: 13.

threatening? If so, these 'peripheral' women, most likely small in number, would be particularly vulnerable to accusations of sorcery and witchcraft.[26]

It is important to acknowledge that no legal documents are known which show that cases of sorcery, or accusations of sorcery, were ever prosecuted in Assyria or anywhere in Mesopotamia. This might be a reflection of the disastrous consequences (i.e., the river ordeal during the Old Babylonian period or capital punishment in the Middle Assyrian period) if the accuser could not prove the charge. Instead, Rollin suggests: "Suspicion of witchcraft in Mesopotamia may therefore have taken more the form of slandering and backbiting, and certain hatreds, anxieties and social tensions may often have been expressed in this manner."[27]

Qadištu

The *qadištu* was another cultic officiant who had a long history in Mesopotamia. She appears in law codes, lexical lists, ritual instructions, incantations and letters from the Old Babylonian through the Neo-Babylonian period. Yet there has been much confusion and misinformation about this particular cultic functionary and the definitions for her do not give explicit information. *AHw* says *qadištu* means "pure, dedicated, a class of women";[28] *CAD* merely says she is "a woman of special status";[29] Gruber says her name literally means "she who is set apart" and denotes "a woman who has been dedicated to the service of a deity, usually Adad."[30]

Although none of these definitions gives specific information about the *qadištu*, texts mention that she had both cultic and non-cultic (secular) activities and that she could marry, have children, inherit and own property.

The *qadištu* is mentioned in connection with wet-nursing and possibly midwifery. Second and first millennium texts document that the *qadištu* was paid for her services as a wet nurse. In an unusual text a *qadištu* adopted a child from the street and nursed it at her breast.[31] Interestingly these texts indicate activities which may have allowed the *qadištu* a degree of financial

---

[26] In her article on women and witchcraft, Sue Rollin says that ideas about witchcraft illustrate the general social disadvantage of women both in Assyria and in Mesopotamia as a whole. Because their social role was more strictly defined than that of men, women who exhibited unusual behavior, particularly actions that prevented them from fulfilling women's functions, could make them suspect (Rollin 1983: 38). Joan Westenholz has suggested that sorcerers and witches can be accounted for by the first-millennium dualistic theory that women were either "good" or "bad." Because they were under their own control, they were considered to be the mediums of evil power, a dangerous, uncontrolled female power (Westenholz 1989a: 253).

[27] But as Rollin also points out, gossip and slander can in themselves be very damaging (Rollin 1983: 44).

[28] "Reine, Geweihte, eine Frauenklasse" (*AHw*, 891).

[29] However, *CAD* includes among the different meanings for the verb *qadāšu* "to make ritually clean, to purify" and "to consecrate, dedicate" (*CAD* Q, 46, 48).

[30] Gruber 1992: 17.

[31] Ana ittišu VII iii 11-14 (Westenholz 1989a: 251).

independence. The reference in the Myth of Atra-hasis to "a house of the *qadištu*" where the midwife assisted the pregnant women giving birth[32] may not parallel reality. There is no mention of the *qadištu* in any of the birth rituals nor is there any reference to women being anywhere but in their own homes when they gave birth.[33]

The known cultic activities of the *qadištu* emphasize her involvement in purification rituals. The most specific example comes from a Middle Assyrian (or possibly Neo-Assyrian) document KAR 154:1-14, which describes a ritual associated with the Adad Temple of Assur. The primary officiants were the *šangû* and several *qadištu* who acted together. In this ritual they processed from the Adad Temple to various other temples and to the harbor gate before returning to the Adad Temple. Throughout this ritual the *qadištu*s periodically performed the *inhu*-song, elevated the statue of the god,[34] brought out offerings, drank and ate some of the same, removed their jewellery and sang more songs with other temple singers.[35]

The association of the *qadištu* with purification rites, in this case sprinkling water in a ritual manner, can also be found in KAR 321 when she performed with the *nadītu*[36] and in the Babylonian fable "The Tamarisk and the Palm" when she sprinkled water in connection with a festival in the city of Kish.[37]

In the Neo-Assyrian period the *qadištu* also participated in exorcistic rituals. In a letter to the Assyrian king Esarhaddon, the chief exorcist reported that during a ceremony which was to occur before Šamaš, the *qadištu* would perform a certain rite whereupon the exorcist would then take over.[38] The *qadištu* is also mentioned in some of the incantations in *Maqlû* (along with the *ištarītu*, *nadītu* and *kulmašītu*) in the company of sorcerers and witches.

References to the *qadištu* as a cultic functionary show that she participated in purification and exorcistic rituals where she was known to carry fir cones (*terinnu*) and the fiber cords (*pilitu*).[39] In one interesting document she was required to use salt to undo a sworn oath.[40] She also functioned as a singer

---

[32] Lambert and Millard 1969: 62-63 I 290.

[33] It is a significant problem that what happens in the myth (i.e., the brick, magic circle, house of the *qadištu*, etc.) is not mentioned in any birth rituals. (Mary Frances Wogec, personal communication, 11 July 2002)

[34] "Elevate" may mean to raise up physically or to exalt or praise.

[35] A complete transliteration and translation of KAR 154 is in Menzel 1981 II: T2-T4. A partial translation can also be found in Westenholz 1989a: 254 and a partial transliteration and translation can be found in Gruber 1992: 29-31.

[36] "The *nadītu*s who with skill heal the foetus, the *qadištu*s with water [per]form purifications" (KAR 321:7; from a rendering by Joan Westenholz [1989a: 253]).

[37] Lambert 1960: 161.

[38] It would be more informative if the chief exorcist specified what rite the *qadištu* performed. (SAA X 246).

[39] *Maqlû* VI 29 and 40, V 54.

[40] Westenholz 1989a: 254 (from Ebeling 1953: 43).

and possibly a sorcerer. But there are no references alluding to any sexual activities.[41]

Mayer Gruber has pointed out that "Tragically, scholarship suffered from scholars being unable to imagine any cultic role for women in antiquity that did not involve sexual intercourse."[42] Sixty years ago, Beatrice Brooks had noted a similar circumstance when she wrote, "… a number of terms in Akkadian texts were arbitrarily translated 'eunuch,' 'harlot,' 'whore,' 'hierodule,' or 'prostitute,' until it seemed that an improbable percent of the population must have been either secular or religious prostitutes of some sort."[43]

Part of the problem lies with the Greek historian Herodotus and later classical writers. Herodotus was the earliest who wrote that all Babylonian women went to the temple of Aphrodite once in their lives to give themselves to a strange man. The women had no choice in a partner and had to go with the first man who threw money in their lap. Once this transaction was completed a woman's duty to the goddess was discharged and she could go home.[44] Strabo and other classical writers reported on the custom and embellished the story.[45] Christian writers like Augustine continued the fiction.

Omens and related literature also contributed to the belief that women officiants were sexually active as part of their cultic offices. Omens such as the *entu* "will die of a venereal disease" or she "will have illicit intercourse" have been used to substantiate the idea of cultic prostitution. That is until recently. The important issue appears to be whether or not the omens were comments on reality or on some type of odd, aberrant behavior that could possibly happen. As a proof for cultic prostitution, they are clearly inadequate.[46]

---

[41] It is very difficult to determine whether any type of sexual activity occurred in Assyrian temples. Some scholars have postulated that artifacts showing actual sexual intercourse are depictions of the sacred marriage ritual. Yet there is no way to prove these artifacts have cultic associations, particularly because the positions, architectural features and numbers of people in a scene do not coincide with textual sources. At Assur, Andrae found six lead figurines depicting sexual intercourse in the area of the New Palace Terrace dating to the time of Tukulti-Ninurta I (1240-1207) (Andrae 1935: 103, Plates 45 & 46). By plotting lead densities, studying assemblages and installations, Julia Assante found that this location was an industrial site that manufactured decorative items for the palace. From other find spots she determined that the lead reliefs were not mass-produced but seem to have been made in limited editions to inlay elite and palatial furniture and therefore were not images of orgiastic cultic occasions (Assante 2000: 12, 3). In his article on Sacred Marriage, Cooper states that "there is no reason to assume that it [cultic sex] was practiced in later Assyria" (Cooper 1972-75: 266).

[42] Gruber 1992: 26.

[43] Brooks 1941: 231.

[44] Herodotus 1954: 94.

[45] Over a 1000-year period at least 15 authors from antiquity wrote on this subject; all of the classical writers were dependent, directly or indirectly, upon Herodotus; and not one of these sources is noteworthy for its disinterested, objective character (Oden 1987: 144-146).

[46] According to Robert Oden (1987: 151), "When read in context, none of these omens provides anything like transparent testimony for cultic prostitution."

The *qadištu* in particular has suffered from the inaccurate portrayal of cultic women and there are several reasons for this confusion. The Akkadian word *qadištu* and the Hebrew word *qĕdēšāh* are clearly cognates and their functions were thus thought to be the same. But recent scholarship has revealed that while the Hebrew *qĕdēšāh* was a prostitute she was not a cultic functionary. The Mesopotamian *qadištu* was a cultic functionary but there is no evidence that at any time or in any place she was a prostitute.[47]

The inclusion of the *qadištu* in the Middle Assyrian laws has also complicated matters. Law 40 states that when the *qadištu* was married she wore a veil in public as did wives, widows, daughters of gentlemen, etc. But when the *qadištu* was unmarried her head had to remain uncovered in public as did that of the *harimtu* (prostitute) and the *amtu* (female slave). Many inferences about women's social status have been made as a result of these Middle Assyrian laws including that they are one more piece of evidence that the *qadištu* was a prostitute. There is not enough information to make a statement such as this with any certainty. The significance or symbolism or legal ramifications of wearing or not wearing the veil in Mesopotamia are complicated and difficult to understand. Van der Toorn has suggested that the primary role of the veil (was) as a symbol of appurtenance and the principal ceremony in which it played a role was the wedding.[48] The few references to the veil do indicate it was often associated with the bride but it also seems to have had a ceremonial use as it was worn by the *entu* at her investiture at Emar.[49] Whether or not veils denoted social status and respectability or even chastity is impossible to say with the sparse information available.[50]

Another misconception has been that the *qadištu* was thought to be part of the cult of Ištar. Because of Ištar's connection to sex and eroticism it was reasoned that the *qadištu* as a functionary of the goddess must have been a prostitute. But it has now been shown that the *qadištu* was not associated with the Ištar cult nor was she a cultic prostitute for Ištar.[51]

Ultimately it has become clear that there is no unequivocal evidence, from either textual or archaeological sources, that various types of prostitution existed in Neo-Assyrian temples. The topic of cultic prostitution appears to be a case of ancient fiction coupled with "…an amalgam of misconceptions, presuppositions and inaccuracies."[52] Hopefully this means that in the future the picture of Assyrian (and Mesopotamian) temple women will be more accurately rendered.

---

[47] Gruber 1992: 28.

[48] Van der Toorn 1995: 339, 330.

[49] Reference from *Emar* VI/3 369:63-64 (van der Toorn 1995: 331).

[50] The fact that there are no examples of women wearing veils in the visual arts is also noteworthy. Joan Westenholz has commented, "… if the married woman wore a veil, why does the visual evidence show none from any period or region of Mesopotamia? The female-worshipper figures, female statues, votive plaques, terracotta reliefs, and stele clearly show their faces and coiffures." (Westenholz 1990: 515).

[51] Renger 1967: 181-184.

[52] Westenholz 1989a: 263.

FEMALE PROPHETS AND PROPHECY

An introduction to prophecy

Prophets and prophecy had long been part of the cultural traditions of the Ancient Near East. Divine-human communication occurred in many ways and one way was through prophecy. In such circumstances a divinity would send a message to one or more humans through an intermediary called a prophet or an oracle. There were various ways the prophet might receive the communication: auditory, audio-visual, visual, dreams, etc. According to the terminology used to describe these events the prophet might become ecstatic, go into a frenzy, scream and shout or possibly go into a trance-like state. That the prophet received the message through spontaneous, non-technical means, however, was crucial. After the divine communication occurred it was passed on to the person(s) for whom it was intended.

In Mesopotamia, prophets were connected with temples, although deities appeared to have freely used prophets who were not necessarily from their own temples. From the beginning prophecy was recognized as a legitimate communication from a divinity if the intermediary was regarded as an authentic medium.[53]

Divine messages are known in Mesopotamia as early as the third millennium BCE. They were communicated through prophets and recorded in letters, economic and administrative texts. During the Old Babylonian period in the second millennium the largest number of prophecies by far are to be found in the letters addressed to the king Zimri-Lim at Mari on the Upper Euphrates River. A few other prophecies addressed to the kings of Uruk and Ešnunna are also known.[54]

More than one thousand years after the Old Babylonian textual attestations of prophecies, records of the same type of oracular activities appeared in the seventh-century BCE royal archives in the Assyrian city of Nineveh, on the Upper Tigris River. These reports list prophetic messages which occurred during the reigns of two Neo-Assyrian kings, Esarhaddon (681-669) and Aššurbanipal (668-627). The majority of these prophecies were addressed to the king, but some prophecies were addressed to the queen mother.

---

[53] This could be tricky and thus various tests were developed and used to assure the prophecy and the prophet were authentic. For example, at Mari a more technical divination, such as extispicy by a *barû*-diviner, might be required to verify the authenticity of the prophet and/or prophecy. Prophets might need to send a bit of their hair and a swatch from their garment. This "hair and hem" would be used to determine the reliability of the prophet and the truth of the prophecy (Huffmon 2000: 50).

[54] A fragmentary and enigmatic text known as the "Old Babylonian Uruk Oracle" (W.19900/1), found in the palace of Sin-kašid at Uruk, contained a message from the goddess Nanaya, a form of Ištar, concerning the future of Uruk. Two texts from the archive of the Kititum Temple in Išchali to king Ibalpiel (II) of Ešnunna called for piety on the part of the king if the goddess Kititum was to support him. (Ellis 1989: 137-140).

During the reign of Esarhaddon there were four collections of prophecies arranged according to chronological or thematic issues which were placed in the royal archives.[55] They were written in the language spoken by the prophets, that is, in Neo-Assyrian.[56] They were recorded as spoken using the first person singular, which indicated that the deity was thought to be personally speaking with the voice of the prophet. Overwhelmingly, the messages preserved in the collections were from Ištar. Only occasionally did other gods such as Mullissu, Aššur, Bel or Nabû send messages through prophecies to the Assyrian royalty.

Further sources of information about prophets and prophecies from the regnal years of Esarhaddon and Aššurbanipal, can be found in royal inscriptions, miscellaneous letters, a lodging list and loyalty oaths.[57] In fact, the inclusion of prophecy in royal inscriptions only occurred during the reigns of these same two kings. Does this indicate that these two kings had a special appreciation for this form of message from the gods? Was prophecy perhaps allotted a higher status during the reigns of these two kings?

The names of many of the prophets and often their city of provenance were recorded. The Neo-Assyrian cities associated with the prophets and prophecy were Nineveh, Kalhu, Assur and Arbail. Prophecies from elsewhere, i.e. Babylonia, were on occasion recorded as well. However the location of the transmission of the prophecy (when the deity spoke through the prophet) is not known. It seems that some prophecies were delivered within the premises of a temple, but they did not necessarily have to occur in the presence of the divine image. Prophecies were also frequently delivered outside the bounds of a temple. Prophets also appear to have accompanied the military on royal campaigns which would seem to indicate that a deity might speak to a prophet anywhere.

The Neo-Assyrian word for prophet was either *raggimu* (m) or *raggintu* (f) which literally meant "shouter" or "proclaimer." It was a specifically Neo-Assyrian designation for prophets replacing the older *mahhû/mahhûtu* which derives from *mahû* meaning "to become crazy, to go into a frenzy." Interestingly, both terms literally describe the ecstatic activities of the prophet. While the term *raggimu/raggintu* is only found in Neo-Assyrian texts, it is the term consistently used in the prophecy corpus and in other texts such as administrative documents and personal letters. The term *mahhû/mahhûtu* is

---

[55] In SAA IX, Parpola includes 28 prophecies. Of these 28, approximately 21 are by 13 prophets whose names are known and of these, nine are women and four are men (Parpola 1997).

[56] According to Parpola, the prophecies were written in pure Neo-Assyrian with numerous phonological and morphological details indicating that the prophets spoke it as their mother tongue. The occasional Aramaic loanwords coincided with the general characteristics of Neo-Assyrian (Parpola 1997: LXVII).

[57] Nissinen, in his study, discusses 16 texts: five excerpts from royal inscriptions, nine letters, a Neo-Assyrian lodging list and paragraphs from two loyalty oaths (Nissinen 1998: 10-11).

attested only twice in purely Neo-Assyrian texts, otherwise it was retained as a synonym restricted to literary use.[58]

Among all the Neo-Assyrian deities Ištar appears to have preferred communicating through prophecy and thus the role of prophet was an important one among her temple personnel. Most likely the prophets of Ištar lived their lives closely connected with her temples in Assyrian cities.

There is evidence to suggest that prophets may not have had the same status as other divinatory practitioners even though they had a similar function. One reason may have been that long years of schooling and training were not necessary to become a prophet while extensive training was necessary to become a credible astrologer, $b\bar{a}r\hat{u}$-diviner, etc. It is not known if there were any requirements to fulfill before one might become a prophet but that humans could somehow regulate this ability to speak for the deity seems very unlikely. Furthermore, prophets behaved in ways uncharacteristic of the rest of society by being ecstatics (i.e., shouting, going into a frenzy, etc.). The other diviners or "scholars" were part of an elite class who helped advise the king on political as well as personal matters. Any political advice from the prophets who were thought to be directly speaking the words of the deities was generally much more oblique and indirect.[59] A final yet important distinction between prophets and other diviners which should be emphasized is that the majority of known prophets were women while all the known scholars were men. And the social status of the two sexes in Assyrian society was not equal.

When comparing prophecy with other forms of divination, it seemed to lack the stature of astrology or extispicy. This impression is substantiated in a few of Esarhaddon's inscriptions (e.g., *Assur A* and *Nineveh A*). When the king discussed his rise to power he began by giving astrological portents in great detail while dreams and speech omens only got a brief mention. It has been suggested that this might possibly indicate a lower ranking of prophecy. In another instance a Babylonian astrologer in a letter to Esarhaddon expressed disbelief and astonishment that the king would summon prophets rather than himself, a skilled Babylonian astrologer. What is implied in his remarks is that prophets should not be so honored by the king, especially if they substituted for skilled professional scholars.[60]

The goddess Ištar and her cities

The goddess Ištar exhibited many different manifestations and she acquired different attributes and characteristics in the many places she was worshipped. In Assyria she was known as Ištar of Assur, Ištar of Nineveh and Ištar of Arbail, just to name a few. These different forms of Ištar had

---

[58] Parpola 1997: XLV-XLVI.
[59] Nissinen 2000: 108-109.
[60] SAA X 109.

connections with each other and the character and associations of one manifestation could color and influence the character of another. At various times her close association with the national god Aššur, her powers as mediator in the divine council, her warlike qualities, her healing skills or her prophetic abilities might take precedence.

Ištar also appears to have had a very close association with the goddess Mullissu. In a few of the prophecies the two goddesses were of such a like mind that they seemed to be speaking in the same voice:

> The word of Ištar of Arbail, the word of Queen Mullissu: I will look, I will listen, I will search out the disloyal ones, and I will put them into the hands of the king.[61]

Certainly by combining their message to the king, the looking, listening and searching out became even more powerful and convincing. The two goddesses were also closely involved in ministering to the king. They were at times referred to as his "mother" or his "nurse" that suggests a very personal and intimate relationship, possibly going back to the king's early childhood. Yet the mother and the nurse of royal children were rarely, if ever, the same woman.

The pairing of these two goddesses has given rise to a certain amount of speculation as to whether they were actually viewed as one and the same goddess.[62] There are four prophecies, one hymn and one psalm which hint this could be a possibility.[63] But these documents are ambiguous, vague and even incomplete so they are not conclusive. The pairing of Ištar of Arbail with Mullissu and Ištar of Nineveh with Mullissu might instead indicate that the two goddesses were both worshipped in the Egašankalamma in Arbail and the Emašmaš in Nineveh.[64]

The question then is how seriously the fusion of the two goddesses should be taken. Was it meant in a literal sense? Or, in the case of Urkittu-šarrat's prophecy, did the words of the two goddesses get combined in order to become more powerful and truthful? And if, as has been suggested, in the Neo-Assyrian period the name of Ištar was a generic term for a female divinity and not a proper name at all, are these questions even meaningful?[65]

The earliest connection between Ištar and prophecy in Mesopotamia is mentioned in a document from the third millennium BCE and in Assyria in a text from the thirteenth century BCE.[66] Ištar, who is generally thought to be

---

[61] SAA IX 2.4.

[62] Parpola says that in Urkittu-šarrat's prophecy "Mullissu ... is clearly only a synonym or another designation of Ištar" (Parpola 1997: XVIII); Nissinen claims in a more general sense that "in Neo-Assyrian texts, Mullissu cannot be separated from Ištar as a divine being" (Nissinen 2000: 95), while Menzel mentions that in the later period (the reign of Aššurbanipal) Ištar of Nineveh and Mullissu fused into one goddess (Menzel 1981 I: 64-65).

[63] SAA IX 2.4, 5, 7, 9; SAA III 7, 9.

[64] Possibly there were statues of both Ištar and Mullissu in each of these two temples which became very popular and were well known.

[65] Wolfgang Heimpel, personal communication, 22 October 2001.

[66] The third millennium reference to prophecy is in an Old Akkadian text dating to the reign of Naram-Sin. The Middle Assyrian administrative document specifically lists the prophets

a goddess of special importance to the Neo-Assyrians, spoke the largest number of prophecies. According to Parpola "the close connection of Assyrian prophecy to the cult of Ištar ... cannot be stressed enough."[67] Many of the names given to the prophets emphasize her importance. For instance, *Ilūssa-āmur*, "I have seen her godhead," *Issār-bēlī-daʾʾini*, "Ištar, strengthen my lord!" and *Issār-lā-tašīyaṭ*, "Do not neglect Ištar!" illustrate this point nicely.[68] Her major cult centers in Assyria were at Assur, Nineveh, Kalhu and Arbail, and of these temples associated with prophecy, Arbail took preeminence.

Arbail was on the eastern edge of the Assyrian heartland and was one of the four cities demarcating its boundaries (the other three being Assur, Nineveh and Arrapha). Because of its geographical position it had political as well as religious significance to the Assyrians. Located at the base of the Zagros Mountains, it was situated on roads which led to the Iranian plateau and would appear to have been renowned for its fortifications.[69] According to Pongratz-Leisten, "... at the moment when the city was rebuilt into a military garrison, the cult of the city god also experienced a special financial and theological promotion."[70]

Arbail was clearly an important city for both religious and secular celebrations. When the *akītu*-festival was celebrated at Arbail it focused on the goddess Ištar who triumphed over chaos.[71] But most interestingly, the *akītu*-festival in Arbail was sometimes associated with extraordinary military achievements. Royal inscriptions and letters of Esarhaddon and Aššurbanipal reveal that when the goddess Ištar returned from the temple in Milqiya to the temple in Arbail "her re-entrance into the city, was combined with the presentation of captives and booty to the cheering public."[72] It seems significant that Arbail was one of the few Assyrian cities during the reigns of Esarhaddon and Aššurbanipal where triumphal processions after military victories took place. In one instance, records recount that the head of the Elamite King Teumman was displayed by Aššurbanipal in Arbail. These

---

of Ištar along with other cultic personnel of the Ištar temple as recipients of food rations thus emphasizing the close connection of Assyrian prophecy to the cult of Ištar (Parpola 1997: XLVII-XLVIII).

[67] Parpola 1997: XLVII.

[68] Parpola 1997: L-LII.

[69] While there is much textual information about Arbail, there have been no excavations of the site due to the fact that the modern city of Erbil is directly over the ruins of the old city (Menzel 1981 I: 6).

[70] Pongratz-Leisten 1997: 251.

[71] The *akītu*-festival was introduced in Assyria when Sennacherib reorganized the cult of Aššur, demoting the god Marduk. When celebrated in the city of Assur, the procession back to the city symbolized the triumph of the national god Aššur over Tiamat (in Babylon Marduk triumphed over Tiamat). However, the *akītu*-festival is attested in other Assyrian cities and various deities replaced Aššur (or Marduk) to symbolize the victory of order over chaos. In both Arbail and Nineveh the deity was Ištar. At Kilizi and Kurbail the god was Adad, at Harran it was Sin (Pongratz-Leisten 1997: 245-246) and in Kalhu the god was Nabû (J. and D. Oates 2001: 119-123).

[72] Weissert 1997: 348.

victory celebrations would have begun in Milqiya-Arbail, continued on to Nineveh and finished in Assur where prisoners and booty were turned over to the Assyrian national god.[73]

Aššurbanipal seems to have had a particularly strong regard for Ištar of Arbail as some of his inscriptions accord her an extraordinarily high rank. He refers to her as "greatest of ladies" and "honored queen" and mentions how her compassion for him assured his military victory over Teumman.[74] This is a good example of Ištar of Arbail becoming known for martial qualities as well as her prophecies.[75]

There must have been a long association of Ištar of Arbail with prophecy. This assured the prestige of her prophets in Arbail as well as herself. Of the 15 Neo-Assyrian prophets known by personal names, seven were based in Arbail.[76] Even when a prophet was from another temple, she/he still might speak the words of Ištar of Arbail. It is no wonder that the kings listened when Ištar of Arbail spoke.

Female prophets: who they were and what they said

It is striking that there were so many women among the prophets of Assyria and that they even may have outnumbered the male prophets.[77] The popularity of female prophets was particularly true for the cult of Ištar, especially at Arbail. Did the goddess Ištar actually prefer to speak through female mediums? Was it possible that women had a special proclivity toward this type of oracular activity? Did prophecy have an inferior status compared to the other types of divination in Assyria and therefore women were more accepted and tolerated in this field? Certainly if no academic training or schooling was required, then women could not be kept out by intercepting them with these prerequisites.[78]

---

[73] Nineveh was the main capital of Assyria and home of the Assyrian king, Arbail was an important center for the cult of Ištar and Assur was the home of the state god of the same name. These three cities demarcated the boundary of the heartland of Assyria. Thus the Assyrian victory processions in Nineveh, Arbail and Assur could symbolize the security of the interior and the strengthening of the boundaries.

[74] Weissert 1997: 347 and nn. 23-24.

[75] Beckman 1998: 7, nn. 82-83.

[76] Nissinen 2000: 98.

[77] Parpola claims that the high number of women prophets in Assyria is paralleled at Mari and in the Old Testament, as well as in Gnosticism and early Christianity (Parpola 1997: XLVIII).

[78] Higher institutions of learning, trade schools, guild associations, etc. have long been a notoriously effective way of withholding the prerequisite training from anyone regarded as undesirable in a profession. If social pressures, class distinctions, conservative sex roles and public opinion are added, this could easily eliminate even more candidates. Therefore it comes as no surprise that not one woman is known among the Assyrian scholars who were required to spend a considerable amount of time in specialized studies, while many women are known among the prophets, a profession which appears to have required no training.

Clearly women with a strong spiritual bent and/or who heard divine voices had a community they could join within the cult of Ištar. There they could live together with others who had the same interests, skills and abilities and they could do their work and make their contributions without feeling ostracized. Even the kings and queens came to them for advice and information from the goddess. The names of nine women prophets are found in the collections of prophecies which have survived: Ahat-abiša, Bayâ, Dunnaša-amur, Ilussa-amur, Issar-beli-da"ini, Mullissu-kabtat, Remutti-Allati, Sinqiša-amur and Urkittu-šarrat.[79]

It is known that Esarhaddon listened to both female and male prophets and honored them with royal audiences as soon as he ascended the throne of Assyria.[80] Aššurbanipal reiterated this attention and respect given to the words of the prophets in his "Hymn to the Ištars of Nineveh and Arbail":

> A word from their lips is blazing fire! Their utterances are valid forever ...
> In their pure mouths [voic]ed the endurance of my throne.[81]

And it was not beneath the dignity of prominent members of Esarhaddon and Aššurbanipal's scholarly inner circle to give additional weight to their advice by directly quoting a prophecy.[82]

The prophecies which have survived give the impression that an important role of the prophet and thus the message from the goddess was to reassure, to nurture, to console, to comfort and to give confidence to the king or the king's mother or the crown prince. Since the known prophecies are mainly addressed to either Esarhaddon or Aššurbanipal, both of whom were younger sons chosen to be the heir to the throne, it is no wonder that heavenly help would either be solicited or at the very least be greatly appreciated. Who better to verify and substantiate the choice of successor and a successful reign than a powerful and capable goddess who was thought to be able to persuade the council of gods of the validity of her position?

The imagery in the prophecies suggests that the relationship between the goddess and the king was a personal one and may have extended back to when the king was a child. The goddess may refer to herself as being the parent or the nurse of this child which suggests that the royal princes may have been raised in the temples of Ištar. In one instance Ištar of Arbail told Esarhaddon,

---

[79] Two of these prophets have both feminine and masculine references which have caused considerable confusion. The name Bayâ has a feminine determinative before the name but she is referred to as a "son" of Arbail. The name Ilussa-amur also has a feminine determinative but the gentilic adjective is in the masculine gender (Parpola 1997: IL-L). There exists the possibility that these two prophets were men turned into women or women made to behave like men, a metamorphosis that Ištar was apparently capable of implementing. But there is no hard evidence to suggest that these two prophets were transgender in any of its manifestations (i.e. transsexuals or transvestites); therefore, in this study they are regarded as females.

[80] Parpola 1997: LXVIII, SAA X 109, Nissinen 1998: 89 (5.2).

[81] SAA III 3.

[82] Bel-ušezib, an astrologer, quotes a prophecy of Bel (SAA X 111) and Nabû-nadin-šumi, the chief exorcist, quotes a prophecy of Ištar of Nineveh and Ištar of Arbail, in both cases to clinch a position (SAA X 284).

"When you were small, I took you to me."[83] In another instance through the prophet Sinqiša-amur she told him, "I raised you between my wings."[84] Aššurbanipal was told by the prophet Mullissu-kabtat who quotes Mullissu:

> You whose mother is Mullissu, have no fear. You whose nurse is the Lady of Arbail, have no fear. I will carry you on my hip like a nurse, I will put you between my breasts (like) a pomegranate. At night I will stay awake and guard you; in the daytime I will give you milk … my calf, whom I (have) rear(ed).[85]

This reoccurring image of the goddess who held the child-king to her breast, wrapped her arms around the child to protect him and crooned comforting words to him could very likely mean these occasions literally had taken place. The god Nabû told Aššurbanipal:

> You were a child, Aššurbanipal, when I left you with the Queen of Nineveh; you were a baby, Aššurbanipal when you sat in the lap of the Queen of Nineveh.[86]

Aššurbanipal even called himself the "product of Emašmaš and Egašankalamma," the temples of Ištar of Nineveh and Ištar of Arbail. He claimed "I knew no father and mother. I grew up in the lap of my goddess."[87]

Parpola and Nissinen both believe that the mother-child image was not just meant metaphorically.[88] They believe that Assyrian princes were entrusted to the temples of Ištar "almost certainly to be suckled and nursed by hierodules who impersonated the motherly aspects of the Goddess."[89]

Another important subject in the prophecies was the protection of the king. Phrases such as "have no fear" and "I will keep you safe" were frequently used for reassurance. The goddess often adamantly declared she would protect the king by putting both the earth and the heavens in order. If the gods were troublesome, she would "reconcile the angry gods with Assyria." If the king's enemies were troublesome, she would "deliver (them) up … for slaughter" or put them "in neckstocks" or "shed (their) blood."[90] More specifically, Aššurbanipal was reassured by Queen Mullissu that she would "finish the land of Gomer like (she finished) Elam" and that Egypt would be conquered as well.[91]

---

[83] SAA IX 1.4.

[84] SAA IX 2.5.

[85] SAA IX 7.

[86] SAA III 13.

[87] SAA III 3.

[88] Othmar Keel and Martti Nissinen have noted that this imagery was not limited to Neo-Assyrian prophecy but well attested all over the Ancient Near East (Parpola 1997: XXXVI).

[89] Nissinen 2000: 104, Parpola 1997: XXXIX. Parpola also cites many examples of the use of the word *piqittu*, which he says should be defined as "a charge associated with a god or a court, specifically an infant member of the royal family." The letters which mention "the *piqittu* of the Queen of Cults" (certainly an Ištar figure) refer to him as being very well or as being feverish because he was teething, etc., and on occasion the king was reassured that he would one day "lift his grandchildren in his lap" (Parpola 1983: 123).

[90] SAA IX 1.2:30-35, 2.5:21-25.

[91] SAA IX 7.

However the goddess appears to have recognized that the enemy could be within or without Assyria. Ištar of Arbail told Esarhaddon she would "search out the disloyal ones and put them into the hands of the king" and that she would "cut the conspiring weasels and shrews to pieces before his feet."[92] With these statements she indicated that she was on his side in the succession controversy.

Prophets and prophecies were also directly involved in important rituals concerning the person of the king. There is evidence which indicates that prophecies played an important part in the coronation of Esarhaddon and were probably proclaimed by a prophet throughout the ceremony.[93] The same appears to be true regarding the coronation rituals of the substitute king.

In the Nineveh royal archives there was a letter addressed to Esarhaddon regarding a particularly controversial substitute king ritual (SAA X 352). In the month of Tebet in 671 there was a total lunar eclipse. Because Esarhaddon was king of both Assyria and Babylonia the substitute king was first enthroned in Nineveh and then a week later in the city of Akkad in Babylonia. Unlike other times when someone of no social value (a prisoner of war, a criminal, an idiot) was chosen to be the substitute king, this time Damqî, the son of an important Babylonian official, was chosen. Mar-Issar, the representative of Esarhaddon in Babylonia, wrote the king a letter and reported that the enthronement of the substitute king, his death and that of his queen and the accompanying rituals had taken place. In this letter he also mentioned that a prophet (an unnamed woman) had prophesized to Damqî while he was still alive: "You will take over the kingship."[94] Although not specifically stated in the letter, the prophecy related by the woman probably came from Ištar of Akkad. Mar-Issar quoted this prophecy because it provided additional justification for the unusual choice of Damqî and emphasized that his kingship had divine sanction. Clearly this choice of a substitute king had been heavily criticized and had also unnerved the general public and Mar-Issar was relating all of these events to the king and reassuring him that all was fine in Babylonia.

In the same letter, Mar-Issar also mentioned that the prophet prophesied a second time, this time to the assembly of the country: "I have revealed the thieving polecat of my lord, and placed (him) in your hands."[95] The assembly was most likely a part of the substitute king ritual, but a separate occasion from the one when the first prophecy was delivered. What seems significant is that a prophet was actively involved in the substitute king ritual and in this

---

[92] SAA IX 2.4, 1.7.

[93] Parpola feels that "The Covenant Tablet of Aššur" (SAA IX 3) gives an indication of this. It records prophecies from Aššur and Ištar of Arbail which were delivered publicly to Esarhaddon on a special occasion that took place on the grounds of Aššur's Ešarra Temple in Assur. Various activities were mentioned including a procession led by the king and a ritual banquet during which these "oracles of well-being" (šulmu) were delivered. Later the tablet was left on display at the temple (Parpola 1997: LXIV).

[94] SAA X 352.

[95] Nissinen 1998: 68 (4.1).

instance the prophet was a woman. Unfortunately this letter is the only reference to a prophet participating in this ritual, therefore it may or may not have been common practice.

Another letter (SAA XIII 37) appears to refer to the substitute king ritual, possibly the exact same one as in the above-mentioned letter (SAA X 352). In this case Adad-ahu-iddina, a temple administrator, wrote to Esarhaddon that the prophet Mullissu-abu-uṣri had taken the king's clothes to Akkad and wanted the king's throne as well. He had refused to give the throne to her and instead wrote to the king asking for his instructions. Because the king's throne was kept at the Ešarra Temple in Assur and this was also where Esarhaddon was crowned, it is very conceivable that Adad-ahu-iddina was a temple administrator in Assur. What seems significant with regard to this letter is that (1) it was to Akkad that the prophet was going with the king's clothes, presumably for someone else to wear; (2) in order for the substitute king to truly become the king he must have the real king's clothing and royal paraphernalia;[96] and (3) the temple administrator was doubtful or suspicious enough of the prophet to query the divine message regarding the transport of the throne to Akkad.

Assyrian records indicate that during stressful and uncertain times the prophets, along with the scholars, were much in demand. One such time was in the chaotic period when Esarhaddon's accession to the throne of Assyria was in doubt. He was forced to leave Nineveh and go into exile. His father, Sennacherib, was murdered by his other sons who then rose up against Esarhaddon with a military force. During this period his mother Naqia consulted with various divinatory practitioners resorting to extispicy, astrology and prophecy as she sought favorable signs regarding her son's safety and succession. Among those consulted was the female prophet Ahat-abiša from Arbail. Speaking for Ištar of Arbail, the prophet reassured Naqia and Esarhaddon that although he was currently out roaming the steppe, the kingdom and the power would most definitely be his.[97] The goddess even referred to Esarhaddon as 'king,' which undoubtedly was meant to reassure Naqia and Esarhaddon that he was the chosen heir. Issar-beli-da"ini, a votary of the king, also reassured Naqia and Esarhaddon telling them the goddess would "cut the conspiring weasels and shrews to pieces before his feet."[98] In other words, the rightful order concerning the succession would occur and the conspirators would be cut down before Esarhaddon. Sinqiša-amur of Arbail also assured Esarhaddon that Ištar of Arbail would deliver up his enemy and keep him safe in his "Palace of Succession."[99] Finally Remutti-Allati from Dara-ahuya, a town in the mountains, told Esarhaddon that both

---

[96] In his discussion of this letter, Nissinen mentions another letter (SAA X 189) which itemized the royal paraphernalia necessary for the substitute king ritual: the clothes of the king, the garments for the statue, the necklace [of go]ld, the scepter and the throne (Nissinen 1998: 80).

[97] SAA IX 1.8.

[98] SAA IX 1.7.

[99] SAA IX 1.2.

the goddess and Arbail rejoiced with him.[100] As prophesied, Esarhaddon was victorious and most likely none rejoiced more than Ištar of Arbail and her prophets who had encouraged and supported his kingship.

At two later times in his reign when Esarhaddon recounted these perilous times and described these evil events, he confirmed the important participation of the prophets. In the *Assur A* inscription, composed in 679 soon after his ascension to the throne, he stated very clearly, "Messages of prophets concerning the establishment of the foundation of my sacerdotal throne until far-off days were constantly and regularly conveyed to me."[101] In 673/2, much later in his reign, Esarhaddon again acknowledged the importance of prophecy during that trying period. In the *Nineveh A* inscription he reiterated once more, "Oracles of prophets, messages of the gods and Goddess, were constantly sent to me and they encouraged my heart."[102]

But these two brief mentions of prophecy are the only ones in the extensive inscriptions of Esarhaddon. This lack of attention to prophecy might indicate its lower status and minimal importance among the oracular arts, but it turns out that in contrast to all earlier Assyrian kings, Esarhaddon was the only one who even mentioned prophecy in his inscriptions at all. This would seem to mean that prophecy had a higher standing during his rule than it had had before. And the fact that these passages mentioning prophecy coincide very nicely with extant prophecies (in Esarhaddon's collections) cannot be accidental according to Parpola and Nissinen. They feel it very likely that the writers of the inscriptions had access to the collections of prophecies spoken at the time of the civil war and Esarhaddon's rise to power.[103]

Conclusion

The methods of deity-human communications in Mesopotamia had long included prophecy and prophets. Within the age-old religious tradition of prophecy there had always been a place for female prophets. In Assyria there were many known women functioning as prophets in the temples, especially the Egašankalamma, Ištar's temple in Arbail. This temple was a very active one and became so well known that it was not uncommon for royalty to travel there and receive prophecies from the prophets of Ištar of Arbail.

Information on prophets and prophecy during the Neo-Assyrian period comes entirely from the reigns of Esarhaddon and Aššurbanipal. These two kings made collections of important prophecies for their royal archives. The earliest collection consisted of prophecies which went back to the period of time when Esarhaddon's accession to the throne was very much in doubt. Possibly it was because the prophets of Ištar relayed messages from the goddess in full support of his candidacy that Esarhaddon, from the beginning

[100] SAA IX 1.3.
[101] Nissinen 1998: 14 (2.1).
[102] *Ibid.*
[103] Parpola 1997: LXIX, Nissinen 1998: 30-31.

of his reign, allowed prophets to have access to his person through royal audiences. The presence of female prophets in these audiences is well documented.

While the social position of prophets appears to have been lower than that of other diviners (especially the inner circle of scholars close to the king) prophets were certainly accorded respect and their prophecies were actively sought by members of the royal family. But was it because of this lower social status or because rigorous training was not required that women had such easy access to this profession/activity? At present this question is unanswerable.

There is no evidence to suggest that there was any differentiation made between female and male prophets. Seemingly, a prophet was a prophet. The goddess Ištar was comfortable speaking through women mediums and this certainly did not lesson the impact of the message. The messages consistently expressed support for the crown prince or king and protection against his enemies. The tone of the messages was always nurturing and loving, sometimes expressed quite personally by the goddess.

In many cases the names of the female prophets are known and occasionally even some of their responsibilities. Interestingly there are also hints of them coming up against what might be termed an "old boys" network. Documents exist which indicate that temple administrators attempted to thwart these women from fulfilling their responsibilities and tasks and/or questioned their credibility.

Of course there is much that is not known about these female prophets. For instance, did they live full-time in the temples? Were they married or were they required to be celibate? Were they taken care of in old age? Were they respected or ostracized when beyond the bounds of the temple community? Were they initially encouraged or discouraged in developing the facility of speaking for the deity?

What is noticeable is that these women were able to find a niche for themselves outside of the family structure. They had a paying job and functions to fulfill. They were not sheltered or hidden away in the temple grounds. They had a public persona even to the extent of appearing before the king of Assyria, participating in important public rituals, i.e., coronations, traveling for the state and being entrusted with important temple and governmental tasks.

Female prophets in Assyria played an active role in established, respected and powerful institutions, especially the Cult of Ištar. Their names and their words were recorded on clay and placed in the royal archives to be remembered and referred to. At home and abroad, from the lowest echelon of society to the highest, the voices of these prophets were heard and acknowledged.

CHAPTER II

MUSICAL WOMEN

Both textual evidence and visual representations exist in Assyrian documents and art to show that women provided music in the temples and in the palaces. Female musicians were mentioned in the royal annals, lists, hymns, ritual instructions and administrative documents. The logogram MÍ.NAR, Akkadian *nārtu* was used to denote a female musician whether an instrumentalist or a singer. On palace reliefs and ivory carvings female musicians were depicted playing music at victory celebrations, banquets and religious events.

The musical instruments played by female musicians were typical of those mentioned in the texts and those found in the art of the first millennium BCE. They might be plucked, blown into, struck of shaken to produce a musical sound. In order to differentiate musical instruments from each other, modern musicologists classify them according to how the sound is produced.[1] Chordophones are instruments with strings which are plucked or bowed or strummed. Examples in the Neo-Assyrian world would be harps, lyres, lutes and zithers. Aerophones are instruments which produce sound when air is blown through the instrument, such as pipes, flutes and trumpets. Membranophones produce a sound when a skin or hide stretched over a frame is struck. Examples would be drums of various shapes: frame, conical, kettle and cylinder. Idiophones produce a sound if beaten or shaken, such as cymbals, clappers and rattles. Images of female musicians performing on all four types of musical instruments are known.

It is worth noting that foreign female musicians dominate both the written documents and the works of art. Their exotic appearance and the exotic musical sounds their instruments made were highly prized by the Assyrians. The texts almost always mention their place of origin and the visual depictions of these female musicians clearly differentiate them from the Assyrians. There are only two visual examples of female musicians in palace relief scenes in which the musicians appear to be Assyrian women.[2]

---

[1] Sachs 1940.

[2] It seems highly probable that royal and upper-class women were given musical training. In earlier periods of Mesopotamian history there are examples of kings advocating musical training for princesses (Šamši-Adad) and even evidence of a musical academy attended by princesses (Kassite Letters) (Harris 1990: 10 n. 40).

Textual Evidence

Textual references pertaining to female musicians heavily emphasized foreign women, not Assyrian women. Two Assyrian kings, Aššurnaṣirpal II and Sennacherib, proudly mentioned in their royal inscriptions that female musicians were received as tribute from foreign rulers. Aššurnaṣirpal listed 10 female musicians collected from the royal city of Kunulua ruled by Lubarna, the Patinu. In order to save his own life Lubarna gave as tribute to Aššurnaṣirpal: 20 talents of silver, one talent of gold, 1,000 oxen, 10,000 sheep, his brother's daughter with her rich dowry, 10 female musicians and many other valuable objects.[3] As a result of these gifts Lubarna was shown great mercy by Aššurnaṣirpal. Female musicians were also listed on the Rassam Obelisk along with linen garments and male servants as part of unidentified tribute received by Aššurnaṣirpal.[4]

The Assyrian king Sennacherib twice mentioned the acquisition of female musicians in his royal inscriptions. After defeating Merodach-baladan of Babylon in his first campaign, Sennacherib reveals that he joyfully entered the Babylonian king's palace and took valuable objects from his treasure house as well as his palace women, his courtiers, his male and female musicians, his artisans and his servants. In a later campaign Sennacherib defeated Hezekiah of Judah and received extensive tribute from him. Hezekiah sent to Nineveh 30 talents of gold, 800 talents of silver and all kinds of treasure from his palace including his daughters, his palace women and his male and female musicians.[5]

The fact that two Assyrian kings specifically included female musicians on lists displayed publicly illustrates that they were held in high regard. That these women were listed with extremely valuable items and along side royal women and palace personnel is another indication of their status and importance. It is also worth noting that in both campaign accounts Sennacherib carefully distinguished the female musicians from the male musicians.[6]

Numerous female musicians were included on palace lists of female personnel. On one such list (ADD 827+914) amidst female scribes, barbers, bakers and stone-borers, a total of 61 female musicians were recorded. Of these 61, three were Aramean women, 11 were Hittite women, 13 were Tyrian

---

[3] RIMA 2 A.O.101.1 iii 72-76IMA 2{r};A.O.101.1 iii 72-76{r}. Also, The Final Edition of the Annals: 477 (Luckenbill 1927 I: 165).

[4] RIMA 2 A.O.101.71IMA 2{r};A.O.101.71{r}. Reade has suggested that these female musicians may likely be the same ones received by Aššurnaṣirpal from Patinu even though the name of the tributary is missing on the obelisk (Reade 1980: 18-19).

[5] The Oriental Institute Prism Inscription: The Final Edition of the Annals: Col. I 32-33, Col. II 46-47 (Luckenbill 1924: 24, 34). Also, The Final Edition of the Annals: 234 (Luckenbill 1927 II: 116); The Account of the First Campaign: 260 (Luckenbill 1927 II: 131); Records Written After the Sixth Campaign: 312 (Luckenbill 1927 II: 143).

[6] In his study of Assyrian music and musicians, Jack Cheng states that "The clear identification of female musicians when a more ambiguous plural could have sufficed is a conscious choice that reflects the significance and symbolic importance of female musicians" (Cheng 2001: 56).

women and nine were Kassite women. On another list (828) 10 female musicians were noted.[7]

Among the archival materials of the Neo-Assyrian state are a group of texts called the Nimrud Wine Lists. Found in three separate rooms at Fort Shalmaneser (the *ekal māšerti*) in Kalhu[8] they listed the specific allotments of wine disbursed to various groups and classes of people in the royal household, beginning with the queen. In some cases personal names were given, in other cases professional titles and for foreigners often only place names. Many foreigners clearly visited and/or lived at court and as many as 26 different groups of foreigners were mentioned in the wine lists.[9] Among the foreigners were two groups of female musicians.

The Nimrud Wine Lists were originally thought to date from 791-799, spanning portions of the reigns of Adad-nerari III and Shalmaneser IV.[10] Subsequently the dates have been revised to 792-774[11] and then expanded to include most of the eighth century.[12] All the texts (with one exception) were dated to the beginning of the Mesopotamian solar year (either the month of Addaru or Nisannu). Kinnier Wilson feels the lists represented the *per diem* allotments of wine for a 10 day period of time,[13] while Parpola believes the lists represented the daily allotments for a one year period.[14] Fales, however, demonstrates that the quantities of wine mentioned in the NWL were (1) far too great for storage in the palace wine cellars (i.e., 1095 liters per day and 400,000 liters per year) and (2) were an unrealistic amount for yearly Assyrian consumption.[15] Instead the most likely explanation is that the NWL indicated the wine allotments for the personnel of the court, army and administration in Kalhu for an important ceremonial occasion.[16] Wine, it seems, was a commodity that denoted rank and status and was primarily for the use of the members of the higher echelons of State.[17]

---

[7] SAA VII 24, 26.

[8] In 1957, 11 tablets were found in the wine magazine SW6. In 1961, 46 tablets and fragments were found in NE48 and NE49 (Kinnier Wilson 1972: 1).

[9] These groups "... range from Palestine through Syria, Anatolia and Iran: Gutians, Elamites, Arameans, men of Sumaria, Egyptians, Kushites, Medes and Mannaeans figure among them ..." (M. Mallowan *apud* Kinnier Wilson 1972: xi).

[10] Kinnier Wilson 1972: 2.

[11] Parpola 1976: 170.

[12] Dalley and Postgate 1984: 24.

[13] Kinnier Wilson 1972: 72.

[14] Parpola 1976: 171

[15] The quantity of wine "exceeds *by twenty-five* times the estimated capacity of one of the few discovered wine cellars...SW6" and it would certainly have put the Assyrians "on an equal footing with the (non-rationed) wine-drinking habits of the modern Italians and French" (Fales 1994: 369).

[16] Fales 1994: 370.

[17] Stronach 1996: 177, Fales 1994: 369. Stronach (1996: 177) adds, "Indeed ... there are many reasons to think that the possession of wine, and the disbursement of wine, each came to be counted as telling elements in the expression of royal authority, not only in Assyria but in other adjacent and especially upland areas of the rest of the Near East."

In the NWL the quantities of wine allotted to the various groups of people varied considerably. The measurements of *qû, sūtu* and *homer* were used but their exact quantities cannot be stated with absolute certainty. Kinnier Wilson believes the table for liquid measures works out to be: 10 cups = 1 *qû*, 10 *qû* = 1 *sūtu*, 10 *sūtu* = 1 *homer* and estimates that the *qû* was the equivalent of about 1.84 or 1.83 liters.[18]

In the NWL there were two groups of female musicians mentioned in two different lists. In ND 10047 and in ND 10054 each group of female musicians was allotted 6½ *qû* or 5½ *qû* of wine. On ND 10047 it is thought that one group was from Hatti and the other group was from Arpad. On ND 10054 it is not possible to determine where the first group of female musicians was from but the second group was definitely from Arpad. Their wine allotments of 6½ *qû* and 5½ *qû* are rather unusual. Kinnier Wilson remarks that these amounts lack symmetry but somehow must be significant.[19] If, as he suggests, a standard wine portion was ⅒ *qû* then this could mean that there were as many as 120 female musicians in the royal household.

The NWL are unique documents which reveal the complexities of the Neo-Assyrian state record-keeping. They point to an extremely large royal household that is estimated to number as many as 6,000 people. The lists are important because they indicate which household members received wine and also what quantity they received. They hint at the social structure (i.e., the queen comes first) and who were the most privileged. To even be included on these lists seems significant. And this is precisely the situation of the female musicians: they were listed separately and received their allotment of twelve *qû* of wine on these festive occasions.

In Assyrian temples, the many references to music indicate that female musicians performed in this venue regularly. Musicians both sang and played instruments such as "the lyre, the small harp, the clapper, the flute, the oboe, the long (pipes)."[20] In a fragmentary list of female temple staff a female musician is listed next to female stewards.[21] On many occasions the cultic officiants themselves made the music. In the "Hymn to the City of Arbail" while various instruments were tuned, the songs of the *kulmašitu* were performed.[22] In KAR 154 a complicated ritual associated with the Adad Temple of Assur is described. Of primary importance in performing this ritual were the *qadištu*s who sang the *inhu*-song.[23]

Visual Evidence

Pictorial examples of female musicians have been found on stone reliefs in Assyrian royal palaces and on decorative ivory objects. The female musicians

---

[18] Kinnier Wilson 1972: 117 & 114.

[19] Kinnier Wilson 1972: 120.

[20] SAA III 4.

[21] SAA XI 152.

[22] SAA III 8.

[23] Menzel 1981 II: T2-T4.

typically performed in groups, sometimes mixed and sometimes all women. These groups performed at victory celebrations, entertained at banquets and participated in religious rituals.

There are three examples of female musicians playing music in palace relief scenes. In two examples female musicians participated in victory celebrations and in the third they were part of a royal/religious procession between palace and temple. In all three instances the relief scenes date to the reigns of two later Assyrian kings, Sennacherib (704-681) and Aššurbanipal (668-631).[24] These reliefs potentially could have been viewed by anyone visiting or living in the palace.

There are six examples of female musicians playing musical instruments on ivory carvings. The ivories have been dated to the ninth, eighth and seventh centuries. While the majority of the ivories were carved by foreign craftsmen in foreign styles, it is not known whether they were carved within Assyria or in a foreign land. These ivories would have constituted valuable personal items in the homes of the Assyrian elite. They were either decorative plaques on furniture or small containers called pyxides.

The garden musicians – stone relief

In a large room in the west corner of the North Palace in Nineveh, William Loftus, excavating in 1854, discovered many wall-relief fragments strewn about in a fashion suggesting to him that they had fallen from an upper chamber. Among these fragments was the garden scene of Aššurbanipal and his queen. Today this scene exists in a fragmentary state. While many of the relief fragments have survived, some are now lost. Fortunately William Boutcher's original drawings have survived. Together the stone fragments and the drawings indicate that an ensemble of female musicians approached the king and queen from the left (Fig. 1 [next page]).

The scene appears to be set in a garden at the queen's residence as all the attendants are women. A procession of food-bearers, fan-bearers and musicians approaches the king and queen. The existing relief fragments and Boutcher's field drawings together reveal that there were at least seven women instrumentalists serenading the king and queen in the garden: four harpists, one lute player, one drummer and one piper.[25] The musicians, viewed in profile, play their instruments while sedately strolling toward the royal couple. The harpists' two hands pluck the strings, the double pipes are in the mouth of the piper, both of the drummer's hands are positioned for beating the drum while the lute player holds the lute with one hand and with the other strums or plucks the strings.

---

[24] The eighth- and seventh-century palace decorations were much more secular with a focus on actual events. In the ninth century, palace decorations tended to focus on religious subjects and in a more general way on the king.

[25] Only part of the harp of the leading harpist but not the harpist herself is visible in Boutcher's drawing of the musicians.

Fig. 1 Drawing of a relief of a procession of musicians in a garden scene, Room S, North Palace, Nineveh (BM Or. Dr., V 46, courtesy Trustees of The British Museum)

The harpist leads the group of musicians into the presence of the royal couple. The harp she carries is a large triangular-shaped vertical harp. It is tucked under her left arm and thus only partially visible. While 12 strings can be seen it is generally thought that Assyrian vertical harps had 17 or 18 strings.[26] The harpist plucks the strings with the bare fingers of both hands as she walks along in the procession. The right hand is placed low on the strings and close to the horizontal arm of the harp, most likely to help steady it. The left hand, which can be seen through the strings, plucks them higher up and closer to the sounding box. Rimmer believes it is entirely possible that because one hand was prominent and mobile, and the other subsidiary and less mobile the sound produced by the vertical harp would have been polyphony in its true sense of 'several soundingness.'[27]

The sounding box forms the upper arm and projects upward at an angle in front of the harpist. One edge is straight and the other curved. The sound holes on the box are clearly visible. One end of the strings is attached to the sounding box which is the longest arm of the instrument. The other end of the strings winds around the shorter horizontal arm; however, the ends are allowed to fall beneath the lower arm and thereby provide a decorative but uniform fringe. The harp is large: the highest end of the sounding box is well above the head of the harpist, the lower arm of the instrument is horizontal at her waist and the lower ends of the strings are at the level of her knees.

---

[26] Rimmer 1969: 32. Cheng 2001: 23 & n. 11.

[27] Rimmer 1969: 33.

The harpist is followed by a drummer. The small conical drum the woman carries looks light and portable. The drum is suspended by a shoulder strap and hangs at the waist of the woman rather like a snare drum in a modern marching band. However, in this example the drum is not struck with drum sticks but with both of the woman's hands which are raised and poised to do so. What looks to be a decorative design near the top of the frame are probably the nail heads which attach the skin or hide to the frame of the drum. The conical shape of this drum is unique in Neo-Assyrian art.

The pair of harpists who follow the drummer are in turn followed by the lute player. She holds the lute at a 45 degree angle to play. Although not visible in the drawing, there would have been two or three strings stretched along the neck and across the resonator. The lute has a long thick neck and a small round bulbous resonator.[28] Although the instrument could be strummed or plucked with the fingers or a plectrum, in this picture the lute player appears to be strumming the lute with her fingers.

The musician playing the double pipes follows the lute player. The pipes project horizontally from the mouth of the piper. The two pipes are not held parallel but divergent, appear to be of equal length and are quite short. The left hand of the piper on one pipe and the right hand on the other pipe cover (unseen) finger-holes which would produce the pitch of the tone as the pipes are blown.[29]

The musicians, like all of the other women who attend the royal couple, are dressed in imitation of the queen. Their hairstyle is essentially the same as hers: the hair is wavy on the top of the head, falls behind the ears, covers the nape of the neck and rests on the shoulders. Each woman wears a plain wide headband in contrast to the mural crown worn by the queen. The dress of each musician has a roll-collar at the neck, three-quarter-length sleeves with decorative cuffs and is ankle-length. A shawl which is draped over the dress has a visible fringe. The fabrics of the dress and shawl are noticeably plain while those of the queen are intricately patterned. Each woman wears foot coverings. And each woman wears elaborate earrings and bracelets. The style of the clothing, the covering of the feet and particularly the beautiful jewellery help define the social status of the women who personally attend the queen.

The relief fragments and the drawing hint at an unusual arrangement of figures in this scene. All attending figures stand on the same ground line, are shown in profile, are approximately the same size and of course face the royal couple. However, those figures closest to the queen and king are paired and overlap each other in such a way that one figure is only partially visible. All

---

[28] Although the shape of the lute can vary considerably, the small round body is thought to be typically Mesopotamian (Collon and Kilmer 1980: 14).

[29] The two silver pipes from the Royal Cemetery of Ur (c. 2600 BCE), although badly damaged, look to be of equal length. Interestingly, one pipe has four finger-holes and the other only one finger-hole indicating that the tuning of each pipe would have been different. Rimmer suggests it is possible that the melody might have been produced by the pipe with four finger-holes while the one-holed pipe might have functioned as the drone pipe with only a one note change (Rimmer 1969: 35-36).

the remaining attendants are shown in their entirety but the farther away they are from royalty, the more distinct they are as individual figures. Because the musicians follow behind the fan-bearers and food-bearers, there is considerable space between each one. Each musician is thus depicted as a soloist and as a member of the musical ensemble. It seems probable that their instrumental music could have been heard in the same way.

In this relief scene the musicians are present to entertain the queen and the king as they enjoy a drink and each other's company in the garden. The musicians add to the ambience by creating beautiful sounds. It is a unique scene in many respects: it is the only known palace relief scene depicting an Assyrian queen; it is the only relief scene thought to be set in the queen's residential gardens and it is one of only two surviving examples of female musicians who look to be Assyrian and not foreign.

The Elamite musicians – stone relief

Huge slabs of fossiliferous limestone found by Austen Henry Layard in 1850 in Room XXXIII of the Southwest Palace at Nineveh portray one of the campaigns of Aššurbanipal against the Elamites.[30] Outside the city walls of Madaktu in Elam a contingent of Elamite citizens approaches the victorious Assyrian army with male and female musicians playing instruments and with women and children singing and clapping (Fig. 2).

Fig. 2 Relief of a procession of Elamite musicians, Room XXXIII, Southwest Palace, Nineveh (BM 124802, courtesy Trustees of The British Museum)

Room XXXIII was in the southwest wing of the Southwest Palace. It was a hall or vestibule which appeared to open off a terrace platform on one side and led into Room XXX on the other side. Given the richness of the decoration and the formal plan of the southwest wing, it was evidently of considerable importance. Not only were reliefs from the reign of Aššurbanipal found in this area but also a major part of his library.[31]

---

[30] The exact date of Aššurbanipal's war against Teumman and the Elamites is uncertain but it would have occurred between years 663 and 653 (Curtis and Reade 1995: 77).

[31] Barnett, Bleibtreu and Turner 1998 I: 27-28.

Military, political and geographical information regarding this scene is clarified by three epigraphs on Slabs 5 and 6. A lengthy epigraph identifies Aššurbanipal, "the king of the world, the king of Assyria," who with the encouragement of Aššur and Ištar had conquered and humiliated his enemies in Urartu and Elam.[32] Another epigraph identifies Ummanigash, the Elamite fugitive, who was brought by the Assyrians to Susa and Madaktu. He was set on the throne of Teumman by Aššurbanipal after Teumman had been defeated. The city depicted on slab 6 is clearly labeled "Madaktu," an Elamite city thought to be approximately 30 kilometers to the northwest of Susa.[33]

Amidst the arrival of the conquering Assyrian army Elamite musicians add their homage. Outside of the city walls of Madaktu and beside the Ulai River which is crammed with dead bodies and discarded military equipment, Elamite warriors bow and scrape before the Assyrian cavalry and chariotry. Behind them the Elamite musicians play instruments, dance and sing. First in the musical procession are five male musicians, then six female musicians and at the end are six women and nine children who look to be either clapping rhythmically or applauding. One of the women with her hand to her throat appears to be either singing or making some sort of expressive sound. It is impossible to determine if it might be joyful or mournful.

As in the Aššurbanipal garden relief scene the leading musicians of both the female and male instrumental groups play a vertical harp. Noticeably the vertical harps far outnumber all the other musical instruments. The long history of the vertical harp in the ancient Near East certainly attests to its popularity.[34]

The vertical harps of the female and male musicians look essentially identical to each other and to the Assyrian vertical harps depicted in other scenes. The only visible difference is decorative. The strings or tassels which hang from the lower horizontal arm differ depending on whether the harp is played by a man or woman. The tassels on the harps played by men have four knots or beads at the end. The women play harps with tassels knotted or beaded from the top to the bottom. The one exception is the harp played by the last woman which has undecorated strings.

Of the 11 musical instruments being played in this procession, seven are vertical harps, two are divergent double pipes, one a cylindrical drum and one a horizontal harp.[35] The musical instruments played by the female musicians

---

[32] Russell 1999: 176-178.

[33] Parpola and Porter 2001: map 16.

[34] Votive plaques from Khafaji, Ešnunna and Ur that depict vertical harps date to the early second millennium (Rimmer 1969: 21 and Pl. Va). A Middle Assyrian ivory comb from Assur which shows a woman playing a vertical harp in a ceremonial procession dates to the late fourteenth century (Harper *et al.* 1995: 85).

[35] The horizontal harp in the Elamite procession has elicited much comment and controversy because the relief was already damaged when found by Layard and further damaged in transit to The British Museum in London. The accuracy of the extensive restorations has since been questioned (see Mitchell 1980: 33-36, Pls. 14-25). The Elamite horizontal harp was shaped and decorated differently than its contemporary in Assyria and was depicted as having ten strings instead of the seven or nine strings shown on an Assyrian instrument. Both Assyrian and Elamite horizontal harps were struck or plucked with a stick or plectrum and only male musicians were ever depicted playing them (Cheng 2001: 24-26, 65).

are the vertical harps, the double pipes and the drum. An almost identical combination of instrumentalists can be found in the Aššurbanipal garden scene where Assyrian female musicians play for the queen and king.

Following the female instrumentalists is a group of six women and nine children. With the one exception 14 of these figures have their hands positioned together in a way which indicates that they are clapping or applauding. As part of the procession they are clearly participating either in the music or the act of welcoming or acknowledging the victors. Although it has been has suggested that these women and children are dancers[36] there is no visual evidence to support this idea. The posture of their bodies and the fact that both feet are firmly on the ground negate this suggestion.

The woman with her hand to her throat however presents a puzzle. Is she producing a sound or not? Rimmer thinks she could be producing a form of "wordless vocalize" by gently beating on her throat to produce a slow tremolo. This sound would produce a pathetic effect entirely appropriate to the circumstances.[37] Cheng suggest "she could just as easily be wounded or making a gesture which is no longer understood."[38] But she is in the midst of the Elamites who are engaged in producing musical and rhythmic sounds. In front of her instrumentalists are playing music, around her women and children are clapping their hands, therefore it stands to reason that she too is an active participant in the musical program.

Although there is not visual evidence that the women and children at the end of the procession are dancers, a case can be made that at least three male musicians are engaged in some sort of dance-step. Two of the vertical harpists and the horizontal harpist are presented quite differently than the other musicians. For one thing they are taking much larger steps. Each has his right leg thrust forward and lifted high in the air with a bent knee. Much more energy is expended with these movements than in ordinary marching and as a result the hems of their skirts are flung up near their right knees.[39] Frankfort has suggested that the men "are pervaded by the rhythm of their music and fall into a dance-step."[40] It certainly seems plausible that the ensemble of musicians might play music and do a dance-step as part of their performance.

Because female and male musicians perform together at the same event, it is important to determine if gender specific details do in fact distinguish one group of musicians from the other. The five musicians in the front are taller, bearded (with one possible exception), flat-chested and wear a different style attire than the six musicians who follow. The latter group of musicians is noticeably shorter and, where not obscured from view by their instruments, have pronounced breasts. Interestingly the hairstyles of all the instrumentalists are identical in that they all have short curls which reach the nape of the

---

[36] Rimmer 1969: 36-37.

[37] Rimmer 1969: 37.

[38] Cheng 2001: 45 n. 88.

[39] If this is the case then the raised hem would not be an implied feminization of the man as Cheng (2001: 62) has suggested.

[40] Frankfort 1970: 181.

neck and which are held in place by a headband which ties at the back of the head.

The clothing of the second group is different. The neck lines are higher and have decorated collars or the women are wearing necklaces. Both groups wear long tunics which are belted but the belts of the women are a different style than those of the men. The women's elbow-length sleeves have a stripe which runs from the shoulder to the cuff which is also striped. There is considerably less musculature delineated on the arms of the group of women. The hems of their skirts are slightly higher in the front but ankle length in the back. The entire procession is marching barefoot.

The clapping and singing women and children at the end of the procession wear similar attire to the women instrumentalists although the skirt lengths of the children are considerably shorter. The hems of their skirts are above the knees in the front and mid-calf in the back. Although there is uniformity in the hairstyles of the female and male instrumentalists the same is not true for the last six women. Their hairstyles seem to illustrate more individuality and personal preference. Only one woman has a hairstyle similar to the instrumentalists. One woman has very short cropped hair and could even be wearing a hair net. Three women have longer hair that touches their shoulders. One woman has extremely long hair that is worn up in a knot at the back of the head. Only one of the women wears a headband.

The uniform appearance of the female and male instrumentalists points to the possibility of an organized group of professional musicians who, when they performed, dressed identically. If they were Elamite court musicians there may even have been dress regulations. The opposite impression is given by the final group of women and children. Their disparate appearance may indicate that they were commoners or at the very least a more miscellaneous and spontaneously-assembled group of sound-makers.

The larger scene reveals that the Assyrian army victoriously approached the city of Madaktu with the Elamite Ummanigash in tow. They were met by the defeated and humbled citizens of the town. The Elamite soldiers bowed and prostrated themselves before the victors. The remaining procession made music. It is impossible to determine what type of music the Elamites were performing. Was it ceremonial and formal? Was it a dirge and mournful? Was it energetic and joyful? And was the music a major part of the proceedings or was it merely background accompaniment? The fact that the musicians comprise a large group in the welcoming continent of Elamites must surely point to the importance of their contribution at this event.

The epigraphs on these stone slabs and the annals of Aššurbanipal specifically mention that the king placed the Elamite Ummanigash on the throne after defeating Teumman. This scene shows the welcome that the Assyrian soldiers and Ummanigash received from the Madaktu citizens. The musicians are clearly not displaced captives about to be marched off to parts unknown.[41]

---

[41] Cheng states that these musicians are "Elamite captives being led from their conquered city" (Cheng 2001: 75), but in fact no one is leading them anywhere. They are accompanying the bowing and prostrating soldiers who go out from the city to meet the conquerors.

If this were so many other citizens would be part of the procession. In this scene only the musicians and other sound-makers accompany the defeated Elamite soldiers out of the city to acknowledge the arrival of the victors.

Although the city of Madaktu can be seen in the distance, all the figures are clearly outside of the city and at a considerable distance from the city walls. The Elamites proceed along the banks of the Ulai River where they are unprotected and vulnerable. This reality is emphasized by the decapitated and dead human bodies, horse carcasses and damaged military equipment that floats by them. An epigraph on another Assyrian palace relief reiterates their situation:

> I dammed up the Ulai River with the bodies of the warriors and people of Elam. For three days I made that stream flow full of bodies instead of water.[42]

There is much that is undecipherable about the musicians in this scene. For instance, was it an unusual occurrence for these particular musicians to perform in the public arena as they are shown to do? It is impossible to determine who they are but if they are court musicians this performance would be quite extraordinary and possibly even demeaning. Can the same be said for female and male musicians performing together? Even though the male musicians walk together and the female musicians do the same, nevertheless they are two units of a larger group. Unfortunately next to nothing is known (although much has been surmised) about customs pertaining to the mixing of the sexes. It may also be true that what was standard conduct in Elam may have differed considerably from what was permissible in Assyria. Other relief depictions of Elamites indicate they may have had very different social and family structures from the Assyrians. In deportation scenes men and women walk together as they are forced to leave their homeland. On occasion it is the adult men who carry the small children on their shoulders.[43]

This Elamite scene is one of the few Assyrian palace relief sculptures that shows foreign musicians on their own soil. Not only are the musicians and their instruments carefully depicted with many precise details but so are the surroundings. In Elam clusters of dates hung from the date palms, numerous fish swam in the waters, most houses had two stories and the city walls were studded with many towers.

The reliefs of Aššurbanipal are known for their density and complexity. Irene Winter has observed that in the reliefs of Aššurbanipal "human and animal figures decrease in proportion and scale to permit greater peopling of the pictorial field."[44] John Russell has noted that the reliefs of Aššurbanipal contain many registers and there is much more overlapping of figures than in the reliefs of other Assyrian kings.[45] Amidst the many registers, scenes,

---

[42] Text A. Russell 1999: 159, 176.

[43] Pauline Albenda (1987: 19) suggests that male participation in child care in the Elamite deportation scenes might hint at a social structure in which adult males actively participated in domestic situations.

[44] Winter 1981b: 26.

[45] Russell 1991: 134.

events, figures and epigraphs on the reliefs in room XXXIII of the Southwest Palace the Elamite musicians are rendered in a manner that nicely illustrates the fact that the Assyrians paid attention to and were fascinated by foreign musicians.

The Ištar Temple Procession – stone relief

In 1853 Hormuzd Rassam working about 65 meters to the north of Forecourt H of Sennacherib's palace in Nineveh discovered a remarkable series of sculptures. Eight stone reliefs depicting a royal procession(s) lined each side of a slightly sloping corridor. This corridor very likely connected Forecourt H of the palace with the Ištar Temple.[46] If this was the function of the corridor the relief scenes would have matched the actual passage of the king and his entourage between his palace and the temple.

Fig. 3 Detail of relief of musicians in an Ištar Temple procession, passage to Ištar Temple, Southwest Palace, Nineveh. The figures lean slightly backwards because the relief was originally mounted on a slight downslope. (VA 953c, courtesy Vorderasiatisches Museum)

The figures in the procession include the king who is seated in a hand-drawn chariot, the crown prince, court officials, eunuchs, soldiers, priests and female and male musicians.[47] The stone slabs on one side of the corridor show the king, his attendants and bodyguards heading uphill while on the other side the priests, soldiers and musicians move downhill. As less than half of the reliefs from each side of the corridor are thought to survive it seems likely that each side showed a complete procession. On the one side the procession moved away from the palace toward the temple and on the other it returned.[48] Today this magnificent procession must be imagined from the extant slabs

---

[46] Russell 1991: 168.
[47] Rassam 1897: 8.
[48] Barnett, Bleibtreu and Turner 1998 I: 133; Reade 1967: 48.

which are to be found in museums in Great Britain, Germany and Iraq[49] and from the drawing of Charles Hodder who assisted Rassam.

Although there are no visible texts accompanying the procession, one stone slab is reported to have one of Sennacherib's palace inscriptions on the back side. This text read:

> Palace of Sennacherib, great king, king of the world, king of Assyria, the mighty one, the lord of all kings.[50]

The placement of such an inscription on the stone slab would indicate that the corridor was regarded as being part of the palace.

The sequence of the figures in the procession is unknown. Rassam only wrote that two officers and two eunuchs pulled the king in his chariot and that elegantly dressed ministers seemed to be walking before the king. The other three slabs have four figures on each slab: soldiers with female and male musicians, including a male horizontal harpist who wears a tall fishtail-shaped hat.[51]

The musicians follow a group of spearmen. The first three are male musicians with frame drums. Next are two female musicians, one with cymbals and one with a large drum which she is carrying on her shoulders (Fig. 3 [preceding page]). Another stone slab (which now exists only as a drawing) shows three female musicians with cymbals and frame drums (Fig. 4). A stone slab which depicts four male musician playing horizontal harps is thought to follow the female musicians.

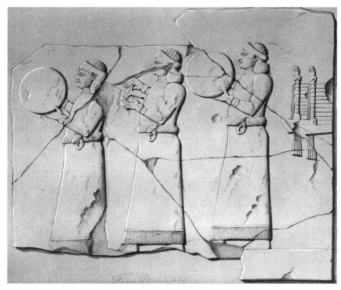

Fig. 4 Drawing of musicians in an Ištar Temple procession, passage to Ištar Temple, Southwest Palace, Nineveh (BM Or. Dr., VI 45, courtesy Trustees of The British Museum)

---

[49] These stone slabs were eventually 'excavated' by the British army during World War II when digging a large pit to accommodate a storage tank (Barnett, Bleibtreu and Turner 1998 I: 7). They were divided between The British Museum, The Royal Geographical Society, The Staatliche Museen of Berlin, The Nergal Gate Museum at Mosul and The Mosul Museum (Reade 1967: 48 n. 22).

[50] Russell 1999: 127, Gadd 1936: 94.

[51] Rassam 1897: 8.

It is not clear whether the musicians are palace musicians or temple musicians or a combination of the two. Dominique Collon has suggested that they are part of the temple personnel who were coming to meet the king.[52] But this is not really clear and they could just as easily be part of the entourage of prominent palace personnel who accompany the king. Perhaps the female musicians were even royal women.

The female musicians have a distinctly different appearance from any of the men in the procession. The women are the only figures whose shoulder-length hair is kept firmly in place with a headband. Although individual strands of wavy hair are visible on the top of their heads the hair below the headband is indistinct and forms a rounded shape as though it was being kept in place by a hair net. The women wear ankle-length dresses which have a fringe around the lower edge. The wide belts at their waists are of an entirely different material from that of their dresses. The belts are tied on the left side ending in a loop. The women are the only figures in the procession who wear slippers on their feet.[53] No male musicians wear jewellery but all the female musicians wear one or two bracelets on each wrist. The woman who carries the drum on her shoulders also wears an elaborate double-strand necklace from which many pendants hang.

There are only three types of musical instruments carried by the musicians: frame drums, cymbals and horizontal forearm harps. There are two different shapes of frame drums in the procession. Square-shaped frame drums are carried by the male musicians while the female musicians carry the round drums. The woman who balances the frame drum on her shoulders is unique. It is very unusual for a musician to carry an instrument in a position where it cannot be played. Why is she doing this? Interestingly only male musicians carry the horizontal forearm harps[54] and only female musicians carry the cymbals (double metal disks).

The two cymbal players hold their cymbals in quite different positions which suggest that the sounds produced from hitting the two disks together would be quite different. One woman holds the cymbals by the two handles and carries them vertically. By moving the disks up and down and clashing them together with considerable force she would create a clanging sound. The other woman holds the cymbals by their edges with her two thumbs on the bottom disk and her fingers on the top disk. She carries them at an oblique angle and most likely creates a clapping sound by moving them rapidly between her thumbs and fingers.

---

[52] Collon 1999: 24.

[53] The crown prince and one spearman clearly wear sandals and a few of the foreign-looking soldiers wear high military boots. All the other men, whether court official, palace servant, soldier or musician, are barefoot.

[54] Jack Cheng has noted that the horizontal forearm harp is depicted more often in Assyrian art than any other musical instrument, is shown in pairs and is always played by male musicians. He also suggests that because these harps appear to have a close relationship to the king they may function as a national symbol (Cheng 2001: 106-117).

In the procession the female and male musicians do not play the same musical instruments but they do walk and play music together. Was this quite common or was this an exceptional circumstance? Would it make a difference if this event was a public occasion or a private (royal) one? Although it has been surmised that female and male musicians never performed together and it has even been asserted that female musicians only played for female audiences, this procession would indicate otherwise.[55]

It should be noted at this point that some writers have been reluctant to commit themselves as to the gender of the five musicians under discussion and a few writers have stated that they are definitely male. Rassam, the original excavator of these stone slabs, wrote that there were "male and female musicians … bearing Assyrian instruments of music …" represented on these reliefs.[56] He was clear about their gender and other writers have followed suit. However of the two stone slabs with female musicians on them only one survives today while the other is known only through one of Hodder's drawings. This definitely adds to the confusion. The stiffness and inaccuracy of Hodder's drawing have been commented upon and it is known that excavators at the time were quite unhappy with him.[57] Thus to not have the actual stone slab with the three female musicians on it is very unfortunate.

Women on the city walls – ivory pyxis

In 1953, while excavating private houses next to the town wall on the acropolis at Kalhu, Max Mallowan found a number of remarkable ivories in room 43 of TW.53. The ivories were discovered in a disturbed upper level of the room, which had been reoccupied briefly by refugees after the sack of the city in 614 BCE. Mallowan thought the ivories probably had been acquired in this later period from damaged or even looted furniture.[58] The ivories are in different styles and range in date from the ninth to the seventh century. Mallowan felt that the eclectic nature of the ivories showed "… that the wealthy householder coveted ivories and collected them, no doubt for their intrinsic as well as for their ornamental value."[59]

Among these various ivories are three fragments of an ivory pyxis (ND3599) probably from the ninth century. It is approximately 4.8 cm in height, has three circular dowel holes drilled into it and two of the fragments join. The ivory pieces are lightly engraved in the Assyrian style. They show an elaborately crenellated city wall with massive doors and at least five towers. Four women can be seen up on the battlements, three hold frame drums and one claps her hands together. Outside of the city walls stands an

---

[55] Cheng 2001: 57.
[56] Rassam 1897: 8.
[57] Barnett, Bleibtreu and Turner 1998 I: 16-17.
[58] Mallowan and Davies 1970: 7.
[59] Mallowan 1966 I: 196.

Fig. 5 Two views of an ivory pyxis showing musicians on the battlements, private house, Kalhu (ND 3599; courtesy The Metropolitan Museum)

impressive warrior, possibly the king, with mace, sword, bow and a spiked shield (Fig. 5).

Ivories engraved in the Assyrian style date to the ninth and eighth centuries. Most of these ivories have been found at Kalhu but it is not known whether the ivory carvers were Assyrian or foreign. The designs were cut or scratched on the ivory with a fine metal tool or carved in high or low relief. Many motifs go back to second-millennium traditions and some ivories show the influence of Middle Assyrian glyptic art. Assyrian-style ivories are consistent in iconography and technique with Neo-Assyrian stone wall reliefs. They often show real events in great detail. The ideology of the king and the Assyrian empire is a subject found on these ivories as well as on the palace reliefs. However, regardless of the subject, Assyrian-style ivories present a "highly-charged space."[60]

On one of the pyxis fragments, three women can be seen on the city battlements. One woman is above the city gates. She faces to the left and holds the frame drum in front of her at chest height. The other two women stand in two separate towers. They face the opposite direction and one woman beats her drum while the other claps her hands. On another fragment a woman stands on the battlements, faces the figure of the warrior and beats her drum. The warrior, fully armed stands in front of her and faces the same direction with the city walls behind him. The large size of the warrior in relation to the city wall and the women in the towers is very noticeable. That the victorious Assyrian warrior is shown in his entirety and the women (foreigners, possibly enemies) as only partial figures also reiterates the ideology of the scene.

---

[60] Renee Dreyfus, lecture on "Ivories in the Assyrian Style," Department of Near Eastern Studies, University of California, Berkeley, 18 March 1994.

The four women wear short-sleeved, belted dresses. The ornate patterns on one of the dresses are clearly indicated. The women have long tresses of hair which flow down their backs and they wear a floppy style cap. This same style of cap is worn by different people to the west of Assyria: Phoenicians, Syrians, Israelites and Hittites.[61]

The bearded warrior (possibly the king) is depicted in great detail. His headgear is damaged but some of his hair can be seen beneath it. He is fully bearded. His tunic is short-sleeved, of richly designed fabrics and has a fringe at the hem. A shawl is wrapped diagonally over it. He carries a bow in his left hand and a mace in his right hand. Part of the spiked shield he carries is visible as is his sword.

The scene is given a distinctive setting by the careful rendering of the architecture. The exterior of the city wall is shown with its ornamentation. Individual features such as double doors in an arched gateway flanked by two towers, the stepped battlements and towers which project above the main wall are clearly delineated. The city walls closely resemble those of two North Syrian cities depicted on the Balawat Gates.[62] The fact that the crenellations on the city walls are perfectly intact and the female musicians appear to be welcoming the Assyrian king suggests that a siege with the eventual destruction of the city will not be necessary.

Comparing the scene on these three ivory fragments to some of the scenes of Shalmaneser III's Balawat Gates assists in determining the date of the ivory pyxis. The spiked shield, for instance, is not portrayed in Assyrian art after the reign of Shalmaneser III (859-824). The Balawat Gates also illustrate the tradition of depicting women on the battlements of fortified cities during the military campaigns of Shalmaneser III.[63]

Celebrations of successful Assyrian military events characteristically included music whether in foreign lands or at home. In their annals Assyrian kings mentioned that musicians accompanied the soldiers on campaigns and that singers performed and music was played when they returned home and entered their cities in triumph.[64] The palace relief scene of the Elamite musicians outside of their city Madaktu welcoming the victorious Assyrians carries a similar message to that on the ivory pyxis. Everyone celebrates an Assyrian triumph, even foreign musicians.

Three musicians in a procession – ivory pyxis

Many ivories were found in the Burnt Palace at Kalhu by both Loftus in the nineteenth century and Mallowan in the twentieth century. The pyxis frag-

---

[61] Wäfler 1975: Abb. 35-42, 47, 54-56, 63, 64, 87.

[62] King 1915: Pl. XXV Band V.1 and Pl. XXVII Band V.3.

[63] Mallowan 1966: 195. King 1915: Pl. XVI Band III.4, Pl. LXIII Band XI.4, Pl. LXXVII Band XIII.6.

[64] Esarhaddon, Broken Prisms B and S: 514; Aššurbanipal, Cylinder B: 865 (Luckenbill 1927: 206, 334).

Fig. 6 Drawing of ivory pyxis with three musicians in a procession, Room 7, Burnt Palace, Kalhu (ND 1642, drawing by R. Hall)

ments depicting three musicians in procession (ND 1642) were found by Mallowan when he excavated room 7 near the entrance to the throne room of the Burnt Palace.

The pyxis is carved in the Syrian style and is about 6 cm in height. It portrays three musicians in profile who face to the left. A male musician plays the lyre, a female musician plays the frame drum and a second female musician plays the double pipes (Fig. 6). The fragments of this pyxis do not indicate whether there would have been more musicians in the procession and toward whom or what they were processing. If the scene is similar to the one on the pyxis found by Loftus the musicians would be proceeding toward a seated female figure.

The male musician wears an Egyptian style wig that reaches his shoulders. He wears a short-sleeved, fringed garment that is belted at the waist. It is longer at the front and the back, where it falls to just above the ankle, but it is considerably shorter at the sides. Mallowan described the clothing of the three musicians as "fashionable linen raiment"[65] and the robe worn by the man has a beautifully detailed lozenge-patterned design. The musician is playing his lyre while he walks along.

The frame drum player who follows the lyre player also wears a short-sleeved, fringed garment that is belted at the waist. It is longer at the back than at the front, which would seem to be a common style of dress worn by foreign women. The garment almost seems to touch the ground at the back but in the front the hem comes just above the ankles. Wavy, vertical stripes constitute the design on the fabric. The woman's hair is pulled back from the

[65] Mallowan 1966: 216.

forehead to behind her ears and falls in one long curl over the nape of the neck to just below her shoulders. Individual strands of hair are visible. She carries the frame drum in front of her chest with her right hand gripping it at the lower edge and beats the drum with her left hand.

Only the head and shoulders of the third musician have survived. She appears to be wearing the same style clothing as the other woman and her hair style is identical. She plays the double pipes which she holds out in front of her at different angles. Her right hand looks to be covering the sound holes in the middle of the one pipe but interestingly her left hand seems to be covering the end of the second pipe.

Separating the three figures are waist-high voluted palmettes with fronds. A guilloche band runs along the top and bottom borders of the pyxis.

The carvings on this pyxis are in deep relief and of the highest quality. These three figures are clearly foreigners and they are depicted in the Syrian style of carving. This means that the physiognomy of all the figures whether female or male is the same. Seen in profile the figures have a flat forehead, large almond-shaped eyes, large nose and small mouth. These features parallel those of other figures from the same region. This pyxis also illustrates that female and male musicians played music together, and most likely in public.

Musicians at the banquet – ivory pyxis

Among the ivories found in the Burnt Palace at Kalhu by Loftus in the 1954-55 seasons were the fragments of a badly burned pyxis (BM 118179). It is 6.7 cm high and carved in the Syrian style. The scene around the exterior of the container depicts a procession of musicians who approach a seated figure (Figs. 7-8). The seated figure is in front of a table piled high with food. On the under side of the pyxis there is an obscure West Semitic alphabetic inscription which may indicate that the pyxis originally belonged to an important personage in Arpad in north Syria.[66]

There are at least five musicians in a procession which moves to the right. The first two musicians play double pipes, the next plays a frame drum and the final two play a mysterious musical instrument which may be a zither, psaltery, xylophone or some type of percussion instrument, possibly even a square frame drum.

All the musicians wear Egyptian style wigs with tight curls. Although the figures all move to the right in a procession, the musicians who play the double pipes and the frame drum are seen in profile, while the two who play the zithers (?) have their heads turned and are viewed in a frontal position. The first and third female musicians wear identical clothing. The garments are short-sleeved, belted ankle-length dresses that are pleated down the back. The second female musician wears a belted, ankle-length dress with a criss-

---

[66] In his discussion of the ivory pyxis, Curtis mentions that E. Puech (1978) believes the inscription can be read 'belonging to ... of Bīt Gusi,' i.e., Arpad. The missing part would be the name of the owner (Curtis and Reade 1995: 150).

Fig. 7 Ivory pyxis with musicians at a banquet, Burnt Palace (BM 118179, courtesy Trustees of The British Museum)

cross pattern. The final two musicians however may be uniquely clothed. In the fragment that survives they wear a short-sleeved garment with the criss-cross pattern. But the lower parts of their bodies are missing, thus it is unclear what the length of their skirts might be. In the reconstruction by Barnett they wear mid-thigh length skirts or pants.[67] This would seem to be pure conjecture and is quite odd. Certainly only men are ever depicted wearing kilt skirts that end above the knees. Women are always shown wearing long garments. Thus it seems entirely possible that these last two musicians could be male in which case this pyxis is one more example of female and male musicians playing together in procession at a ceremonial event.

Fig. 8 Drawing of ivory pyxis with musicians at a banquet (drawing by R. Hall, after Burnett 1957: Pl. XVI, S.3)

---

[67] Barnett 1957: Pl. XVI.

The first musician in the procession has only partially survived. Only the end of the double pipes she plays and the lower part of her dress and feet are visible. The second double pipe player is visible in her entirety. She holds the double pipes out in front of her at an angle, with one end in her mouth. The third musician plays a circular frame drum. She holds it at the bottom with her left hand and beats it with her right hand. The last two musicians hold rectangular-shaped musical instruments with their left hands and appear to manipulate what look like strings arranged horizontally on the instrument with their right hands.

The musicians approach a figure seated in a round-back chair in front of a table piled high with delicacies. The seated figure has two attendants. One stands on a stool arranging the food. The lower portion of a final figure can be seen between the attendants and the musicians. She wears an ankle-length dress with an overskirt that trails behind her. There are either palm or lotus plants between many of the figures and there is a chevron pattern border at the top and the bottom of the pyxis.

It is difficult to interpret this scene without being able to identify the seated figure. Was she royalty? Was she a priestess? Was she a goddess? Was this occasion a religious or a secular celebration? Whatever the event the music clearly played an integral part.

Frame drum player and stag – ivory pyxis

Among the ivories found by Loftus in the Burnt Palace were the fragments of a pyxis (BM 126515) burnt blue by fire. The pyxis is carved in the Syrian style and is 6 cm high. In one panel a female musician facing right plays a frame drum or possibly a tambourine, and in the panel directly behind her is a galloping stag (Fig. 9). The woman has an elaborate coiffure. Beautiful long, wavy hair flows down past the nape of her neck and rests on her

Fig. 9 Drawing of ivory pyxis with frame drum player and stag, Burnt Palace, Kalhu (BM 126515, drawing by R. Hall, after Burnett 1957: Pl. XVI, S.9a-d)

shoulders. Her dress is short-sleeved with a wide belt. The top half has a rectangular pattern on it while the skirt is pleated and has a multi-tiered border design around the hem. Typically, the skirt is longer at the back and shorter at the front. She walks barefooted toward a lotus plant. She holds the drum in front of her with her left hand and beats it with her right hand. Chevrons separate the female musician from the stag and also form the top and bottom bands of the pyxis. Because only two figures on the pyxis survive it is not possible to determine if the scene depicted is a hunting scene. If it is, it is of great interest that a female musician would be involved in such a male-dominated activity.

Double pipe player with figures carrying provisions – ivory plaque

While conducting rescue excavations at Til Barsib (Tell Ahmar) in Syria, excavators from the University of Melbourne discovered 12 carved ivories during their 1993 and 1994 seasons. The ivories were found in a large domestic structure (building C1), which dated to the seventh century. The procession ivory with the double pipe player was found in a pit sunk beneath the floor of room XV. Because it is not clear exactly when the pit was dug the exact date of this ivory is problematic. However, as the building was abandoned in the years around 600 BCE at least a *terminus ad quem* date can be given.[68]

Til Barsib was in an area dominated by the Assyrians from the ninth through the seventh centuries. Located relatively far to the west within the Assyrian empire it became an important provincial capital. The Assyrian presence was much in evidence and like other inland Syrian cities Til Barsib drew on a Mesopotamian repertoire of subjects and motifs in its arts. Bunnens has noted that the material culture was predominantly Assyrian and that their influence permeated the entire site of Til Barsib.[69]

The provisions procession ivory is a long plaque, carved in low relief. It is 10 cm in height and 32.3 cm in length (Fig. 10 [next page]). It is broken at both ends and at the top.[70] The five figures are shown in profile and face to the right. The four male figures follow the female double pipe player who leads the procession. The top of the head of another figure can be seen in front of the female musician indicating there might have been a group of musicians leading the procession. Each figure is separated from the one ahead and behind by a lotus flower on a tall wavy stem. The lotus plant between the two men carrying the pomegranates and the small birds consists of a two-tiered lotus with the lower flower at the height of the men's knees. All of the flowers are open in a manner which presents a canopy effect. Thus it appears that each figure is enclosed in her or his individual niche. A guilloche band runs along the top and the bottom of the plaque.

---

[68] Bunnens 1997a: 435, 438.
[69] Bunnens 1997b: 28.

Fig. 10 Drawing of ivory plaque of double flute player with figures carrying provisions, probably for a banquet, Room XV, Building C1, Til Barsib (TAH 94 C. 48/F. 1789/O. 1708, drawing by R. Hall)

The four male figures wear short kilt skirts which overlap in the front. The skirts appear to have vertical stripes but are probably pleated. They wear Egyptian style wigs which reach their shoulders. Each man in the procession carries provisions in both hands, most likely for a banquet. It is unclear what type of objects the first man is carrying, but the second man carries pomegranates, the third small birds and the fourth fish.

The female musician has on a similar style wig. She wears a long robe which also appears to be vertically pleated. It has a decorative border, sleeves which end at the elbows and is longer at the back than at the front. This type of robe, although usually belted, is a typical garment worn by women and considered Syrian.[71] She plays the double pipes as the group proceeds. With one end of each pipe in her mouth and one hand on each pipe, she holds them horizontally in front of her.

The procession plaque belongs to the North Syrian style of ivory carving. This style can be identified on the basis of details and motifs. In this case, curvilinear floral elements used as fill-ornaments, a scene which includes musicians in a procession, the clothing and hairstyles, the physiognomic features, the large size of the figures crowding the space and the absence of Egyptian elements reveal the North Syrian style of the ivory plaque.[72]

Bands of female musicians in procession were clearly a popular theme on ivory containers which either originated in Syria or were decorated by carvers who came from that area. The figures on this ivory plaque (physiognomy, clothing and activities) closely resemble those on the Syrian style pyxides discussed earlier. The scene on this ivory plaque is one more example of a female musician who plays her instrument in a mixed musical group and probably in public as well.

---

[70] Bunnens (1997a: 442) says that the top of the ivory was intentionally cut, probably to fit a round object.

[71] Bunnens 1997a: 442.

[72] See Winter 1976a: 26, 29. Winter discusses the North Syrian group of ivory carvings as originally defined by F. Poulsen and R. D. Barnett.

Female lyre player – ivory plaque

This ivory miniature of a woman carrying a lyre (ND 7597) was found by Mallowan in room SW37 at Fort Shalmaneser in Kalhu. It is 6 cm high and an example of the Phoenician style in ivory carving. When found she was covered in bitumen that Mallowan thought was an adhesive used to attach gold leaf overlay.[73]

The Phoenician style of ivory carving illustrates a strong adherence to Egyptian art traditions. Egyptian themes and figures abound in this style of carving as well as their canons of proportion, sense of space and ideas of grace and beauty. Winter has observed that Phoenician ivories demonstrate "harmony, elegance and careful design of the plaque as a whole."[74]

The Egyptianized female lyre player is shown in profile facing left (Fig. 11). She wears an Egyptian style wig and a sheer, pleated ankle-length gown. She exemplifies the grace and beauty and elegance associated with this style of carving. She holds the rectangular lyre on the left side at chest level and plays the strings with both hands. The lyre she plays is an asymmetrical or oblique style instrument. The cross-bar is at a slight angle to the sound box and the strings have a fan-shaped arrangement.

Fig. 11 Ivory plaque of female lyre player, Room SW37, Fort Shalmaneser, Kalhu (AM 1959.210, courtesy Ashmolean Museum)

Although no women are portrayed in Assyrian art playing the lyre, it is not uncommon in Egyptian and Syrian art to see women lyre players.

Conclusion

The textual and visual evidence clearly shows that there were many female musicians in Assyria who performed music in different venues and for diverse occasions. Female musicians were mentioned or depicted at victory celebrations, in royal or religious processions, at banquets and in religious ritual

---

[73] Mallowan (1966: 575-576) mentions that, "All the fragments found in this room bore similar traces of this black viscous substance. It seems extraordinary that the lovely detail of the ivory should originally have been obscured in this way, but frequent traces of gold, and the head, ND 8027, still overlaid by its golden covering, prove the point."

[74] Winter 1976b: 8.

events. Occasionally these may have been spontaneous performances, but it is quite obvious that these events, whether political, religious or private, would have required the very best musicians, in other words, professional musicians.

As professionals these female musicians would have had a legitimate position in Assyrian society and been valued for their expertise outside of the household and domestic spheres. They would have needed to spend considerable time training, meeting regularly and rehearsing in order to achieve a high level of competence and musicality. At state or sacred celebrations, the king or the queen or the temple administrators would have required no less.

In most of the examples cited the female musicians are not mentioned or shown alone, but in groups. Some groups had only female musicians but some groups had both female and male musicians which prove that female musicians were not segregated playing only with each other. Nor is it the case that female musicians played only for female audiences.

The references to female musicians in Assyrian documents and portrayals of female musicians in Assyrian art show that there was a distinct tradition of women performing, not only within the palace and temple, but also in public. The Assyrians took advantage of and benefited from these female musicians who were talented and skilled technicians with specialized knowledge.

CHAPTER III

PALACE WOMEN

Information about palace women in the Neo-Assyrian period may be derived from personal names, titles, legal dealings, estates and holdings, contributions to temples, burial sites, personal belongings, reliefs and much more. There were large numbers of palace women at any given time. They included servants, officials and royal women among whom were the king's mother, wives, sisters, daughters and daughters-in-law.

Households

It needs emphasizing that the households of royal women were not "harems" as the word has been used in more modern times. The term "harem" conjures up many inaccurate, unverifiable and inappropriate images that have more to do with the western imagination than with the information from the Neo-Assyrian texts themselves. Orientalist ideas from the Victorian period in the nineteenth century CE have greatly influenced how the Islamic Middle East and even the pre-Islamic ancient Near Eastern world is viewed. This is quite odd because most scholars acknowledge that there is no connection between the ancient and medieval cultures of the Middle East.[1] Because the term "harem" suggests female seclusion or incarceration, eunuch guards and the unlimited sexual pleasures of the male head of house, the word gets in the way of attempting to understand how the Neo-Assyrian royal women's households were organized, how they functioned and what their place was within the larger social, political and economic scene. In this section on the households of royal women the word "harem" will be avoided most assiduously.

The texts make clear that the households connected with the royal women of Assyria were large, well organized, "self-contained and self-sufficient."[2] This was especially true for the households of the queen and the queen mother. These queens had multiple residences. They owned real estate and

---

[1] See, for example, Van De Mieroop 1999: 146.

[2] Van De Mieroop (1999: 155) has pointed out: "Throughout Mesopotamian history we observe the existence of households of rulers' wives, which were self-contained and self-sufficient. They demonstrate the participation of women in the economic sphere separate from their husbands and on the same terms, although on a smaller scale."

had other extensive holdings to finance and maintain their households. They had their own personnel which included both women and men. They also had their own military units for protection.

Residences

Neo-Assyrian palaces had both public and private areas. The *bētānu* or the inner quarter (possibly a specific building inside a palace) was used by members of the royal family. Whereas archaeologists often designate the *bētānu* with its restricted access as the area where the wives and concubines of the king were kept, this residential area was certainly occupied by a more diverse group of people.[3]

Nevertheless, in a few of the Neo-Assyrian capital cities the separate living quarters of royal women and their households are known. In the city of Kalhu both the Northwest palace and Fort Shalmaneser had areas where the domestic quarters of the queen and her household were located. At Nineveh an area in the Southwest palace was occupied by a wife of an Assyrian king.

In the Northwest palace at Kalhu the residential area south of courtyard Y was excavated in the nineteenth century by Layard, in the 1950s by Mallowan and in the 1980s and 1990s by the Iraqi Office of Antiquities and Heritage. According to the excavators, this wing of the palace contained a number of well-constructed and spacious residential apartments. Most had a living or reception room and adjoining bathroom. One set of rooms was particularly grandiose and decorated in a rich and sumptuous style. There was a large reception room together with a large inner room and a bathroom suite. Joan and David Oates believe this residence must have been that of a queen.[4]

The identification of this wing of the building as women's quarters is established by what was found in the rooms and under the floors of the domestic wing of the palace. In a sealed cupboard in room HH, Mallowan found a collection of small female personal belongings that he thought would have been the property of a princess.[5] Under the floor of room DD he found the grave of a woman who was buried with jewellery so valuable and precious he felt this could only be a royal grave. More recently in 1988 and 1989 Iraqi archaeologists discovered queens' tombs beneath the floors of rooms MM, 49 and 57. Two of the three tombs had inscriptions giving the name and title of the queen for whom the tomb was intended. These tombs also contained hundreds of valuable objects.[6] In addition, Muzahim Mahmud Hussein dis-

---

[3] For instance Sennacherib is known to have built a *bētānu* for his oldest son (*CAD* B, 275). It should be noted that as *bētānu* refers to the inner part or interior this term was used either for a palace or temple.

[4] J. and D. Oates 2001: 65.

[5] This collection consisted of a set of mixed beads; a few strips of gold foil; four ivory disc beads, two of which were beautifully engraved; and an assortment of colored shells (Mallowan 1966 I: 114).

[6] Damerji 1999: 3-12.

covered a set of underground chambers beneath rooms 74 and 75 that are thought to have been a treasury or a guarded safe for the valuables of the royal women. "Some 271 objects were found here, including many of great beauty."[7] All in all these objects and tombs reveal the considerable wealth and status of the royal women who occupied these rooms in the Northwest palace.

Residential quarters for the queen and her household were also found in Fort Shalmaneser at Kalhu. This building was called the *ēkal māšarti* which has been translated as 'arsenal' or 'review palace.' It was built in the ninth century by Shalmaneser III and extensively renovated in the seventh century by Esarhaddon. This enormous building was excavated by Max Mallowan and David Oates between 1957 and 1963.[8]

The southwestern corner of the building contained the residential area. It was separated from the more public and formal areas by bolted corridors to give privacy and protection. It contained a complex of luxurious apartments and palatial suites of rooms grouped around courtyards such as S6, S37, and S43. In some of the rooms large numbers of miscellaneous items belonging to women were found.[9] A group of tablets comprising part of the archive of the *šakintu*, the female official in charge of the queen's household, was found in storeroom S10. Certainly it was here that the queen maintained a household. That the queen had more than one residence in Kalhu came as a surprise and may indicate that she had multiple residences in other Assyrian cities as well.

While excavating the residential area of Sennacherib's Southwest Palace at Nineveh Layard discovered a pair of colossal sphinxes flanking the doorway to room LXV. The text inscribed on the sphinxes includes Sennacherib's dedication of this part of the palace "for Tašmetum-šarrat, the queen, my beloved wife."[10] This unusual inscription clearly identifies the west wing of the palace as the residence of the queen.

Textual references give further information on the royal residences of the queens of Assyria. A letter to Sargon from the Governor of Assur discusses the type of labor to be used for the building of the queen's palace in Ekallate.[11] A large ration list from the reign of Sargon (ND 2803) gives the issue of foodstuffs to royal establishments mentioning those of the queens in Arbail, Kilizi, Adian and Kasappa.[12] A survey of *šakintu*s and weavers from the reign of either Esarhaddon or Aššurbanipal names thirteen households with *šakintu*

---

[7] J. and D. Oates 2001: 67, fig 38.

[8] Mallowan 1966: 369-371; J. and D. Oates 2001: 145, 148 n 3.

[9] "... a large collection of women's items in the form of literally hundreds of beads, many of frit and glass, amulets, fibulae, a bone comb and in particular a number of alabaster and rock crystal vessels of the types designed to hold cosmetics" (J. and D. Oates 2001: 190).

[10] This unusual inscription is translated and discussed in Galter, Levine and Reade 1986: 31-32 and Reade 1987: 141.

[11] SAA I 99.

[12] ND 2803 (Parker 1961: 55).

in 9 different cities.[13] References to the residences of Assyrian queens attest to at least 26 households in as many as 20 different cities throughout the empire.

One further intriguing possible residence involves the queen mother Naqia during the reign of her son Esarhaddon. There are three fragmentary copies of a building inscription describing a palace that she had built for her son in Nineveh.[14] Although the site of the palace has not been found Naqia described the location as being "in the midst of Nineveh behind the Sin and Šamaš temple." It is not known whether this palace was ever used as a residence by Esarhaddon and it is entirely possible that Naqia herself may have lived there.[15]

Real estate and wealth

The real estate holdings and other wealth of the Assyrian royal women appear to have been considerable. Records exist which indicate that royal women owned towns, estates with agricultural lands and the people who lived on them.

Two successive queen mothers are known to have owned property in the town of Šabbu. A land grant by Sennacherib has been pieced together from three different fragments. He transferred the estate of the previous queen mother in Šabbu to 'the mother of the prince of the succession house.'[16] Here is an example of property that belonged to one queen mother being transferred to the future queen mother. A property transfer such as this one at Šabbu indicates that the economic benefits of being the mother of the future king were significant. The land grant contains Sennacherib's name and titles (broken), the royal seal, part of the date, a report of an oracular inquiry made with regard to Šabbu, the town of the queen mother, a declaration of people exempted from taxes and something (unknown) which was done for the mother of the crown prince.

The transfer of the property in Šabbu most likely occurred after the death of the earlier queen mother but before the mother of the crown prince actually held the same title. Although there were two different sons (by two different mothers) designated crown prince by Sennacherib during his reign it may be possible to identify the woman who received this property. The queen mother is known to have been alive in 692 (SAA VI 143) and the first crown prince was killed in 694. Melville argues that because the land was specifically given to "the mother of the king's son of the succession house" (AMA-*šú ša* DUMU

---

[13] Nineveh, Nasibina, Šibaniba, Bit-Adad-le'i, Šudu, Te'di, Kahat, Sunê and Tušhan (SAA VII 23).

[14] Borger 1956: 116.

[15] Melville 1999: 38-42.

[16] SAA XII 21-23.

LUGAL *ša* É *re-[du-ti]*) rather than the queen (MÍ.É.GAL) the woman in question is Naqia.[17]

The town of Lahiru which is thought to be in the Diyala region not far from the Elamite-Babylonian border was also part of the land holdings of Naqia when she was queen mother. An economic document regarding the sale of people by "Idu'a, town manager of Lahiru of the domain of the queen mother ..." was dated to the year 678.[18] Interestingly other royal family members also owned property in Lahiru. Šamaš-šumu-ukin, a son of Esarhaddon, resided there when he was crown prince and Libbali-šarrat, queen of Aššurbanipal, owned land there in 668.[19]

The town of Gadisê in the Harran area was also associated with Naqia when she was queen mother. There is a reference to a statue of Naqia placed in the streets of the town which may indicate that the queen mother held land there.[20]

Town ownership and land holdings were not the exclusive domain of individuals of the rank of queen or queen mother. An unnamed daughter of the king owned a town, also unnamed, in which an estate was assigned to the *sartinnu* or chief judge.[21] "Šadditu, daughter of Sennacherib, king of Assyria, and sister of Es[arh]addon, king of Assyria ..." bought property which included a garden, house, land and people.[22] And Abi-rami, the sister of the queen mother Naqia, leased land in the town of Baruri in 674.[23]

In addition to real estate holdings, royal women received tribute and gifts from various sources. In the Nimrud Wine Lists the queen was the first entry in the majority of the extant lists to receive a sizable allotment of wine.[24] In two different wine lists the queen was issued 3 *sūti* which was approximately 300 portions of wine.[25] In a distribution list of miscellaneous commodities to palace personnel at Nineveh the queen received "5 sheep and 5 *šappu*-jars of wine" which would be approximately 250 portions of wine.[26] Both allocations

---

[17] Melville also states: "This document may represent the protocol for dealing with the estates of the deceased queen mother, and the rest of her wealth was probably dispersed in a similar manner" (Melville 1999: 21).

[18] SAA VI 255.

[19] SAA XIV 1.

[20] Melville 1999: 105 n 6.

[21] SAA XI 221.

[22] SAA VI 251.

[23] SAA VI 252.

[24] According to Kinnier Wilson (1972: 6), "The king, however, does not feature in the wine lists, the obvious reason being that he and his table were served from a royal cellar situated in another part of the city. It is thus the queen, entered as SAL É.GAL or *ša ekalli*, who is the first to be mentioned in the lists ...."

[25] Kinnier Wilson 1972: 44.

[26] Whereas there is a tentative agreement that 5 *qû* = 1 *sapputu*-jar, there are a variety of values assigned to the *qû*. Kinnier Wilson suggested 1.842 liters (Kinnier Wilson 1972: 114), while Powell and Gaspa suggested 0.8 liters (Powell 1987-90: 502 and Gaspa 2007: 173-174). This creates a wide variance in the amount of wine assigned the queen and her household. When the queen received 5 *sappu*-jars the amount in liters could vary from 46.05 to 20 liters, either of which is a considerable amount of wine. To complicate matters Powell (1984: 57) has further observed that it is difficult to fix the absolute value of any Assyrian capacity unit.

of wine indicate that the queen had a household of considerable size and that its members were well cared for.

The queens of Assyria were also mentioned first in other accounts of tribute and audience gifts. Tribute from subordinate areas was sent to the king who then distributed it to the palace sector. In a letter to Sargon from his son Sennacherib, who was then the crown prince, the shares to be received by various people in the palace were listed. At the top of the list was the queen who received 18 minas of silver plus other luxury items.[27] Although this list represents only two of the numerous shipments of tribute that flowed into the palace annually, it does indicate that the wealth of the queen would have been considerable.[28]

Precious metals and luxury items would have been an important part of the queens' incomes. Another document recorded silver payments concerning the queen mother and also the daughter of the king.[29] In an account of flax and wool the queen received 20 talents of linen fiber. Only the 'Central City Nineveh' received more.[30]

The gifts, offerings and contributions by the queen and queen mother to various shrines, temples and even the Assyrian military establishment illustrate their wealth and status. During the reigns of Esarhaddon and Aššurbanipal there are many examples of offerings sent by members of the royal family to various Assyrian temples, either on a regular basis or for special events. The queen sent cattle, sheep and ducks to an unknown temple.[31] The queen sent offerings of beer and wine to the Aššur temple for Mullissu on days 17 and 18 of a special celebration.[32] Naqia, the queen mother, also contributed cattle, sheep and ducks to a temple, plus oil, honey and aromatic plants.[33] Naqia, the queen mother, sent one mina of gold to a temple in Babylonia when the king sent valuable jewels. The king's agent there reported that the jewels and the gold would be used for a tiara for Nabû.[34] In another text it is reported that the gifts the queen mother and the king sent to the temple were stolen.[35]

The reports of the 'inspector' of the Nabû temple in Kalhu list the horses and mules supplied to the military. They arrived "from all the major cities in

---

[27] These luxury items included 12 tunics, 13 togas, one potful of iced fish and one creel of 100 fish. Only the *turtānu*, commander-in-chief of the provincial troops, received more silver, amounting to 20 minas, while the crown prince only received 13 minas. Among the other palace officials who received tribute were the Grand Vizier, the Chief Eunuch, the Palace Superintendent, the Scribe of the Palace, the Chariot Driver and the 'Third Man' (SAA I 34).

[28] Mattila 2000: 144-145.

[29] SAA VII 48.

[30] The text (SAA VII 115) comes from Nineveh and most likely from the reign of Esarhaddon or Aššurbanipal. Because it cannot be precisely dated it is not possible to know which queen is referred to. The term 'central city Nineveh' is an abbreviation for 'palaces of the central city of Nineveh.'

[31] SAA VII 175, 181.

[32] SAA VII 183-184.

[33] SAA XIII 76-77.

[34] SAA X 348.

[35] SAA XIII 154.

Assyria and from as far away as Parsua in Iran and Damascus in Syria" and from individuals wealthy enough to make contributions.[36] The only members of the royal family who sent horses were the queen and queen mother. In the existing reports the queen mother contributed 20 Kushite horses and the queen contributed eight Kushite horses.[37] Since the quality of the horses is not defined, it is impossible to know whether these numbers indicate that the wealth of the queen mother was greater than that of the queen.

The evidence points to the considerable wealth of the royal women of Assyria. Not only the queen and queen mother but the daughters and sisters of Assyrian kings had substantial holdings. Royal women owned real estate and they received tribute from subordinate areas as well as gifts from the king. In turn they made contributions and gave gifts to shrines and temples and they supplied valuable horses to the military. Regardless of whether these contributions were voluntary or required they illustrate that the royal women could afford to make them.

Personnel: the šakintu

The *šakintu* was the female chief administrator of the household of the queen or the queen mother. As the head of a queen's household the *šakintu* commanded a large staff of both men and women that included her own female deputy (*šanītu*), female steward, male or female scribe, cook, eunuch, etc.[38] She transacted a large volume of business, could buy and sell land and slaves on her own account and received large amounts of rations from a royal source. This is a good indication of the complexity of her responsibilities and the size and extent of the household of a queen.

Šakintu literally means "appointed woman." This female title corresponds to the male title *šaknu*, yet, in Neo-Assyrian sources, the male official with this title was either a provincial governor or a military officer in charge of chariots, cavalry or foot-soldiers. Thus, while the *šakintu* "... may grammatically be the feminine equivalent of the *šaknu*, there is no equivalence of function."[39]

References to the *šakintu* in Neo-Assyrian documents appear throughout the entire Neo-Assyrian period. The first reference dates from the early eighth century and the last from the post-canonical period in the late sixth century (from 648 to 612). The earliest reference is from 788 during the reign of

---

[36] Those who contributed horses were the commander-in-chief, the palace herald, the chief cupbearer, the governors of Kalhu and Nineveh and the magnates of the province of Bet-kari in Media (Cole and Machinist 1998: XVIII).

[37] SAA XIII 89, 101, 108.

[38] According to Teppo (2005: 53), "The administrators (*šakintu*) and their staff and relatives are the largest autonomous group of women within the Assyrian royal palaces."

[39] Postgate 1980: 69.

Adad-nerari III while the most recent is either from 617 during the reign of Sin-šarru-iškun or from 611 after the collapse of the Neo-Assyrian Empire.[40]

A woman holding the position of *šakintu* might be identified merely by her title or by her personal name, residence and/or city. Thus a document might read: "the *šakintu*" or "Zarpi the *šakintu*" or "the *šakintu* of Assur" or "Ahi-ṭalli the *šakintu* of the central city of Nineveh".[41] In fact, seven personal names of *šakintu*s are known: Addati, Ahi-ṭalli and Zarpi from Nineveh and Amat-Ba'al, Ilia, Šiti-ilat and Amat-Aštarti from Kalhu.[42] All in all, 54 *šakintu*s from 22 separate households in 17 cities are mentioned in Neo-Assyrian documents.[43]

Most references locate a *šakintu* in a capital city (Nineveh, Kalhu or Assur) or cities close to the capital such as Kasappa, Kilizi, Arbail, Adian or Šibaniba. Other sources, however, mention places far afield from the Assyrian heartland: Kahat, Nasibina, Tušhan, Til Barsib and Haurina, all to the west. The location of four cities mentioned as having *šakintu*s are currently unknown: Bit-Adad-le'i, Te'di, Šudu and Sunê.[44]

Three Assyrian cities are mentioned as having more than one palace or residence for the queen and therefore more than one *šakintu*. In Nineveh four are mentioned: the Central City, the Review Palace of Nineveh, the Review Palace of the New Contingent, and the household of the Lady of the House (SAA VII 23). In Kalhu three are mentioned: the Old Palace (ND 2309), the New Palace (ND 2307) and the Review Palace (Fort Shalmaneser) (CTN III 30, 35). There is also a reference to two residences for *šakintu* at Sunê (SAA VII 23). All these references to households where there were *šakintu*s imply that wherever a queen had a residence there would have been a woman with this title managing it.

Documents that pertain to the *šakintu* and her staff were found in 5 Assyrian cities. These were Nineveh, Kalhu, Assur, Til Barsib and Tušhan.[45] The bulk of the texts from the capital city of Nineveh was excavated in the nineteenth century by Layard. He did not give a specific provenance, but merely identified the tablets as being "from Kuyunjik."[46] One of the documents (SAA VI 88), however, was part of the dossier of the *šakintu* Ahi-ṭalli and was found in the Royal Library in the Southwest Palace of Sennacherib. Since many of the *šakintu*'s documents refer to the "central city" household of the queen

---

[40] Teppo 2007: Appendix 1, 268-271.

[41] In *CAD* the discussion of the *šakintu* mentions that "central city" is an ellipsis for "palace(s) of the central city" (*CAD* Š/1, 166).

[42] Teppo 2005: 56.

[43] Teppo 2007: 257-258, 268-271.

[44] With the exception of Bit-Adad-le'i, Te'di, Šudu and Sunê (mentioned in SAA VII 23), the location of all the other cities where *šakintu*s are named can be found in Parpola and Porter 2001.

[45] Teppo 2007: 258.

[46] Although the legal corpus from Nineveh was published at the turn of the twentieth century by C.H.W. Johns, in 1913 by J. Kohler and A. Ungnad and in 1988 by T. Kwasman, this group of texts has most recently been published by the State Archives of Assyria: Volume VI in 1991 and Volume XIV in 2002.

which is thought to have been located in the Southwest Palace, it seems highly probably that most of the queen's household tablets were found there.[47]

In Kalhu the majority of the texts that deal with the queen's household and the *šakintu* and her staff came from Fort Shalmaneser. Eighteen texts were discovered in storeroom S10 and Corridors D and E by Mallowan and Oates in 1958 mixed together with ivories and burnt debris from the destruction of the arsenal.[48] An additional but important document that outlined a marriage contract for the *šakintu*'s daughter was found in the Northwest Palace on the citadel of Kalhu.

Persons holding the title *šakintu* could apparently have children although there is no record of them actually marrying. In one instance a son is mentioned and in another the *šakintu* Amat-Aštarti of the Northwest palace at Kalhu arranged a lucrative dowry and an equitable marriage for her daughter. The tablet containing this marriage contract was found in the Northwest palace and not in Fort Shalmaneser with the other *šakintu* texts. It was discovered during the 1952 excavations in room ZT16 on the ziggurat terrace between the Northwest palace and the ziggurat at Kalhu and can be dated to the later part of the reign of Aššurbanipal in the middle of the seventh century.[49]

Amat-Aštarti, 'the *šakintu* of the new palace' gave her daughter Subeitu to Milki-ramu. A very detailed list of a lavish dowry is included in the document.[50] The dowry of Subeitu included gold plate, silver jewellery, wool and linen garments, copper furniture and utensils and a bronze bed. This legally certified list would obviously have protected her daughter's rights to the property. Postgate has pointed out that "as elsewhere and at other times the woman will have retained a right to her dowry and under normal circumstances have passed it on to her sons."[51]

The final section of the marriage contract lays out the conditions of the marriage, of a divorce if it occurred and the subsequent compensation. There are very specific stipulations regarding what would happen if Subeitu was childless, if her husband took a concubine and if the concubine had children. If Subeitu "hated" her husband she could divorce him but if Milki-ramu wanted a divorce he would need to pay back the dowry two-fold. The witnesses to this contract included a number of high officials, one being the chief magistrate of Kalhu.[52] Interestingly there were two seal impressions on the tablet which indicate that both Amat-Aštarti and Milki-ramu had to agree on the terms of this marriage. Clearly the *šakintu* Amat-Aštarti had the social standing and wealth to negotiate a very favorable marriage for her daughter.

---

[47] Teppo (2007: 262) speculates that the non-literary texts from the reigns of Sennacherib, Esarhaddon and Assurbanipal were located in the Southwest Palace while the texts from the reign of Sargon II and the post-canonical period were from the North Palace.

[48] Mallowan 1966: 434, Dalley and Postgate 1984: 9.

[49] Parker 1954: 29-30.

[50] Mallowan (1966 I: 178) refers to these objects as "a dowry fit for a princess."

[51] Postgate 1979: 97.

[52] Mallowan 1966 I: 178.

The documents found that refer to the *šakintu* or members of her staff indicate that they were an active and affluent household within the palace. They made loans of silver or sheep, they bought property: orchards, estates, fields and houses and they bought people: singly, in large numbers and with land. For instance, among the legal transactions of the *šakintu* Addati was her loan of two minas of silver in 694 to Bibiya the deputy village manager. This was a substantial loan as she received as pledge an estate of 12 hectares of land outside of the city of Assur and seven persons in lieu of the silver.[53] In Nineveh the *šakintu* Ahi-ṭalli bought an orchard with 17 people in 683 and also an estate worth six minas of silver.[54] At a later date the *šakintu* of the central city bought land worth five minas and ten shekels of silver.[55] In Nineveh a *šakintu* bought 20 slaves for eight minas of silver in a single transaction.[56] In the same city the *šakintu* Ahi-ṭalli bought three slaves in 686 and then 17 persons in 683.[57]

Another possible explanation for the wealth, financial transactions and large numbers of women the *šakintu*s managed may have to do with their involvement in textile production.[58] It is known that large numbers of women lived in the palaces and also that large amounts of flax and wool were distributed there (SAA VII 115). Palace textile production was not that uncommon in ancient Near Eastern history and certainly not in Mesopotamia in particular. Given the size of their staff and the innumerable expenses, gifts and contributions that a queen was expected to make and give, it makes good sense that there would be a business operation in her household, run by her chief administrator.

Finally, there is one mention of a woman, Ahi-ṭalli, moving from the position of *sekretu* to *šakintu* (SAA VI 88, 89). Not much is known about who precisely the *sekretu*s were but there were clearly many of them in the palace. It has been suggested that they were the concubines or secondary wives of the king but the term could also mean any women who lived in the palace other than the queen.[59] What is interesting about Ahi-ṭalli is that she changed from being one of many *sekretu*s to the elevated position of *šakintu*, the woman in charge. This change in status reveals fluidity in the queen's household and indicates that it was possible for a woman to advance to the position of *šakintu*. It is the only known example of a palace woman changing

---

[53] SAA VI 81.

[54] SAA VI 90, 93.

[55] SAA XIV 175.

[56] SAA VI 86.

[57] SAA VI 89, 90.

[58] Teppo 2007: 266-268.

[59] The term *sekretu* (MÍ.ERIM.É.GAL) literally means an enclosed woman. Amélie Kuhrt (1995 II: 527) has suggested that a *sekretu* might have been a royal concubine or royal wife or female palace servant. Sarah Melville (2004: 40) states that the *sekretu* was a concubine although in a general sense the term could signify any woman who lived in the palace who was not the queen. Saana Teppo (2007:265) accepts Melville's hypothesis qualifying that "this cannot be proved beyond doubt."

her position and, as it turns out, Ahi-talli is the only *sekretu* whose name has survived in archival documents.

Personnel: the scribes

The household of the queen consisted of a large staff of both women and men. Although her chief administrator was always female, she employed both female and male scribes. The names Aššur-resuwa (eunuch), Issar-duri, Asqudu and Nabû-aplu-iddina which appeared in legal transactions identified each man as a "scribe (LÚ.A.BA.) of the queen."[60]

The queen also employed female scribes (MÍ.A.BA-*tú*). In a Neo-Assyrian survey of female personnel that focused on female musicians, six female scribes were listed.[61] Two queries to the deity Manlaharban that request information on the rumor of an insurrection against Aššurbanipal end with the disavowal (*ezib*), "Disregard that a woman has written and placed it before you."[62] It is impossible to determine whether or not it was extraordinary or unusual for the scribe who wrote out the request to the deity to be a woman, but these two queries reveal that female scribes did function in this capacity. Female scribes were certainly a feature of Mesopotamian culture and evidence for them spans the period from the third to the first millennium BCE.[63] The Neo-Assyrian period was no exception.

Among the tablets from the queen's household that were found at Fort Shalmaneser were two documents in which the queen's scribe Attar-palti loaned a considerable amount of silver.[64] It is not clear whether she did this privately or in her official capacity as scribe in the queen's household. In ND 7088, Attar-palti loaned 52 shekels of silver to Salam-šarri-iqbi, who came from a village outside of Kalhu. His name is the same as a *turtānu* who held the *limmu* office at the time of Sin-šarru-iškun (623-612). The loan document clearly states that the silver came from the temple of the goddess Mullissu. ND 7090 documents a loan of half a mina of silver to Nasî by the queen's scribe Attar-palti. Although this text does not say that the silver came from the temple of Mullissu, Dalley and Postgate suggest that because of the many similarities with ND 7088, the silver most likely did come from the temple. They also comment, "it is particularly interesting to note that the queen's household offered loan facilities to men with silver drawn from the temple of Mullissu."[65] One final element in the text which is confusing is that in ND

---

[60] SAA VI 31, 253, 310, 325; SAA XIV 29.

[61] SAA VII 24.

[62] SAA IV 321-322. A standard disavowal (*ezib*) of this type was a disclaimer intended to "neutralize" any harmful circumstances or unfavorable conditions that might jeopardize the outcome of the extispicy (Starr 1990: LXVIII, n. 1)

[63] Meier 1991: 541.

[64] CTN III 39-40.

[65] Dalley and Postgate 1984: 95, 13.

7088 the masculine determinative before the word for scribe is found but in ND 7090 there is no gender determinative at all.[66]

Personnel: other household members

Among the members of the queen's household and the queen mother's household were members of the military. Their names and positions can be found on palace personnel lists and legal documents. Were they part of the queen's own army or were they merely part of the queen's bodyguard units? Dalley and Postgate have made the suggestion that part of Sennacherib's military reforms involved dividing the 'royal' units of the army into two or three parts among leading members of the royal family. From Sennacherib's reign onward administrative records make reference to the separate military establishments of the queen and queen mother. Dalley and Postgate also consider the possibility that the queen maintained a household at the Kalhu arsenal (Fort Shalmaneser), a palace specifically designed and used for military purposes, because she maintained her own military unit there.[67]

The members of the military identified as 'of the queen' included cohort commanders, chariot drivers, 'third men,' bodyguards and more specifically the cohort commander of chariot fighters. On one personnel list alone the queen mother is identified as having three bodyguards, one cohort commander, one 'third man' and two chariot drivers.[68] While the queens appear to have had reasonably large military attachments assigned to them there is not sufficient evidence to determine whether their military units were an army or merely their bodyguards.

Both the queen and queen mother had eunuchs as part of their households. Seven legal transactions of Milki-nuri, the eunuch of the queen, reveal that he had the necessary resources to purchase slaves and even entire villages. In 668 he bought the village of Nabû-šezib with its fields, orchards and people.[69] In 666 he bought the village of Bahaya including its fields and one farmer with his people in the district of Lahiru.[70] In three undated transactions Milki-nuri bought ten, five and six slaves for what must have been a considerable amount of silver.[71] The queen mother also had eunuchs in her households. In one document alone, a list of officials at court, four different eunuchs are recorded as being part of the queen mother's household.[72] While

---

[66] Meier has noted that in an earlier period there were no gender markings in Sumerian to distinguish women from men in occupations that they both shared and later in Akkadian the feminine determinative was not rigidly applied (Meier 1991: 541). This does not explain the use of the masculine determinative for a female scribe.

[67] Dalley and Postgate 1984: 41, 11.

[68] SAA VII 5.

[69] SAA XIV 1.

[70] SAA XIV 2. Lahiru was a district associated with members of the royal family. The queen mother, the queen and the crown prince are known to have owned property there.

[71] SAA XIV 3-5.

[72] SAA VII 5.

the duties and responsibilities of eunuchs are not clear they must have held important and lucrative positions.

In addition to the *šakintu*, scribes, members of the military and eunuchs, other members of these queens' households appear in palace records. The queen's butler was wealthy enough to acquire land in a village for six minas of copper[73] and in a lodgings list his deputy is mentioned.[74] There were cooks and confectioners in the queens' kitchens in Nineveh and Kalhu or Arbail.[75] There were also weavers, tailors, fullers, a treasurer and a goldsmith.[76] Even a deputy of the queen mother's chief of quays is listed.[77] And in a legal transaction one of the witnesses is the merchant of the queen's house.[78]

Although it is not possible to know the exact size and structure of a queen's household, she clearly had a staff of considerable size. It would seem that each queen's residence whether in Kalhu, Nineveh, Assur, Kilizi, Ekallate or in other Assyrian cities had its own staff. Palace records also reveal that certain positions in the queens' households involved great prestige and wealth. A *šakintu* was able to negotiate an extremely favorable marriage for her daughter even though the future husband seems to have been a man of wealth and prestige himself. The queen's eunuchs had the wealth to buy slaves and entire towns. Other household members owned slaves and even made loans of large amounts of silver.

Royal Women

Centralization and hierarchical structures of power characterized the Assyrian state. At the apex was the Assyrian king, the all-powerful monarch. Among royal women there very likely could have been a similar hierarchy of power with those women closest to the king being the most important. For instance, it is highly conceivable that a woman born into the royal family had a higher rank than a woman who married into it. But did the mother of the king have more status and rank than the principal wife of the king?[79] Perhaps it depended on the woman herself. The evidence indicates that both Sammuramat and Naqia became much more important and influential after their sons became kings of Assyria. The queen mother Sammuramat's name appears beside her son's in royal inscriptions, and she is one of the few queens to have a stele erected at Assur among the stelae of Neo-Assyrian kings. Naqia is known to have corresponded with foreign rulers and important government

---

[73] CTN II 44.

[74] SAA VII 9 i 24-25.

[75] SAA VII 6. Dalley and Postgate 1984: 144-149.

[76] SAA VII 5, 9, 12; Dalley and Postgate 1984: 11 n. 27; SAA XVI 65.

[77] SAA VII 9 r. i 27-28.

[78] SAA VI 140 r. 11-12.

[79] According to Melville (2004: 52), "The highest-ranking woman in Assyria was, *ipso facto*, the mother of the king, although under normal circumstances, the queen mother had no official role and probably lived quietly on her own estate away from the palace."

officials during her son's reign. Naqia is also the only queen known to have the power to impose and enforce a loyalty oath on the Assyrian people after her son had died.

Since a royal woman's relationship to the king was of such vital importance, the terminology that explained it was much more than mere description. It defined her in a way that often made the use of her personal name unnecessary. There are many reports and letters that referred to the 'mother of the king' (*ummi šarri*) during Esarhaddon's reign and this was obviously deemed sufficient identification. The expression *ummi šarri* apparently identified Naqia in the most meaningful way thus her personal name was omitted. However, occasionally the opposite occurs when only the personal name of a royal woman is given.[80]

Daughters and sisters

With the exception of the crown prince very little is known about the children of Assyrians kings.[81] Occasionally their names, general health and activities are mentioned in legal documents, palace lists and personal letters. The names of five of Esarhaddon's children, four sons and his daughter Šerua-eṭerat, are given in a medical report to the king from his exorcist.[82] The names of five of Esarhaddon's children, which include Šerua-eṭerat, are part of the accounts of a ceremonial banquet.[83] Correspondence from a priest to the king mentions offerings made by Esarhaddon and five of his children, including Šerua-eṭerat, during a celebration for Nabû and Tašmetum.[84] Interestingly the name of Šerua-eṭerat is always included among Esarhaddon's offspring, but the names of his sons vary from document to document. Why did she have such a visible presence among Esarhaddon's children? Does this indicate she was a favorite of her father's or that her mother was the principal queen? Did she have exceptional abilities or perhaps a strong personality? Or was she the first born?

Information concerning the daughters of Assyrian kings indicate that they had wealth, owned property and maintained a high status in the court and

---

[80] A few examples when only the personal name of the royal woman is given in a document follow. In a query to the sungod, Šamaš is asked whether Esarhaddon should appoint NN to the service of Naqia. No title for Naqia is included (SAA IV 151). In a letter to the king, the chief exorcist Nabû-nadin-šumi discusses a ritual for Šadditu but never mentions that she is the daughter of Sennacherib (SAA X 273). In an edict giving the schedule for distribution of meat from offerings, the "mausoleum of Ešarra-hammat" is mentioned twice. In both instances Ešarra-hammat's name occurs without any explanation that she had been the queen of Esarhaddon (SAA XII 81).

[81] "The number of royal offspring is rarely known: Sennacherib seems to have had six or seven, Esarhaddon had about nineteen, of whom nine are known by name [Parpola 1983: 117-118], while only two are known for Ashurbanipal." (Kuhrt 1995 II: 528).

[82] SAA X 223.

[83] SAA XI 154.

[84] SAA XIII 56.

society. They also participated in religious rituals and at certain times became part of Assyrian alliances through political marriages with foreign rulers.

Both the administrative records and legal transactions of the royal court refer to property owned by the kings' daughters. In a schedule of estates assigned to court officials and members of the military, one official, the *sartinnu*, received an estate in the "town of the Daughter of the King." In another section of the same document four estates that had previously been owned by members of the military were "given over to the princess of the New Palace."[85] In a legal transaction "Šaddit[u, daug]hter [of] Sennacherib, king of Assyria and sister of Es[arh]addon, king of Assyria" bought property that consisted of a garden, house, land and associated workers for eight minas of silver.[86] Although few in number these documents suggest that the daughters of the king are among the royal women and other members of the royal family who owned considerable property throughout the Assyrian empire.

Royal women participated in and had religious rituals performed for them. The chief exorcist for Esarhaddon, Nabû-nadin-šumi reported a breach of professional etiquette to the king which involved a ritual that the king had requested be done for his sister Šadditu.[87] When Nabû-nadin-šumi had not been able to complete the ritual another exorcist, unqualified according to Nabû-nadin-šumi, had hurried up from Kalhu and performed it. Obviously the chief exorcist was upset but the incident does illustrate the high standing of Šadditu if the king would order a ritual to be performed for his sister by an exorcist of the highest order.

The state god Aššur took on a new importance in the first millennium as he began to embody more and more the interests of Assyria.[88] Royal visits to the sanctuaries of Aššur would have constituted important occasions. During one such visit to the sanctuaries of Aššur and his wives Mullissu and Šerua at Assur, royal women attended and participated in a ritual. The most important role seems to have been played by the king but when offerings of cooked meat were offered to Šerua at one point during the ritual the daughter of the king was supposed to call out her name "Šerua." At another point the sister of the king was to call out "Šerua wife of Aššur."[89] The attendance of female members of the royal family and the participation of the daughter and sister of the king in a ritual at the sanctuary of the state god Aššur must have had political and religious significance.

An Assyrian king's daughter might be used to cement a political alliance with another state through her marriage to its ruler. This is precisely what happened to Ahat-abiša the daughter of Sargon II. Throughout his reign Sargon had problems with the Anatolian frontier to the west. When the king of Tabal died the Assyrians sanctioned the accession to the throne of his son

---

[85] SAA XI 221.

[86] SAA VI 251.

[87] SAA X 273.

[88] Jacobsen 1976: 231-232; also Porter 1993: 65, 143.

[89] BM 121206; van Driel 1968: 99, 101, 103.

Ambaris of Bit-Purutaš. Sargon's daughter was married to Ambaris and correspondence to Sargon indicates that his daughter and her staff made reports to him.[90] But the Assyrian plan did not work as Ambaris aligned himself with the Phrygians and Urartians against the Assyrians and Sargon was forced to take action. Ambaris was deposed and Tabal was made into an Assyrian province. Postgate thinks it possible that Ahat-abiša was left to administer Tabal following her husband's revolt and execution.[91]

Esarhaddon contemplated marrying either one or two of his daughters to foreign rulers for the same reason. Two formal queries made to Šamaš the sungod record that he considered these marriages in order that treaties be upheld and the peace with Assyria be kept.[92] In one query Bartatus king of the Scythians is the potential bridegroom while in the other query the name of the ruler is not mentioned. The Assyrian king must have had strong doubts about these rulers to make these enquiries. While it is not known whether the marriage(s) took place, Starr contends that given "the political situation at that time, it is more than likely."[93]

One of the few pieces of private correspondence between two royal women is the letter written by Esarhaddon's daughter Šerua-eṭerat to her sister-in-law, the wife of the crown prince Aššurbanipal. There have been multiple editions and translations of this letter with widely varying meanings and inferences. Oppenheim's translation suggests that Šerua-eṭerat is complaining about not hearing from her sister-in-law and that she is offended given her status as the daughter of the Assyrian king.[94] Luukko and Van Buylaere's translation shows that Šerua-eṭerat is admonishing her sister-in-law for not writing her tablets and doing her homework. Luukko and Van Buylaere further feel that the tone of the letter "... illustrates the undercurrent tensions between two high-ranking women at court" and suggest that Šerua-eṭerat may have written the letter out of feelings of rivalry and jealousy and fear of loss of influence and status at court.[95] Livingstone's translation suggests that Šerua-eṭerat is reprimanding her sister-in-law for not writing her tablets and reciting her exercises but that she is treating her sister-in-law with respect by addressing her with her royal titles.[96] Furthermore Livingstone sees no evidence for the rivalry and court intrigue that other translators have alluded to with their interpolations. Instead, he stresses that the letter illustrates the

[90] SAA I 31.

[91] In a letter to his father (ABL 197 = SAA I 31), Sennacherib mentions a message from Tabal from the major domo (*rab bēti*) of Ahat-abiša. The letter belongs to the period after Ambaris was removed. Postgate (1973a: 31 n. 19) writes, "It is clear that Bit-burutaš continued to have Ahat-abiša as its nominal ruler, even if the administration was effectively carried on by her *rab bēti*."

[92] SAA IV 20-21.

[93] Starr 1990: LXII.

[94] Oppenheim 1967: 158, No. 97.

[95] SAA XVI 28 (cf. *ibid*. XXVIII).

[96] Livingstone 2007: 103-105.

importance of literacy at the Assyrian court and that young royals were expected to learn to read and write.[97]

That this letter has survived is quite extraordinary and its content is quite insightful. The opening of the letter indicates that it is written by someone of a higher social position than the recipient.[98] It demonstrates a social distinction that existed between the two women in the Assyrian royal court, one born a member of the royal family and the other who married into it. That Šerua-eṭerat feels confident in admonishing her sister-in-law, most likely Libbali-šarrat, who will eventually become queen is quite interesting. But even more important is the evidence that education was advocated and literacy possibly required for life at court. This included the royal women, at least in the court of Esarhaddon. They were expected to be able to read and write and this is quite a revelation.

Queens' titles

The names of eleven women who used the title Mí.É.GAL or Mí.KUR are known.[99] As the title was used by both the principal wife of the king and also by the mother of the king it is not always clear whether the royal woman using the title was actually the principal wife of her husband the king or whether she began using the title once her son became the king.[100]

The title Mí.É.GAL or Mí.KUR (an abbreviated form where KUR means palace) might be used for the woman who was the wife or mother of the Neo-Assyrian king. Literally the term means 'woman + palace.' Transcribed into Neo-Assyrian it is read as *sēgallu* (< *issi ekalli*).[101]

The title Mí.É.GAL was used much more often for a queen or queen mother than the term Mí.KUR.[102] While the use of Mí.KUR generally occurs on archival documents as part of the identification of a profession (e.g., the scribe of the

---

[97] Livingstone (2007: 104) clearly states that "One has the feeling, though, that Oppenheim and other later translators intentionally ignored the plain meaning and tried to twist it because they baulked at the idea of a woman – and that a princess – having personally anything to do with writing at all."

[98] "The word *abutu* at the beginning of any Neo-Assyrian letter clearly marks the letter as sent from superior to inferior, at least from the writer/sender's point of view" (Svärd and Luukko 2009: 285 n. 37).

[99] The names of the women using this title are Mullissu-mukanni_šat_-Ninua, Sammuramat, Hamâ, Yabâ, Banitu, Atalia, Naqia, Tašmetum-šarrat, Ešarra-hammat, and Libbali-šarrat. An eleventh name is known from a limestone vessel fragment in The British Museum. It is inscribed with a name read as [Ana-Taš]metum-taklak. This is the only reference to her, and while it is unclear which Assyrian king she was the wife of, Finkel (2000: 12) suggested she might have been the second wife of Esarhaddon after Ešarra-hammat died.

[100] Melville (2004: 46) feels that "The king's mother was *ipso facto* his father's consort, regardless of past reality. Anything else would be at odds with the ideology of legitimacy."

[101] Parpola 1988: 75 and Postgate 1979: 95 n. 9.

[102] Mí.É.GAL is used 117 times in Neo-Assyrian sources (according to the *Corpus of Neo-Assyrian Texts*) (Svärd 2010: 1 n. 1), while there are at least 13 uses of Mí.KUR where the term refers to the queen (*ibid.* 2)

queen's household), there are two times when MÍ.KUR is specifically used with a named queen. Ešarra-hammat used MÍ.KUR in an inscription on an eye-stone dedicated by her. Naqia used MÍ.KUR in the loyalty oath she imposed on the nation of Assyria for her grandson Assurbanipal (see below). The two terms MÍ.É.GAL and MÍ.KUR appear to have been used synonymously and interchangeably. The most conclusive evidence for this is the document ND 7088. Attar-palṭi, the female scribe of the queen's household, is owed 52 shekels of silver. On the tablet she is referred to as LÚ.A.BA-*tú ša* É MÍ.KUR but on the envelope she is referred to as LÚ.A.BA-*tú ša* É M[Í].É.GAL.[103]

An important question however is whether more than one wife of the king could use the title MÍ.É.GAL or MÍ.KUR at the same time. Dalley and Postgate suggest that because the scribes used the title without any further qualification, it must have referred unambiguously to the king's main wife who was the mother of the heir to the throne.[104] Melville, however, feels that it was entirely possible that while outside the palace there was only one known MÍ.É.GAL, within the domestic quarters, or even the grave, more than one wife of the king could use the title on an informal basis.[105] Clearly the question is still open as to whether more than one wife of the king could use this title at the same time.

Two wives of Sennacherib, Naqia and Tašmetum-šarrat, however, are referred to as MÍ.É.GAL, but it is unclear whether these titles were used simultaneously or sequentially. In fact, there is no evidence that Naqia used the title while her husband was alive, although there are many examples of its use once her son was king. Tašmetum-šarrat is referred to as MÍ.É.GAL in an inscription by Sennacherib so it is certain that she used the title while her husband was alive. If the title MÍ.É.GAL referred to the king's main wife and the mother of the designated heir to the throne as Dalley and Postgate have suggested, Tašmetum-šarrat was an important royal woman. This even suggests that she may have been the mother of the ill-fated Aššur-nadin-šumi, Sennacherib's oldest son, who was sent to rule Babylon and was then betrayed and killed. If the title MÍ.É.GAL was used more loosely for royal women Tašmetum-šarrat could have been "simply a young (politically insignificant) girl ... who happened to catch the fancy of the aging monarch and was never first queen at all."[106]

Another question arises as to whether the title could be used by the mother of the king at the same time it was being used by one of the king's wives? Both Sammuramat and Naqia used the title MÍ.É.GAL during the reigns of their

---

[103] CTN III 39, 39A.

[104] Dalley and Postgate 1984: 11.

[105] Melville 2004: 43, 47. This statement is largely based on the inscriptions found on personal objects such as bowls, jars and a mirror in the recently discovered (1988 and 1989) queens' tombs at Kalhu.

[106] Melville, commenting on a statement by Borger (R. Borger, "König Sanheribs Eheglück," *ARRIM* 6 [1988]: 6), does not feel this situation is likely given the length of the inscription and that palace rooms were actually dedicated to Tašmetum-šarrat (Melville 1999: 18).

sons. But did Adad-nerari III have a wife using this title when his mother Sammuramat used it? Naqia certainly used this title throughout her son Esarhaddon's entire reign and must therefore have used it at the exact same time as his wife Ešarra-hammat. In this one case it seems likely that two women did use the title MÍ.É.GAL at the same time.

The title MÍ.É.GAL clearly gave the woman who used it considerable prestige. But was the title accompanied by official power or was it merely an honorary title? Some of the royal women who used the title were quite powerful and influential, while others appear not to have been. Unfortunately the information regarding what precisely the use of the title MÍ.É.GAL meant is not known. Nor is it known how the woman using the title fit within the hierarchy of the entire royal court.

Queen's symbol: the scorpion

The intriguing symbol of the scorpion has been found on objects that are connected to royal women and their domestic quarters in the palace. The scorpion has been found on small personal objects such as shells, a bowl, mirror, vase and weight. It has also been found on royal seals and clay seal impressions. The Sargonid queens and their households specifically appear to have used the symbol of the scorpion as a form of identification. The object at hand was thus recognized as being either the property of a specific royal woman or from the royal women's residential quarters of the palace. It has been noted that the use of symbols seems to have been a particular favorite of Sargon and his descendants.[107] The Sargonid kings continued the use of the lion being stabbed by the king, the crown prince used the Y-shaped cross (ispillurtu)[108] and the queens used the symbol of the scorpion.

Because the symbol of the scorpion was used by Sargonid royal women it is not surprising that two objects bearing the name of Atalia, queen of Sargon, and another object thought to have belonged to her, have a scorpion engraved on them. The three objects were found in the tomb of Yabâ in the Northwest Palace at Kalhu where Atalia is thought to have been interred. Resting on the chest of the top body in the sarcophagus was a gold bowl with eleven tiny gold flasks in it.[109] Around the outer rim of the bowl is an inscription that reads, "Belonging to Atalia, queen of Sargon, king of Assyria."[110] Between the beginning and the end of the inscription is the image of the scorpion. Lying on the floor of the burial chamber were more objects including an electrum cosmetics container with an electrum mirror as lid. Although the container is inscribed with the name of "Banitu, queen of Shalmaneser, king of Assyria," on the handle of the mirror is the inscription, "Belonging to

---

[107] J. and D. Oates 2001: 220-221.

[108] The seventh-century examples are from the period when Aššurbanipal was the crown prince (Radner 2008: 502-506).

[109] J. and D. Oates 2001: 83.

[110] Kamil 1999: 17, al-Rawi 2008: 137-138.

Atalia, queen of Sargon, king of Assyria,"[111] and at the end of the inscription is the image of the scorpion. The third object is a bronze weight cast in the form of a duck. On one side is an inscription in Assyrian cuneiform and on the other an inscription in Aramaic letters. Next to the Assyrian cuneiform signs is the image of the scorpion. As the other two queens with grave goods in this tomb are pre-Sargonid queens and the only objects with scorpions inscribed on them belonged to Atalia, the queen of Sargon, it is almost certain that the duck weight was hers as well.[112]

Among a collection of trinkets found by Mallowan in the residential area of the Northwest Palace at Kalhu was a large cockleshell decorated with the "spirited engraving of a scorpion."[113] In fact, three large shell beads were engraved with a scorpion design.[114] Mallowan thought this collection of small personal items was probably the property of some princess who kept it on the shelf in Room HH

Tašmetum-šarrat, a queen of Sargon's son Sennacherib, also used the symbol of the scorpion. On an alabaster vase found at Assur an inscription reads, "belonging to Tašmetum-šarrat, queen of Sennacherib,"[115] and next to her name is the image of a scorpion.

Seals and seal impressions use the scorpion either on its own or as a filler motif in the company of other figures. There are at least 65 known examples of seal impressions from Nineveh that have the image of a scorpion on them. In many of the impressions the entire scorpion is visible: the head, thorax, abdomen, curved tail, legs and pincers. The shape of the seal impression is either round or oval. There is usually an ornamental border around the scorpion and occasionally an inscription.[116]

The border designs on the scorpion seals have been one of the principle factors in determining their association with other royal seals. The guilloche border was only used on royal seals, never on private seals. Of the 65 scorpion seal impressions, 50 have the guilloche border design.[117] And the majority of royal seal impressions that have the image of the king slaying the lion also have the guilloche border. Another design, the garland, can also be found surrounding the scorpion on seals. It is unfortunate that the one example of an inscription surrounding the scorpion on a seal impression is too fragmentary for the signs to be read.[118]

---

[111] Kamil 1999: 17, al-Rawi 2008: 137-138.

[112] Al-Rawi (2008: 126-130) suggests the possibility that the scorpion could have been an astrological sign of Sargon II.

[113] Mallowan 1966: 113-114. Although Mallowan only mentions an engraved scorpion on one cockleshell, Joan and David Oates (2001: 79) state that there were three large shell beads that bore engraved scorpions and Parker (1955: 112) states that "Many of these shells were engraved with figures of scorpions."

[114] J. and D. Oates 2001: 79.

[115] Luckenbill 1924: 152.

[116] Herbordt 1992: 136.

[117] *Ibid*.

[118] Radner 2008: 500. Herbordt 1992: 137.

The seal with a scorpion as the main motif is most likely a bureaucratic seal type used by the queens' household. It is often found on textile labels and textile production was likely an important activity and source of income for royal women and their households.[119] Two such textile labels found in the Southwest Palace at Nineveh had seals with an image of the scorpion on them. SAA VII 93 (B.M. 82-5-22,40) derived "from Ibbiya, in the domestic quarters" and was dated 658, that is, from the reign of Aššurbanipal.[120] The seal impression on the textile label shows a scorpion with a flower above it, both figures within the guilloche border.[121] SAA VII 102 (B.M. 83-1-18,567) is only a fragment but contains part of a textile list and part of a seal impression. Part of the scorpion and the guilloche border are clearly visible on the impression.[122] This label is also thought to date from 658. Other examples of textile labels with images of scorpions from Nineveh are known although interestingly none are from Kalhu or Dur-Šarrukin.

Two quite unique sealings were found in Nineveh. One such sealing with multiple impressions was found in the Southwest Palace at Nineveh by Layard. On it are three "Royal Seal Type" designs showing the king facing a rampant lion. These designs alternate with images of scorpions.[123] The other sealing shows a scorpion, king with rampant lion and the Y-shape. These three images are known to be seals associated with the queen, king and crown prince's bureau.[124]

There are other seals and sealings where the scorpion is a filler motif intermingled with other figures, often the king and the queen. An unusual example, however, are three impressions of the same seal found on a small, uninscribed clay sealing ND 808 in the Northwest Palace at Kalhu. The sealing was found on the floor in Room HH in the residential area of the palace where royal women most likely resided. This is the same room where Mallowan found the shells engraved with the image of the scorpion. It is thought that the sealing dates from the year 716 during the reign of Sargon.[125] On the seal impression a woman with her hands raised in prayer stands facing a scorpion. The two figures are encircled by a guilloche band.

Sealings from both Kalhu and Nineveh show the king and queen approaching deities with the scorpion as a filler motif above the scene. In some examples the royal couple face a god and goddess, each standing on an animal

---

[119] An administrative seal containing a scorpion with other figures was found in the Northwest Palace at Kalhu and used during the reign of Sargon II. The sealings had inscriptions demonstrating a connection with sheep (Radner 2008: 509).

[120] SAA VII 93.

[121] Herbordt 1992: 252, Taf. 20.5. It is entirely possible that the flower or rosette may have been connected with Ištar. Some scholars think it possible that during the Neo-Assyrian period the rosette occasionally replaced the star as her symbol (Black and Green 1992: 156-157).

[122] Herbordt 1992: 252, Taf. 20.6.

[123] Mattila 2002: 10, Fig. 3.

[124] Radner 2008: 500; Herbordt 1992: 68, 133, Taf. 35.7.

[125] Radner 2008: 499; Herbordt 1992: 137, 200-201, Taf. 20.4; Parker 1955: 111-112, Pl. XXII.1.

such as a bull or lion or dog (ND 807, ND 1106a, ND 1106b),[126] while in other examples (Fig. 12) they approach a single goddess standing on an animal (BM 84789, BM 84802, BM 50781).[127] These representations are surrounded by a guilloche border.

While most of the examples of the scorpion image on a seal derive from seal impressions, there are two known stamp seals with images that include both the queen and the scorpion amidst other figures.

A white chalcedony stamp seal used late in the reign of Sennacherib[128] shows a scene in which the king and queen approach a goddess, probably Mullissu, seated on a throne on the back of a lion (BM 2002-5-15, 1).[129] In the space above the figures is a scorpion. Surrounding the scene is a guilloche border. There are also sealing impressions thought to have been made by this exact seal (BM 84671, K 348+Ki 1904-10-9, 246).[130] This is the only known case of an original Neo-Assyrian seal and its antique impressions to be in existence today.

Fig. 12 Sealing of queen and king worshipping a goddess with a scorpion between the king and goddess, Southwest Palace, Nineveh (BM 84789, courtesy Trustees of The British Museum)

The other example of an actual seal with the image of a scorpion was found in the Northwest Palace at Kalhu (IM 115644). It was discovered by Hussein in Tomb III. This Royal Seal is made of gold and was likely worn as a piece of jewellery. It shows the queen standing in front of the enthroned goddess Gula who rests her feet on a dog. Behind the goddess is the scorpion. Around the scene is a guilloche border.[131] There is a one line inscription on the rim that reads: "Belonging to Hamâ, queen of Shalmaneser, king of Assyria, daughter-in-law of Adad-nerari."[132]

The symbol of the scorpion was used by Assyrian royal women, predominantly the queens of the Sargonid kings, often with inscriptions to identify an object as the property of a specific queen. The scorpion image also appears to have been used on a bureaucratic level identifying documents as being from

---

[126] Radner 2008: 497; CTN II 257, 260, 261, Pl. 97i, j, k.

[127] Radner 2008: 497-498, Figs. 9, 10, 11; Herbordt 1992: 137-138, Taf. 32.4, 5; Reade 1987: 144-145, Figs. 5, 6.

[128] This dating is based on the textile label K 348+Ki 1904-10-9,246 (Radner 2008: 498; SAA VII 94).

[129] Radner 2008: 498, Fig. 12a-b.

[130] Radner 2008: 499, Figs. 13a-b, 14; Herbordt 1992: Taf. 32.3; Reade 1987: 145, Fig. 7. Although Reade thinks the two figures before the goddess are quite possibly the queen and an attendant, Dominique Collon checked the seal against the impression [BM 84671] and is certain the impression was produced with this seal (Radner 2008: 498 n 33).

[131] Al-Gailani Werr 2008: 155-156.

[132] Al-Rawi 2008: 136.

the queen's household. The decorative border on many of these seals was one used only on royal seals.

The question arises of why the symbol of the scorpion was chosen to be the symbol for royal women. The scorpion certainly figures in Mesopotamian art, especially engraving, from very early times (Sumerian) and is thought to have been "quite clearly connected with fertility."[133] The scorpion is also said to be a symbol of fertility commonly found on seals of the Neo-Assyrian period.[134] Another idea is that because the scorpion mother fiercely protects her young (the ideal mother) and the queen was always the mother of the crown prince, the symbol of the scorpion was appropriate.[135] In addition another aspect of the scorpion that might be relevant in this context is that it is a dangerous animal and "a suitable image of power and protection."[136] An incantation against the scorpion says, "its pincers are extended (like the horns of a wild bull), its tail is curved up (like that of a raging lion)."[137] If the latter image of the scorpion was considered relevant, the Sargonid queens would be fitting companions for the Sargonid kings.

Queens' burials

While it is known that many Assyrian kings were buried in Assur, inscriptions from that city indicate that the queen of Esarhaddon, Ešarra-hammat, was also buried there. Although no specific tomb can be identified as hers, references to the "mausoleum of Ešarra-hammat" are mentioned more than once in connection with the royal tomb complex at Assur. Other Assyrian queens were buried at Kalhu. Their tombs have been found underneath the floors of the domestic quarters in the Northwest Palace. In 1951 Max Mallowan found two graves and in 1988 and 1989 the Iraqi Office of Antiquities and Heritage found three queens' tombs.

The two graves that Mallowan found in 1951 were about five feet below the floor in opposite corners of Room DD in the Northwest Palace.[138] He thought they had been dug no earlier than the end of the eighth century. In the first grave there was only an engraved bronze bowl in the coffin. In the second grave a baked clay bath-shaped coffin was sealed by three slabs of alabaster, two of which were inscribed. The two inscribed slabs consisted of re-used foundation tablets recording the building of the city wall by Aššur-naṣirpal II (883-859). In the coffin was the skeleton of a woman whose body had originally been laid in a sitting or leaning position. Around her neck was a necklace of semi-precious stones and glass beads. Her shroud had been fastened at the shoulder by a bronze fibula with a gold chain and an engraved

---

[133] Parker (1955: 111) cites "Van Buren, A.f.O. 12, where much evidence is collected."
[134] J. and D. Oates 2001: 79.
[135] Radner 2008: 495.
[136] Black and Green, 1992: 161.
[137] CT 38 38:60f. Quoted s.v. *zuqaqīpu*, *CAD* Z, 164.

gem set in gold. This piece of jewellery has become known as the "Nimrud Jewel." The pale mauve chalcedony gem was engraved with a scene consisting of two musicians, one playing a lyre and the other double pipes, on either side of a sacred tree. It is attached by links on a swivel to the gold chain. Mallowan felt that "So valuable and precious a jewel could only have belonged to royalty."[139] Yet no seal or inscription gave the name of the royal woman buried in this grave.

In 1988 the Iraqi Office of Antiquities and Heritage discovered a tomb ('Tomb I') under the floor of Room MM during excavations and restoration. A row of bricks mounted vertically on the floor led to the discovery of the tomb. The entrance chamber contained a terracotta sarcophagus that held the skeleton of a woman approximately 45 to 55 years of age at death. The main chamber was a barrel-vaulted room of baked bricks, some of which were inscribed with the name of Aššurnaṣirpal. It also contained a terracotta sarcophagus with the body of a woman inside. She lay on her back, her skull resting on a silver bowl. She was estimated to have been approximately 50 to 55 years of age when she died.[140] Undyed flax textile fragments in a tabby weave were found near the body. Some were heavily stained from a copper alloy object.[141]

There were numerous grave goods in the sarcophagus with the woman. There were vessels of copper and bronze, flat seals engraved with the Assyrian themes of the sacred tree and winged deities and two frit or faience plaques with erotic scenes.

There were also approximately 200 pieces of gold jewellery.[142] There were necklaces of gold chains, gold beads (some in the shape of pomegranates), and semi-precious stones. There were crescent-shaped earrings decorated with intricate patterns in fine granulation and embellished with gold wires and dangling gold cones. There were armlets and rings, five on her left forefinger alone, and a gold fibula with the shapes of a Pazuzu-demon, a woman, a fish and an eagle molded together. And there was an even finer example of the "Nimrud Jewel." A stone engraved with a scene was encased in gold and decorated with delicate granulated designs with two lions resting on the crossbars. It appeared to be suspended from a gold chain with a looped swivel.

In 1989 a further tomb ('Tomb II') was found by Hussein below Room 49 in the Northwest Palace. It also was constructed of baked bricks and had two barrel-vaulted chambers. The entrance chamber was roofed with an east-west vault while the main chamber had a north-south vault. Double stone doors secured by an iron bar led from one chamber to the other.

In the entrance chamber was an alcove which contained a stone funerary tablet. It gave the name of the tomb's occupant as Queen Yabâ and read:

---

[138] Mallowan 1966 I: 114-115.
[139] Mallowan 1966 I: 115, fig. 58.
[140] J. and D. Oates 2001: 80-81.
[141] Crowfoot 1995: 117.

By the command of Šamaš, Ereškigal and the Anunnaki, the great gods of the netherworld, mortal destiny caught up with Queen Yabâ in death, and she traveled the path of her ancestors. Anyone, in time to come, whether a queen who sits on the throne or a palace lady of the palace who is a favorite of the king, that removes me from my tomb, or places anybody else with me, or lays his hand on my jewellery with evil intent, or breaks open the seal of this tomb – on earth, under the rays of the sun, let his spirit roam outside in thirst. In the Netherworld he must not receive with the Anunnakku any offering of libation of water, beer, wine or meal, but instead may Ningišzida and (unintelligible), the great gods of the netherworld, inflict his corpse and ghosts with eternal restlessness.[143]

The name of Yabâ was inscribed on other objects in the tomb including two gold bowls. One inscription reads, "Belonging to Yabâ, queen of Tiglath-Pileser, king of Assyria."[144]

In the main chamber was a massive sarcophagus of one piece of Mosul marble that occupied the full width of the north end of the room. Directly above the sarcophagus was a vertical terracotta pipe. It is one of the few known examples of a libation pipe through which the *kispu* (funerary) offerings would have been made to the dead queen. This suggests that the rooms above were used for the *kispu* or funerary banquets.[145] These were occasions when the dead were remembered and given food and flowers. In an alcove in the main chamber was an alabaster jar that contained decomposed brown organic material that might be desiccated brain.[146]

It came as a shock to discover that there were two skeletons inside the sarcophagus. Obviously the specific prohibition on the curse tablet not to place another body in the coffin had had no effect. Paleopathological work on the skeletons indicates that both women died at approximately the same age, that of 30 to 35. But they were not buried at the same time, as there were 20 to 50 years between the interments. The first body is thought to be that of Yabâ, the owner of the tomb. Her body was in an advanced state of decomposition and was damaged when the second body was put in the sarcophagus. The second body is thought to be Atalia (wife of Sargon II) as there are at least three objects in the tomb inscribed with her name, one being the gold bowl that was found lying on the chest of the second woman. Necropsis shows that the second body was cooked or exposed for several hours at 150-250° C. One possible reason would be that if the woman had died far from Kalhu her body would then have had to be brought back to the city for burial beneath the palace.

The names of three queens were found on objects inside of the tomb. All three were queens of kings who ruled Assyria in the second half of the eighth century. Their names were inscribed on gold bowls, crystal jars, an electrum

---

[142] Damerji 1999: Abb. 8-15.

[143] George 1990: 29. Also Damerji 1999: Abb. 18.

[144] Kamil 1999: 15.

[145] Postgate 2008: 180.

[146] Although it had originally been thought that the jar contained a cremation burial, the organic material had not been burned, nor had there been any resin used as in Egyptian mummification procedures (Müller-Karpe, Kunter and Schultz 2008: 148).

mirror and an electrum cosmetics container. These objects had belonged to Yabâ, queen of Tiglath-Pileser III (744-727), Banitu, queen of Shalmaneser V (726-722) and Atalia, queen of Sargon II (721-705).[147]

There were many remarkable objects lying on the floor in the main chamber, an electrum cosmetics box with an electrum mirror as lid being one. Inside of the sarcophagus were 157 objects, most of which were jewellery.[148] There was a gold crown of flowers on thin sheets of gold that still had part of a skull in it.[149] There were gold earrings, necklaces, finger rings and anklets, the latter each weighing between 2-2½ pounds. There were necklaces and armlets of gold inlaid with semi-precious stones and colored glass plus many more objects. Donny George has suggested that as a result of the king collecting craftspeople from all over the empire an "Assyrian empire style" developed in jewellery design which reflected the multi-cultural elements of the Assyrian empire.[150]

A group of rock crystal vessels, two with the names of Yabâ and Atalia inscribed on them, were found in the tomb. Lying on top of the bodies was a copper/bronze mirror with a palmette handle made of ivory, gold, carnelian and other semi-precious stones. The linen clothing or shrouding on the bodies had numerous gold objects sewn on them, including 770 tiny gold rosettes, 1,160 convex studs plus stars, discs and hanging balls. Fibulae were pinned to the clothing and hanging from them were seals and brightly colored stones.[151] Most assuredly these grave goods "make this tomb one of the most remarkable ever found in the Near East."[152]

Finally a third tomb ('Tomb III') was found by Hussein in 1989 under Room 57. The inscriptions on the doors between the two chambers and on the lid of the sarcophagus indicated that the tomb had been constructed for the queen of Aššurnaṣirpal II (883-859), who was the original builder of the Northwest Palace. The size and weight of the sarcophagus indicated that it would have been placed in the tomb before its completion and even before the completion of the room above.

The tomb had two chambers but the main chamber had been broken into and robbed in antiquity. It was essentially empty except for the sarcophagus which was set into the floor of the tomb. It was an Egyptian-style sarcophagus with a heavy stone lid upon which was carved, lengthwise, a five-line inscription that reads:

> Belonging to Mullissu-mukanniš at-Ninua, queen of Aššurnaṣirpal, king of Assyria, and Shalmaneser, king of Assyria. No one later may place here, whether a

---

[147] Kamil 1999: 18.

[148] Damerji 1999: Abb. 21-32.

[149] Muzahim Mahmud Hussein in a lecture on "The Discovery of the Tombs," The Nimrud Conference, The British Museum, London, 12 March 2002.

[150] D. George in a lecture on "The Craftsmanship of the Nimrud Jewellery," The Nimrud Conference, The British Museum, London, 12 March 2002.

[151] Collon 2008: 114.

[152] J. and D. Oates 2001: 82.

palace lady or a queen, nor remove this sarcophagus from its place. Whoever removes this sarcophagus from its place, his spirit will not receive the *kispu*-offerings with the other spirits. It is the taboo of Šamaš and Ereškigal! Daughter of Aššur-nirka-da"ini, chief cup-bearer of Aššurnaṣirpal, king of Assyria.[153]

This inscription is important because it is the only specific piece of evidence that reveals that Assyrian kings did marry into Assyrian nobility. Another less complete but similar inscription on a tablet reads, "Anyone later who removes my throne from before the shades of the dead, may his spirit receive no bread!"[154] Both inscriptions indicate rituals and beliefs which can be placed firmly within Mesopotamian burial traditions.

The double stone doors between the two chambers were found closed, blocked with bricks and replastered. While the main chamber in the tomb had been found virtually empty, the same was not true of the entrance chamber. It held three bronze coffins, one of which held an even larger collection of royal treasure than had been found in the second tomb.

The bones of at least 13 persons, some of secondary deposition, were found in the three coffins. The first coffin contained the skeleton of an adult woman, four children and a fetus. The second coffin contained the skeletons of two females, one an adult and one a child. The third coffin contained the skeletons of five adults: three men and two women.[155] Many unanswerable questions have arisen concerning the many skeletons in the three coffins. Were the skeletons all members of the royal family? Was one of the skeletons Mullissu-mukanniṣat-Ninua who might have been reburied in the entrance chamber after the desecration of her main burial chamber? Why were adult men and women buried together in the same coffin?

Among the 449 objects found in the tomb, of which the gold and silver alone weighed 50 pounds, were two cylinder seals, a spouted ewer, gold plates and bowls and many exquisite pieces of jewellery. An adult-sized gold crown was found resting on the child's head in the second coffin. It was made of numerous pieces of gold that had been welded and hammered together. Pomegranates or poppies, flowers, grape leaves and four-winged clothed figures of a Phoenician or Etruscan type decorated the crown. It had been inlaid (although only the bitumen that was used for the gluing remained) and lapis lazuli grape clusters hung from the rim.[156] Pieces of textiles, all heavily stained with bronze, were found.

In the tomb were inscribed objects that ranged in date from the ninth through the eighth century. The seal of a eunuch courtier is thought to date to the reign of Adad-nerari III (810-783); a gold bowl belonged to a *turtānu* who was commander-in-chief during the reigns of Shalmaneser IV (782-773), Aššur-dan III (772-755) and Aššur-nerari V (754-745); and a 15-mina duck weight came from the time of Tiglath-Pileser III (744-727). Thus it is evident

---

[153] J. and D. Oates 2001: 85; also Damerji 1999: Abb. 36-37.

[154] Al-Rawi 2008: 124.

[155] Müller-Karpe, Kunter and Schultz 2008: 144.

[156] Damerji 1999: Abb. 41-45.

that many of the objects in the tomb postdate Mullissu-mukannišat-Ninua, queen of Aššurnaṣirpal II (883-859).[157]

The queens' tombs found below the residential section of the Northwest Palace at Kalhu are unique. They are the only tombs found that still contained the coffins, bodies and grave goods of Assyrian royal women. These tombs complement the tombs of the Assyrian kings. The kings were buried below the palace at Assur whereas the queens were buried below the palace at Kalhu. The queens' tombs might even have been preplanned as was the case for Mullisu-mukannišat-Ninua. Fittingly the title for queen, MÍ.É.GAL, literally 'woman of the palace,' appears to have been accurate even after death as the queens were buried beneath 'their house.'

The grave goods have also provided hitherto unknown information. Objects of gold, crystal, electron, ivory, semi-precious stones and colored glass reveal high levels of craftsmanship. Examples of Assyrian jewellery, previously known only from the carved stone reliefs and sculptures, were found in abundance. They illustrate an eclectic 'Assyrian empire style' that reflects the Assyrian proclivity for adopting the artistic ideas of other cultures. In addition, extremely rare and fragile textiles of linen and flax surrounded many of the bodies discovered in these tombs.

Sammuramat

Sammuramat was the wife of the Assyrian king Šamši-Adad V (823-811) and mother of the Assyrian king Adad-nerari III (810-783). Much has been written about her and her story became steeped in the myths and legends which surrounded the classical heroine Semiramis.[158] The Greek writer Herodotus and the Roman historian Diodorus added to the legend with their stories of Semiramis. Somehow the two women became identified with each other even though the classical Semiramis story bears virtually no relationship to the historical Sammuramat.[159]

Because there is a scarcity of records from the reigns of her husband and son, the historical personage Sammuramat is elusive. It is therefore even more important to look closely at the evidence and information that does exist to attempt to obtain a more accurate picture of this queen who "caught the imagination of the ancients."[160]

---

[157] J. and D. Oates 2001: 86.

[158] In the legend, Semiramis was born in Palestine to a goddess. Eventually an Assyrian officer fell in love with her and took her to Assyria. There the king fell in love with her and was able to marry her when her husband committed suicide. Not long after the birth of a son the king died and left the Assyrian throne to Semiramis. She became a warrior queen who led Assyrian troops into Media, Egypt and Ethiopia. She also was credited with rebuilding the city of Babylon. Finally she abdicated in favor of her son who was conspiring against her and either committed suicide or changed into a pigeon and flew away. In a provocative article Lewy has attempted to show that Semiramis was ultimately a combination of two powerful Assyrian queens, Sammuramat and Naqia (Lewy 1952: 264-286).

[159] Levine 1973: 260.

[160] *Ibid.*

There are four known public monuments in different locations of the Assyrian empire that bear the name of Sammuramat. The monuments include two stone statues found in the Nabû Temple at Kalhu, a boundary stele in the Pazarcik area in southeastern Turkey and a stele for Sammuramat that was erected in a row of royal stelae at Assur. At Kalhu the two statues were erected in the Nabû Temple and dedicated to the god Nabû by Bel-tarṣi-ilumma, a governor of Kalhu. The statues most likely represent the governor and were put in the temple to show his devotion to and trust in the god Nabû. The texts on the statues specify that the statues were dedicated for the life of Adad-nerari III, king of Assyria, and for the life of Sammuramat, the queen (MÍ. É.GAL). According to Grayson the inscriptions on the two statues are essentially identical.[161]

Sammuramat's high profile during her son Adad-nerari's reign and the inclusion of her name on public monuments and in royal inscriptions is as noteworthy as it is unusual. The fact that the names of the king and his mother are found on the two statues underlines the importance of Sammuramat during her son's reign. If Sammuramat had acted as regent for her son at the beginning of his reign, the continued references to her are more understandable.

The stele discovered in the Pazarcik region in Turkey states that it is a boundary stone of Adad-nerari and Sammuramat. It was erected to resolve a boundary dispute on behalf of Ušpilulume, king of the Kummuhites with Qalparuda, son of the king of the Gurgumites. The text explains that on behalf of Ušpilulume, Adad-nerari and Sammuramat crossed the Euphrates River and fought a battle with Ataršumki of Arpad.[162] It illustrates the active involvement of Sammuramat in the affairs of the Assyrian empire during the reign of her son Adad-nerari. Interestingly it is the only known instance when a queen is reported to have accompanied an Assyrian king on a military campaign.

A stele to Sammuramat was erected in a double row of stelae placed between the inner and outer city walls at Assur. The monuments were found by Walter Andrae in the early part of the twentieth century. These stelae are unique as nowhere else in Assyria have long rows of stelae been found. One row consisted of the monuments of officials while the other row contained the monuments of nine kings and three queens.[163] Although the stelae were set up over a 700 year period of time, the kings stopped erecting them in the ninth century, the officials stopped in the eighth century, but the queens continued well into the seventh century. It is not clear why queens continued

---

[161] "The inscriptions on the two statues are identical, with two minor variants, and therefore no scores are given ... the two inscribed statues were removed to the British Museum, where they are registered as BM 118888 and 118889" (Grayson 1996: 226-227).

[162] Grayson 1996: 204-205.

[163] There is a general chronological sequence for the stelae; however Claudio Saporetti has shown that the individual stelae of the official row do not follow a chronological order (Canby 1976: 122, 114, referring to Saporetti 1974).

the tradition of erecting stelae at Assur after the kings and officials had stopped, but among the queens' monuments was the stele for Sammuramat.

The large limestone stele was almost three meters high with the usual oval-shaped top. Although the stele has no visual depiction of Sammurat, near the top is a seven-line text which reads:

> Stele of Sammuramat,
> queen of Šamši-Adad,
> king of the universe, king of [A]ssyria,
> mother [of Ad]ad-nerari,
> king of the universe, king of Assyria,
> daughter-in-law of [Sha]lmaneser,
> king of the four quarters.[164]

Sammuramat was the first Neo-Assyrian queen to have a stele placed among the monuments at Assur. The function of these monuments is not known and the inscriptions are not particularly informative, yet they are clearly dedicated to powerful and important persons in the Assyrian government.

A question that remains unanswerable about Sammuramat is whether she acted as regent for her son Adad-nerari at the beginning of his reign. It has been surmised that he was too young to rule on his own and therefore his mother acted as co-regent. But no proof actually exists that Adad-nerari was a minor when he ascended the throne. Tadmor has pointed out that "no queen mother in Mesopotamia is known to have been formally considered as reigning jointly with her son or her grandson."[165] The idea that Sammuramat was co-regent for four years stems from the misreading of the Saba'a stele that was erected in the desert south of the Sinjar hills. The translation that Unger and Luckenbill read as "In (my) fifth year of reign, when I took my seat on the royal throne"[166] has now been corrected to read "In my fifth year after I sat down majestically on the royal throne."[167]

The fact remains that Sammuramat did occupy an unusual position during the reign of her son Adad-nerari. Ben-Barak claims that the power and influence she wielded began during the reign of her husband Šamši-Adad.[168] Tadmor states that Sammuramat "seems to have meddled in the issue of Succession" and afterward she dominated her son.[169] Lambert feels that she is one of the two well-known cases "in military Assyria ... of a female power behind the throne."[170] Grayson suggests that Sammuramat's rise beyond the traditional station of a queen mother and her spheres of influence are an

---

[164] Andrae 1913: 11; cf. RIMA 3 A.O.104.2001IMA 3{r};A.O.104.2001{r}.

[165] Tadmor 1973: 147.

[166] Luckenbill 1927 II: 260-262.

[167] Tadmor 1973: 147.

[168] Ben-Barak 1987: 37.

[169] Tadmor 1983: 54.

[170] Lambert 1987: 125.

indication of Adad-nerari's lack of ability to rule effectively.[171] Reade stresses that,

> Clearly she [Sammuramat] was able, after her husband's death, to brush aside conventional obstacles and exercise a range of choices that were normally the prerogative of men.[172]

It is truly regrettable that few documentary materials survive from either the reign of Sammuramat's husband Šamši-Adad or her son Adad-nerari. While her son's reign may have had some atypical aspects including the high profile of the queen mother, the reasons for her prestige and visibility are not known. That Sammuramat played an active role in Assyrian politics is, however, irrefutable.

Tašmetum-šarrat

Tašmetum-šarrat was the wife of the Assyrian king Sennacherib (704-681). Although very little is known about her, two inscriptions clearly identify her as MÍ.É.GAL. One inscription on an alabaster vase from Assur identifies her by name as the wife of Sennacherib and next to her name is the image of the scorpion.

Two colossal sphinxes discovered by Layard during his second campaign at Nineveh sat in the doorway of room LXV in Sennacherib's Southwest Palace. The text inscribed on the sphinxes identified this area of the palace as the residence of the queen Tašmetum-šarrat. This text, unparalled in Assyrian history, reads:

> And for Tašmetum-šarrat, the queen (MÍ.É.GAL), my beloved wife (*hīrtu narāmtu*), whose features Belit-ili has made perfect above all women, I had a palace of loveliness, delight, and joy built and set *apsasātī* of white limestone in its doorways. At the command of Aššur, father of the gods, (and) of Ištar, the queen, may she be granted days of health and happiness within both these palaces, may she have her fill of well-being, may the favorable *šēdu* and the favorable *lamassu* turn to these palaces forever and never leave them[173]

This inscription is unique in that Assyrian kings did not ordinarily express personal feelings in their official inscriptions. In this text an unknown aspect of Sennacherib's character is revealed. What is also striking about this text is its eloquence and sensitivity. Reade comments that it is totally unexpected to find "in the stern context of Assyrian propriety ... such a paean of praise for a woman incorporated in an official inscription."[174]

Nothing more is known about Tašmetum-šarrat.

---

[171] Grayson 1999: 268.
[172] Reade 1987: 139.
[173] Galter, Levine and Reade 1986: 32.
[174] Reade 1987: 141.

Ešarra-hammat

Ešarra-hammat was the wife of the Assyrian king Esarhaddon (680-669). It has been argued that because Ešarra-hammat was Babylonian, her son Šamaš-šumu-ukin was made the ruler of Babylonia by Esarhaddon.[175] But there is no reliable evidence to support a Babylonian connection for Ešarra-hammat.[176] Nor is there any evidence that she was the mother of Šamaš-šumu-ukin, or any other children of Esarhaddon for that matter.

What can be said with certainty is that Ešarra-hammat was the principal wife of Esarhaddon as both titles MÍ.É.GAL and MÍ.KUR were used in documents or on objects next to her name.

One inscription with the name and title of this queen is on a roughly circular banded agate eye-stone. The two-line inscription with the first line cut around the pupil and the second cut around the white band, reads:

Of Ešarra-hammat, Queen of Esarhaddon, king of the land of Assyria.[177]

The inscription is of particular interest because the names of kings, not queens, were more commonly inscribed on eye-stones. Also of interest is the less commonly used term for queen, MÍ.KUR.

The eye-stone, roughly 16 millimeters in diameter, has a white base, a mottled brown pupil and is pierced from side to side. It is similar in shape to an eye-stone of Sargon II. Yet because no eye-stones have been found *in situ*, their function remains unclear. It can be said that "the shape of the agate votives makes them quite unsuitable as beads in ordinary necklaces,"[178] but they could easily have been dress ornaments, part of a tiara worn by a divine statue,[179] the eyes on a divine statue, part of the Assyrian regalia,[180] or they may have had no function or special significance other than that of a votive. Lambert feels this particular eye-stone was a votive and from its presence in a temple would be understood to be a gift of Ešarra-hammat.[181] Another inscription with the name and title of Ešarra-hammat was found on a broken stone from Assur. It reads, "... of the house ... mausoleum of Ešarra-hammat, his queen ... ..."[182]

Ešarra-hammat died in the year 673/2 which was in the eighth year of Esarhaddon's reign. Her death was recorded in the Babylonian Chronicle (iv

---

[175] Grayson 1991b: 139.

[176] Brinkman 1984: 71 n. 343.

[177] Lambert 1969: 65.

[178] Lambert 1969: 71.

[179] See SAA X 41 in which a letter from an astrologer to the king described the beauty of the eye-stones that were to become part of the crown of the god Nabû.

[180] H. Galter (1987: 17 n. 31) suggests a comparison with a "scepter of banded agate from the hoard found in a Parthian house in Babylon, which might have come from either the palace or from Esagila."

[181] Lambert 1969: 66, 69.

[182] Borger 1956: 10.

22) and the Esarhaddon Chronicle (line 23)[183] and therefore it must have been regarded as a significant event.

Ešarra-hammat was undoubtedly buried in Assur. Above all else, a broken stone inscription from Assur mentions her mausoleum. Further evidence can be found in an administrative document from Assur that provides a schedule for the distribution of meat destined for temple personnel and the royal tomb complex. The list specifically mentions "ribs" and a "haunch" that were to be left at "the mausoleum of Ešarra-hammat."[184] It is known that many Assyrian kings were buried in vaulted tombs underneath the Old Palace at Assur and that many Assyrian queens were buried in vaulted tombs underneath the Northwest Palace at Kalhu. The question therefore arises as to whether or not Ešarra-hammat was given a distinction not normally accorded to Assyrian queens.

Two letters sent to the king from the chief exorcist describe funerary rituals that Parpola believes were performed for the dead queen Ešarra-hammat after her burial.[185] The proposed dates of the two letters are thought to directly follow her death. In these two letters the king is kept informed, the Inner City (Assur) is mentioned, women are lodged in an unsuitable house and are involved in the performance of the ritual. The house of mourning where the king resided in isolation during the period of mourning is specified. These facts all emphasize and point to ritual which followed a royal burial.[186]

Not long after the death of the queen Ešarra-hammat, Esarhaddon designated his two sons Aššurbanipal and Šamaš-šumu-ukin as heirs to the Assyrian and Babylonian thrones respectively and had the country swear an oath of allegiance.[187] Although this decision must have been controversial, a letter from the king's personal exorcist explains how the crown prince of Assyria (Aššurbanipal) reported that he had been ordained "because of her (= the dead queen's) righteousness" and that "her ghost blesses him in the same degree as he has revered the ghost."[188] This letter "proves beyond doubt that the possibility of summoning spirits of the dead to act as 'political witnesses' was not at all unthinkable at the Assyrian imperial court."[189] The letter also reveals the stature of the dead queen and the respect given her even after her death.

Libbali-šarrat

Libbali-šarrat was the wife of the Assyrian king Aššurbanipal (668-627). Textual references indicate that she followed in the royal tradition of owning

---

[183] Brinkman 1984: 82 n. 400.

[184] SAA XII 81.

[185] SAA X 233-234.

[186] Parpola 1983: 195, 197.

[187] Brinkman 1984: 82, Tadmor 1983: 43-44, J. and D. Oates 2001: 206-207.

[188] SAA X 188.

[189] S. Parpola in Tadmor, Landsberger† and Parpola 1989: 45.

property at Lahiru in the Diyala region. An economic transaction of the queen's eunuch was witnessed by "the mayor of the Lahirean village of the queen" in 668 when Aššurbanipal was the Assyrian king.[190]

A dedication made by Libbali-šarrat included interesting wording, as it states:

...for the life of Aššurbanipal, her..., his throne and for her own life, length of days and the stability of her rule...[191]

Fig. 13 Drawing of Libbali-šarrat on
Assur Stele (Stele 15756/8, Assur, drawing by
R. Hall, after Börker-Klähn 1982: 227)

Prior to Libbali-šarrat the only queen who referred to her rule or term of office using the word *palû* was Naqia. While there has been considerable discussion about a queen using the word "rule" (*palû*) in reference to herself, it would designate the time when she was queen.[192]

Pieces of a stele belonging to a queen of Aššurbanipal were found among the double row of monuments at Assur.[193] The inscription reads:

Stele of
Libbali-ša[rrat]
queen
of Aššurbani[pal]
king of the universe, king of Assyria.[194]

At the top of the oval-shaped stele is a relief of the queen seated on her throne (Fig. 13). The queen sits erect facing right with part of the highly decorative throne back visible behind her. She wears the mural crown, favored by Assyrian queens, that resembles the battlements of a city. Three

---

[190] SAA XIV 1.

[191] AR 17:4-6.

[192] W. Heimpel, personal communication, July 2001.

[193] Andrae 1913: 6-8 and Taf. X.

[194]For a line drawing and photograph of the inscription see Andrae 1913: 8 and Taf. X; for the revised transliteration of line 2, see PNA 2/II, 661 s.v. Libbāli-šarrat b.

multi- crenellated towers project above the main wall. The mural crown is elaborate, formal and likely an official part of the queen's royal regalia.[195]

The queen's hair can be seen below the crown on her forehead. It falls behind her ears but the length cannot be determined due to a missing section of the relief picture. She has a finely arched wide eyebrow, almond-shaped eye, straight nose, rounded cheeks and thick chin and neck. In her left hand she grasps a bulbous plant with a thick stem; her right hand is raised with fingers extended upwards. Her dress has short, pleated or striped sleeves and is decorated with rosettes that might be embroidered or metallic.[196] Only the very top part of her body can be seen in the surviving pieces of the stele. Andrae commented more than once on how the representation of the queen on the stele is very similar to that of the queen with Aššurbanipal in the garden relief scene.[197]

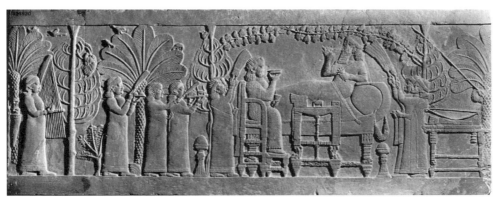

Fig. 14 Detail of relief of queen and king in garden, Room S, North Palace, Nineveh (BM 124920, courtesy Trustees of The British Museum)

The garden scene relief (Fig. 14) that shows a queen with the king Aššurbanipal was found at Nineveh by William Loftus in 1854. It was discovered among many wall relief fragments lying in a large room (S), connected by a passageway to the North Palace. It is extremely rare to have a portrait of the queen with the king and this is the only example in which the two are shown in the privacy of a garden. Because the scene is thought to be set in a garden

---

[195] One additional and quite confusing example of a possible queen wearing a mural crown occurs on a ninth century glazed tile from the Ištar temple at Nineveh. Thought to date from Aššurnaṣirpal's reign it shows a figure wearing the mural crown and a long plait, both characteristics part of the portrayal of seventh century queens. Another broken tile has been joined to the first one and it contains a beard. Do the two tile pieces really belong together and who are they supposed to represent: a king, a queen or someone else? Although the two pieces were joined when displayed in Baghdad, Reade feels the relationship between the hair and beard seems slightly wrong and he questions whether the two pieces really belong together (Reade 1987: 139).

[196] In Tomb II of the queens' tombs found at Kalhu in 1989, the linen clothing or shrouding on the bodies had gold rosettes, stars, circles and triangles sewn onto the garments (see above, discussion on queens' burials).

[197] Andrae 1913: 7, 8.

on the grounds of the queen's residence it is an even more unusual subject for an Assyrian palace relief and a rare glimpse into the private accommodations of a royal woman. Surely the woman must be the principal wife of Aššurbanipal, that is, Libbali-šarrat.[198]

One of the many unique elements in this relief scene is the depiction of Aššurbanipal reclining on a couch. Although decorative couches are known in Assyrian art they are generally shown as being carried off as valuable spoils of war by victorious Assyrian soldiers.[199] Here Aššurbanipal wears no kingly or ceremonial attire nor does he wear the crown of the Assyrian king. In no other relief scene is a king shown lying on a couch dressed so informally with a blanket covering him.

In contrast the queen is seated facing the reclining king. Although the queen fills the foreground space she is noticeably lower than the king but higher than the servants. The height and placement of the figures nicely illustrates court hierarchy. Both the queen and king hold a drinking bowl in their right hand and a flower in their left hand.

The queen is shown in profile facing to the right and toward the king. On her head she wears the mural crown in the shape of the battlements of a city. Six towers with three crenellations on each project above the main city wall. Traditionally in ancient Near Eastern art either women or goddesses wear the mural crown.[200] The queen's wavy hair can be seen above and below the crown. Unfortunately the nose and lower part of the queen's face have been mutilated (as have the face and right hand of Aššurbanipal.[201] However the same arched eyebrow, almond-shaped eye, round cheek and chin that were

---

[198] In a controversial 1997 article entitled "Ashurbanipal Banqueting with his Queen? Wer Throhnt bei Assurbanipal in der Weinlaube?" (*Mesopotamia* 32 [1997]: 289-308), Constanze Schmidt-Colinet identifies the figure on the throne beside Aššurbanipal as a eunuch and not his queen. This proposed change in gender has been more than adequately refuted by Pauline Albenda (1998). By examining the iconography and artistic style, Albenda illustrates how the identity of the enthroned, mural-crowned figure is the Assyrian queen. In his article "Ashurbanipal's Feast: A View from Elam," Javier Álvarez-Mon suggests two other possibilities for the identity of the enthroned female depicted: She could be "a female member of the royal Elamite house captured by Ashurbanipal during his conquest of Elam" or she could be his grandmother, Naqia (Álvarez-Mon 2009: 147, 156).

[199] Javier Álvarez-Mon (2009: 145) suggests that it is no accident (1) that the couch that Assurbanipal reclines on is similar to the one shown plundered from the Elamite king Humban-Haltas III's royal cities and (2) that the relief slab showing this plundering is in close proximity to the garden relief scene.

[200] The goddess Hepat wears a mural crown in a relief at Yazilikaya, a Hittite sanctuary (Barnett 1985: 2); the goddess Cybele is said to have placed the walled city of Gordion on her head indicating that she wore a mural crown (Barnett 1976: 56); the queen Ahat-milku of Ugarit appears to have possessed a mural crown made of gold (Barnett 1985: 2). In addition there are at least three other depictions of Assyrian queens wearing the mural crown.

[201] Since the faces of both the king and queen were mutilated while the surrounding attendants were left unharmed, Zainab Bahrani believes the destruction was deliberate and must have taken place when Nineveh fell in 612 BCE. Because an image was thought to ensure a person's immortality, its destruction or mutilation truly meant the cessation of existence. To damage a royal image was thus much more than merely an insult (Bahrani 1995: 365-367, 380-381).

noted on the queen's face on the Assur stele, characterize her face in the garden relief scene.

The dress and shawl worn by the queen are intricately patterned with wide borders and long fringes. The dress has a high neck, three-quarter length sleeves and is floor-length. The shawl is wound around her body with an edge falling vertically from her right shoulder. The queen's footwear (and that of her female attendants) has soft soles that are appropriate for interior or domestic spaces.

The high regard that Assyrian royalty had for jewellery made of various metals and precious stones can be seen not only on their images in art but also in the royal burials recently discovered at Kalhu where literally hundreds of pieces of jewellery were found in the queens' graves. In the garden scene the jewellery worn by the queen and the king is essentially identical. Both wear crescent-shaped earrings decorated with fine granulation and embellished with lotus buds and flowers. This style is unknown in Assyria before the seventh century and, according to Maxwell-Hyslop, "marks the apogee of the technical skill of Assyrian jewelers."[202] The bracelets worn by the queen and the king feature the rosette pattern, a long-standing favorite motif in Mesopotamia. In Neo-Assyrian art the rosette bracelet is worn not only by humans but also winged apotropaic figures. Typical of the more complicated design patterns preferred during the reign of Aššurbanipal, the bracelet of Libbali-šarrat has a series of small rosettes (instead of the single rosette style favored in the ninth and eighth centuries) attached to a flat gold strip with thick borders.[203]

The necklace suspended from the curved end of Aššurbanipal's couch is an enigma. It most likely did not belong to Aššurbanipal as he is never depicted wearing any type of necklace in a relief. Did the necklace then belong to Libbali-šarrat as the couch belonged to the queen? Pauline Albenda comments that stylistically the necklace resembles the *menat* necklace worn in Egypt and that it might constitute one of the many objects brought back from Aššurbanipal's Egyptian campaigns.[204]

In the garden scene relief, both the queen and the king hold drinking bowls. The bowl of the king has been gouged out, but the finely fluted bowl of the queen, most likely of gold, is perfectly preserved. In both cases the bowl is shown "elegantly balanced on the fingers of the right hand in front of the body and at the level of the face."[205] Drinking bowls were made of various materials but the ones held by the royal pair were most certainly of gold. Metal bowls must have been highly prized since gold bowls were found in the

---

[202] Maxwell-Hyslop 1971: 243-244.

[203] Maxwell-Hyslop 1971: 248.

[204] Albenda thinks that because the necklace looks Egyptian it was part of the war booty or even a gift from the reigning Egyptian king. She speculates that it may even be an example of the "gold of honor," a gold collar traditionally presented by pharaohs to their favorites (Albenda 1977: 33-36).

[205] Stronach 1995: 177.

queens' tombs at Kalhu and bronze bowls were discovered in the Northwest Palace at Kalhu.[206]

Administrative records reveal that large quantities of wine were consumed by the royal households, and in the extant *Nimrud Wine Lists* the queen's ration of wine is usually listed first.[207] Grapes were cultivated in Assyria and wine would have been available for drinking. Thus it seems highly probable that in the garden scene the queen and the king are drinking wine, a commodity that could denote rank and status.[208]

The queen sits on a chair that has a high back and armrests. Three stretchers with two opposed volutes are visible between two legs that have decorated conical feet. Decorative chairs were prestige items used by royalty at banquets, ceremonial and ritual events and even on military campaigns. Their basic structure was of wood but they were often decorated with bronze, ivory, gold and inlays of colored pastes and precious stones. In addition to artistic representations numerous furniture pieces have been found by excavators in Neo-Assyrian palaces. The description by Layard of a throne found in the Northwest Palace at Kalhu is particularly revealing:

> With the exception of the legs which appear to have been partly of ivory, it was of wood, carved or overlaid with bronze .... The metal was most elaborately engraved and embossed with symbolic figures and ornaments .... As the woodwork over which the bronze was fastened by means of small nails of the same material, had rotted away, the throne fell to pieces, but the metal casing was partly preserved.[209]

In the garden scene relief the queen's feet rest on a footstool that is similar in design to the throne. In Assyria only royalty use footstools at banquets. In other banquet relief scenes all the guests are left with their feet dangling above the ground. A footstool appears to have been one way of distinguishing a royal person from others of lesser rank. In the garden scene both the throne and footstool have fabric cushions. Another piece of fabric rests on the throne back and may have been a shawl or lap robe for the queen's use.

It is striking that the queen is the figure who wears the crown, is formally dressed and sits quite regally while the king casually reclines on a couch. Does this scene hint that the queen had a visible role in the Assyrian government hierarchy, particularly if the king was ill? There was a precedent for an Assyrian queen being a visible presence as Aššurbanipal's grandmother, the

---

[206] Assyrian kings recorded lavish gifts of metalwork in the form of tribute from numerous neighboring lands. In 1849 Layard found eighty bronze bowls in the Northwest Palace at Kalhu. Names in Phoenician, Aramaic, Hebrew and Lydian were inscribed on some of them. If these were the names of previous owners, they may have been tribute offered from these places to the Assyrian king (Barnett 1974: 16-17).

[207] Kinnier Wilson 1972

[208] Stronach 1996: 177. Julian Reade has commented that even in modern times what one drinks is felt to denote rank and status. He writes, "In my own country, England, there is often a social distinction: wine for the urbane, beer for everyone else" (Reade 1995: 36).

[209] Baker 1966: 188; quoted from A. Layard, *Discoveries among the Ruins of Nineveh and Babylon* (1853): 198-200.

queen Naqia, had certainly been such a presence during the reign of her son Esarhaddon.

The garden scene is thought to be set in the grounds of the queen's residence because all of the attendants are female. The royal couple takes refreshment and enjoys each other's company while framed within a grapevine arbor. The vines are shown twisted around a pair of conifers and pruned in such a way that they come together to form a natural canopy for the queen and king.[210] Beyond the grapevine arbor, birds perch on date palms and pine trees while female attendants fan the royal pair and female musicians play music.

The garden scene is the central focus of a much larger three-register setting. Albenda believes that each of the three registers indicates a landscape that existed progressively further and further from the palace. In the upper register, the restricted scenery is the queen's garden. In the middle register, the grove of pine trees with pomegranate and flowering shrubs could have represented a park or wooded area within the palace grounds. In the lower register, a millet field appears to designate an agricultural area beyond the palace complex.[211]

The political context for this garden scene is revealed by the severed head of the Elamite king Teumman which hangs in one of the pine tress. Further to the left in the top register is a group of Elamite princes who prostrate themselves or walk toward the royal couple. According to the epigraph above their heads, they must bring a royal meal prepared by their own hands to Aššurbanipal the Assyrian king.[212] Since no male attendants are visible within the immediate vicinity of the queen, an interesting question is: would the Elamite nobles be the ones to personally serve the king in the queen's garden? Furthermore, is the political content of the scene another reference to the queen's active participation in Assyrian politics?

Conclusion

Royal women in Assyria were wealthy, having extensive land holdings throughout the empire. They also had multiple residences within a city as well as in different Assyrian cities. Their households were large, well-organized and contained personnel which included women and men and also military units. The woman who was the chief administrator (the *šakintu*) commanded a large staff, transacted a sizable volume of business, had considerable responsibilities and was often a powerful and wealthy woman in her own right.

In addition to real estate holdings royal women received tribute and gifts. Distribution lists indicate that the amounts the queens and princesses received were extensive. However it is clear from their *šakintu* holdings that royal

---

[210] Albenda 1974: 6.

[211] Albenda 1976: 61.

[212] Russell 1999: 204, Gerardi 1988: 25, Gadd 1936: 180.

women were required to give gifts and make contributions to temples and to the state.

Royal women could become important and influential, not only with respect to the king, but also with other government officials. This appears to have been particularly true for the wives and the queen mothers, many of whom had considerable prestige. The daughters of kings, on the other hand, might be used to cement political alliances by marrying rulers of neighboring states and then reporting back to their father, the Assyrian king.

Assyrian queens had their own symbol, the scorpion, which was engraved on personal objects or used in their royal seals. The recently discovered tombs of some Assyrian queens beneath the Northwest Palace at Kalhu illustrate the prestige and great wealth in jewellery and personal objects that queens accumulated over a lifetime. Objects of gold, silver, semi-precious stones and rock crystal accompanied these women into the afterlife. Even the tombs themselves, some of which appear to have been pre-planned, were clearly designed for important royalty.

Specific information allows glimpses into the lives, activities and abilities of a few of the Assyrian queens. Sammuramat was included on public monuments displayed in different locations throughout the empire. Statues in temples were dedicated to her. A stele in Turkey indicates that she went on military campaigns with her son the king and was thus actively involved in affairs of state. She was also the first Assyrian queen known to have a stele placed among the monuments at Assur. Clearly she held a prominent position and had extraordinary abilities.

Tašmetum-šarrat is the only known Assyrian queen to have inspired her husband the king to place an inscription in the palace where he praised her and called her "his beloved." Ešarra-hammat is the only known queen to have been buried at Assur along with the Assyrian kings. Two visual images of an Assyrian queen have survived which are thought to be of Libbali-šarrat. One image is on a stele at Assur and the other shows the queen entertaining the king with food and music in the privacy of the garden at her residence. The garden scene relief is unique in many ways not the least of which is that it is the only image of an Assyrian queen on a palace relief to survive.

By examining the written documents, the visual depictions and the material evidence a fascinating, if not surprising, picture of Assyrian palace women unfolds. This is especially true if one avoids preconceived notions of gender roles and stereotyped images of women in ancient Near Eastern society.

CHAPTER IV

NAQIA/ZAKUTU – QUEEN EXTRAORDINAIRE

The queen who was the wife of Sennacherib, daughter-in-law of Sargon II, mother of Esarhaddon and grandmother of Aššurbanipal, four kings of Assyria, is known either by the name Naqia or Zakutu. In many ways she is a mystery, as her family, origin and status when she entered the royal household are unknown.

What is known is that her name Naqia is West Semitic as is the name of her sister Abi-rami.[1] She became a wife of Sennacherib while he was still the crown prince[2] although nothing is known about her until 683 BCE when her son Esarhaddon became the crown prince. Whether she had any other children is not known for certain, although a sister to Esarhaddon, Šadditu, is mentioned in a few documents. Šadditu was treated in such a special manner that it is thought she must have been his full sister and thus a child of Naqia.[3] How important Naqia's position was as one of the wives of Sennacherib is not known as the only mention of her while he was the king is a reference to "the mother of the king's son of the succession house"[4] when she was granted an estate in the town of Šabbu, traditionally the town of the queen mother. Naqia's correspondence with women prophets regarding the plight of Esarhaddon when he was in exile around the time of the assassination of his father Sennacherib also indicates that she must have been present in the palace at that time and concerned about her son's situation.[5]

---

[1] A document exists in which "Abi-rami, the sister of the queen mother" leased land in the town of Baruri in the year 674 (SAA VI 252).

[2] "Based on the estimated chronology for other members of the family, it is most likely that Naqia bore her son, Esarhaddon, between 713 and 711. Thus Naqia must have entered Sennacherib's household by at least c. 713." (Melville 1999: 13) Sargon II, Sennacherib's father, ruled in Assyria from 721 to 705.

[3] For example, "Šadditu, daughter of Sennacherib, king of Assyria, and sister of Esarhaddon, king of Assyria ..." bought land (SAA VI 251) and her brother, the king, ordered a special ritual performed on her behalf in 672 (SAA X 273).

[4] SAA XII 23 r. 6-7.

[5] One such prophecy was, "I am the Lady of Arbail. To the king's mother: Because you implored me, saying: 'You have placed the ones of the (king's) right and left side in your lap, but made my own offspring roam the steppe' – Now fear not, *my* king! By the mouth of the woman Ahat-abiša of Arbail." (SAA IX 1.8:12-23).

All the correspondence to and about Naqia comes from the period when her son Esarhaddon was king. There are letters from Assyrian scholars and officials, Babylonian officials and one from her son, the king, although no correspondence from Naqia herself has survived. There is also a bronze relief fragment of Naqia with an Assyrian king as well as two dedicatory inscriptions, one building inscription, two inscribed agate beads and a loyalty oath which Naqia imposed on the Assyrian people for her grandson, Aššurbanipal. Various economic and administrative documents also exist. One text survives from the reign of Aššurbanipal which mentions a queen mother who could have been Naqia, but that identification is not conclusive.[6]

It is important to distinguish between what is actually known and verifiable about Naqia and the great amount that has been written about her which is strictly conjectural and is at times negative to the extreme. Even though "in fact there is no text identifying Naqia by name and title that securely dates to Sennacherib's reign"[7] much has been written about her undue influence on her husband and that she held more power than was normal or proper for a queen. Ben-Barak claims her "... influence was already in evidence in the lifetime of her husband ..."[8] and Reade states "... it is plain that Sennacherib listened to Naqia's advice."[9]

Clearly queen mothers are viewed by many writers as irritating meddlers or even dangerous women. Frame, when discussing Naqia, makes the very general statement, "It is well attested in the ancient and mediaeval world that a resourceful and energetic queen or queen mother could become a power behind the throne."[10] Wiseman concludes that Naqia's actions had "... considerable sway in the state affairs of Assyria and Babylonia," and that they were "... a further indication of the influential part played by queen-mothers in the ancient Near East."[11]

Many scholars also feel that the succession of Esarhaddon was really Naqia's idea. Lewy asserts that the succession which caused Sennacherib's assassination "...was inspired into him by a woman...,"[12] meaning Esarhaddon's mother Naqia. Parpola says that after the death of Sennacherib's eldest son Aššur-nadin-šumi, Esarhaddon out-maneuvered the second-eldest son to become crown prince as he was "... the favorite son of Sennacherib thanks to his mother Naqia ...."[13] Reade comments that "Naqia/Zakutu has long been

---

[6] Remanni-Adad, chariot driver to King Aššurbanipal, bought Dannaya, an entire town, in 663 and one of the seals on the document belonged to "... Asqudu, scribe of [the queen] mother" (SAA VI 325:2). Asqudu would be the scribe of Naqia if Aššurbanipal's mother was Ešarra-hammat who had died in 672. Unfortunately, there is no document which gives the name of the mother of Aššurbanipal so that it cannot be stated for certain whose scribe Asqudu was.

[7] Melville 1999: 23.

[8] Ben-Barak 1987: 37.

[9] Reade 1987: 142.

[10] Frame 1992: 93.

[11] Wiseman 1958: 6, 9.

[12] Lewy 1952: 272.

[13] Parpola 1980: 175.

recognised as responsible for the promotion of her own son Esarhaddon to the position of crown-prince late in Sennacherib's reign, a move that apparently led to the king's murder by the demoted elder son ...."[14] As if all this was not harmful enough, Tadmor claims that Naqia "... meddled in the issue of succession and acted as co-regent ... in the case of Esarhaddon and Aššurbanipal ...."[15] Grayson comments "... her influence increased even farther with the accession of her grandson."[16] Van De Mieroop states that "As queen of Sennacherib, she was instrumental in the rise of her son Esarhaddon to the throne of Assyria ...."[17] And Leichty says "there can be little doubt that the hand of Naqi'a was behind this appointment ...."[18]

No evidence exists to verify these declarations. There are no documents that indicate Naqia had any type of overwhelming influence on her husband or son or grandson or even that she behaved in an excessively forceful manner. She certainly would have found herself in a better situation once her son was declared the crown prince, but that she was responsible for Sennacherib's decision to choose Esarhaddon to succeed him cannot be proven by the available evidence.

Two Names: Naqia and Zakutu

The name Naqia was certainly an Aramaic name (Naqqi'ā). It means "pure, clean, innocent." Some scholars have thought that because she had a West Semitic name she was either a foreigner coming from outside Assyria proper or more specifically that she came from Babylonia. There is certainly no convincing proof that either of these suggestions is valid. Having a West Semitic name during the eighth and seventh centuries in Assyria was not uncommon[19] and "... may simply reflect the linguistic diversity of the empire in which Akkadian and Aramaic were both current."[20] The name Naqia, when translated into Akkadian, was Zakutu, which was an artificial name that would not have seemed particularly Assyrian.[21]

Naqia used both names while she was queen. Yet it is difficult to draw any conclusions concerning how and when she used each name, particularly as only eight texts survive which mention her by either name. The numerous remaining texts referred to her as "mother of the king"

The queen's name "Naqia" is used in five surviving texts. Two texts were queries placed before the sun god Šamaš by his priests who were diviners.

---

[14] Reade 1987: 142.

[15] Tadmor 1983: 54.

[16] Grayson 1991b: 140.

[17] Van De Mieroop 1993: 259.

[18] Leichty 1995: 951.

[19] Fales has noted that a text from Nineveh, K 8434, contained a long list of the personal names of women and approximately one half were West Semitic. (Fales 1979: 56).

[20] Kuhrt 1995 II: 527.

[21] Melville 1999: 16.

Both were written when her son Esarhaddon was the king of Assyria. A bronze relief fragment (now in the Louvre) shows an Assyrian queen following an Assyrian king and an epigraph, although incomplete, descends from the queen's shoulder with the name "Naqia."[22] A banded agate bead, which likely belonged to a necklace placed on the statue of a deity, has an inscription on it which reads "Naqia, queen of Sennacherib (...)."[23] Of the two copies of dedicatory inscriptions written on a single clay tablet, 645, the dedication to the Lady of Nineveh used the name "Naqia" while the other dedication to the goddess Mullissu of Assur used the name "Zakutu."[24]

Besides the second dedicatory inscription quoted on tablet 645, a second bead of banded agate, deltoid in shape, was inscribed with the name "Zakutu ... for the life of Esarhaddon, king of the land of Assur, her son and for her own life, has donated."[25] Finally, in the loyalty oath she imposed on the nation of Assyria regarding the kingship of her grandson Aššurbanipal, she used the name "Zakutu."

Why and when she used which name is puzzling. Did she use the two names interchangably? Or did she change from using the Aramaic name "Naqia" to the Akkadian "Zakutu" sometime during the reign of her son Esarhaddon? Unfortunately it is impossible to fix specific dates to these documents and objects – only that they date to the period after her husband Sennacherib had died and all but two of the inscriptions mention her son Esarhaddon as the king of Assyria.

It is, however, worth commenting on the possibility that two uses of the Assyrian name "Zakutu" might point to something more. In the one surviving political document, the loyalty oath for Aššurbanipal, she might have used the Assyrian name "Zakutu" as a strategic reminder and potent reinforcement of the position and power she wielded at this point in her career as queen in Assyria. It has also been suggested that the use of her Assyrian name "Zakutu" in the dedicatory inscription to Mullissu, the consort of the god Aššur, might have implied "some parallelism between goddess and queen, each in alternative manifestations ...."[26] However, she instead might have thought it more appropriate to use her Assyrian name when she made a dedication to the wife of the state god of Assyria.

Titles

The titles associated with Naqia are those commonly used by the women who were wives and mothers of Neo-Assyrian kings. References to these royal women in Neo-Assyrian documents or inscriptions written logographically are MÍ.É.GAL or MÍ.KUR. Both terms mean 'woman + palace' and they appear

---

[22] Parrot and Nougayrol 1956: 155-157.

[23] Galter 1987: 22.

[24] Melville 1999: 43.

[25] Van De Mieroop 1993: 259.

[26] Reade 1987: 143.

to have been used interchangeably (see Chapter III – Palace Women, *Queens'
titles*).

In the case of Naqia, there is no evidence that she used the title MÍ.É.GAL
while her husband Sennacherib was the king. In fact, it should be questioned
whether or not she was actually ever his principal wife. There are, however,
five examples of her use of MÍ.É.GAL during the reign of her son Esarhaddon
and they occur on objects which were of religious and political importance.
MÍ.É.GAL was used on the building inscription for a palace she had built for
her son the king, on the two dedicatory inscriptions on jewellery and precious
stones dedicated to goddesses in the temples at Assur and Nineveh and on
two inscribed beads (which were most likely meant to be part of jewellery
placed on religious statues).

MÍ.KUR was used much less frequently by 'palace women' and is found on
only one document associated with Naqia and that is the loyalty oath she
imposed on the nation of Assyria for her grandson Aššurbanipal. This is a
unique document in that it represents the only loyalty oath that is known to
have been imposed by someone other than the king. Moreover, this document
illustrates one of the few times she used her Akkadian name Zakutu. Was
there a strong political reason why she used Zakutu and MÍ.KUR together?
Was it a coincidence that MÍ.KUR was used on a document originating late in
her life, one written after her son Esarhaddon had died?

Most documents, however, referred to Naqia as the 'mother or the king'
which was written logographically as either AMA.LUGAL or AMA.MAN, or, if
written syllabically in Neo-Assyrian, *ummi šarri*. Letters written to her or
about her, the omens from oracles, exorcists or haruspices and the economic
transactions by Naqia or her household staff all tended to use 'mother of the
king' without actually citing her name.

Religious Activities

"In Assyria, the political and religious spheres were not distinct …"[27] and
acts of piety were a serious responsibility of royalty. Both the visual and the
textual materials give evidence of Naqia's religious activities. A picture
emerges of Naqia as queen-mother showing reverence for the deities by
participating in religious ceremonies, having her own image displayed in
temple cellas, giving gifts and provisions to various temples throughout the
Assyrian empire and corresponding with priests and high temple officials

Visual evidence of Naqia playing a role in religious ceremonies can be
found on the bronze relief fragment showing her following an Assyrian king,
in a scene where both she and the king can be seen carrying ritual objects. It
is thought that on the missing part of the relief there was an image of the deity
which the two figures would have been approaching.[28] The inscription on the
bronze relief mentions a mouth-washing and mouth-opening ceremony

---

[27] Melville 1999: 42 n. 54.

thought to have been performed on a statue of Ea (the inscription is incomplete). Regardless of the temple or city in which the ceremony took place, Naqia as a high-ranking royal family member clearly was an active participant. The bronze relief itself most likely was intended for display in a temple either on an altar base or on a divine throne dais.

Two seal impressions from Sennacherib's 'Palace without Rival' in Nineveh may reveal a similar religious occasion.[29] An Assyrian queen wearing a mural crown with a cone projecting from the top stands behind an Assyrian king in front of a goddess who is standing on an animal. There is no way to date these seal impressions and thus to know if the queen shown is actually Naqia, but the composition may be essentially identical to the bronze relief in its entirety. In each case the statue of the goddess was most likely displayed in a temple cella.

It is well known that the Cult of Aššur received much attention and elevation in status during the reign of Naqia's husband Sennacherib when the temple precinct at Assur was enlarged and changed. Documents of rituals for the god Aššur and his entourage survive, including BM 121206, thought to have been discovered during the excavations at Assur.[30] Although the document is puzzling (inasmuch as it contains sections which do not appear to go together), a definite description of a ritual which occurred during a royal visit to the sanctuaries of Aššur and his wives Mullissu and Šerua[31] was described. "Female members of the royal family" are mentioned as being on hand and participating in the ceremony (which may well have taken place following the completion of Sennacherib's structural enhancements). It is unfortunate that more is not known concerning the involvement of royal women in Assyrian religious rituals but isolated clues such as those revealed in BM 121206 show that they were present and they did participate.[32] Surely Naqia would have been among these women.

Textual evidence exists that some temples would actually have had a visual reminder of the important position and religious role Naqia played by having statues of her along with her son Esarhaddon, the king of Assyria, within their sanctuaries. Whereas statues of Assyrian kings, occasionally accompanied by their sons, are known to have been placed in temples, Naqia is the only queen whose image is known to have been privileged in this manner. In Kalhu, a functionary of the Temple of Nabû wrote to the king requesting that the 200 kilograms of gold sent by the king be made available for the royal statues and the statue of the queen mother.[33] "At Assur ... her image may have been

---

[28] Parrot and Nougayrol 1956: 147.

[29] Reade 1987: 144-145.

[30] Van Driel 1969: chapter IV.

[31] According to Lambert (1983: 82), the jury is still out as to whether Šerua was a wife or daughter of Aššur.

[32] A further reference to a queen participating in a religious ritual can be found in KAR 215. During an offering ceremony in the New Year's temple of the king (bīt akīti), the queen carried "the weapons" (Henshaw 1994: 23; quoted from Ebeling 1951: 401-405).

displayed in one of the sanctuaries in Ešarra."[34] Statues of her are mentioned in a letter from Harran,[35] although whether these statues were to be placed in a temple or outside in a public area or both is indeterminable due to the poor condition of the text in question. Thus images and statues of Naqia would appear to have been erected in the three cities of Kalhu, Assur and Harran and images of her are likely to have existed in other temples in other cities throughout the rest of the empire.

Naqia gave gifts and provisions to temples in at least five cities throughout the Assyrian empire: Kalhu, Assur, Nineveh, Harran and Borsippa. In Kalhu her activities are identified with the sanctuary of Tašmetu in the Temple of Nabû. Two letters to Naqia from a temple official discuss what ingredients were necessary for a ritual and also what animals would be sacrificed.[36] Either Naqia was providing the necessary objects or she was the administrator in charge of rituals for Tašmetu, the consort of Nabû. At Assur Naqia gave a gift to Mullissu at her sanctuary in Ešarra "for the life of Esarhaddon and for herself, her own life, the length of her days, the stability of her reign (and) her well-being." The gift was "a piece of gold jewellery, covered with obsidian, carnelian and *papardillu* stone, weighing 7½ mana, 5 shekels."[37] To "the lady" of the Emašmaš temple in Nineveh, Naqia dedicated a "pectoral of red gold set with precious stones weighing 3¾ mana," again for the life or Esarhaddon and herself.[38] Naqia also made donations and sponsored work at temples outside of Assyria proper but within the Assyrian empire. At Harran, a fragmentary letter from an unknown temple official to Naqia cites decorative work being done on a temple. It mentions the tail of a lion, an inlaid bed and statuary of the queen mother. In Babylonia, most likely Borsippa, Naqia provided gold for the crown of Nabû and sponsored rites connected with an eclipse.[39] Finally, there are two inscribed agate beads which were probably part of the jewellery placed on statues of deities in a temple somewhere in the empire. One inscription reads, "Naqia queen of Sennacherib" while the other reads, "To the god [...], Zakutu the queen of Sennacherib, king of the land of Assur, for the life of Esarhaddon, king of the land of Assur, her son and for her own life, has donated."[40]

The visual presence of Naqia in Assyrian temples, her participation in religious rituals and the many cult objects she provided demonstrate that she

---

[33] SAA XIII 61 r. 1-4.

[34] Melville 1999: 59.

[35] SAA XIII 188 r. 8-13.

[36] Nergal-šarrani from Kalhu reports to the queen mother, "What is going into the ritual? – These are its constituents: sweet-scented oil, wax, sweet-scented fragrance, myrrh, cannibis, and *sadīdu*-aromatic .... [On the xth] day, they will perform the whole-offerings: one ox, two white sheep, and a duck" (SAA XII 76). And "Concerning the offerings .... They are all made before Tašmetu: a bull and 2 rams, and a duck. This is all" (SAA XIII 77:7-12).

[37] Melville 1999: 43.

[38] Melville 1999: 43.

[39] SAA X 348:15, 313 r. 1-7.

[40] Van De Mieroop 1993: 259.

took her religious responsibilities very seriously. Perhaps, as Melville has suggested, "we must regard such widespread participation as extraordinary."[41]

Political Arena

A comment often made about Naqia is that "she behaved like a king." Records survive which illustrate that there were times during the reign of her son Esarhaddon when she successfully assumed royal attributes and responsibilities. Whether Naqia was one of the lone Assyrian queens to have behaved in this manner or whether other queens commonly did these things is not known, but the records certainly point to her exceptional abilities. That these abilities were recognized throughout the Assyrian empire can also be verified.

One of Naqia's most startling accomplishments was the construction of a palace for her son on "a piece of empty land in the midst of Nineveh behind the Sin and Shamash temple ..."[42] This action was totally unprecedented. There are no other known examples of anyone building a palace for an Assyrian king. There are, of course, many examples of the opposite being true as Assyrian kings are known to have built palaces for their queens. Naqia commemorated the completion of the palace with offerings to the gods, a celebratory banquet and a building inscription in the royal style of the Sargonid kings.[43] She began the inscription with her name and titulary, then followed with praise of the gods who put her son on the throne and mention of the captive laborers (her war booty) who constructed the palace. Next, the location of the palace, some details on the materials and furnishings, the offerings to the gods and the inaugural banquet were mentioned. Finally the inscription ends with how the building and its luxurious furnishings symbolize the kingship of her beloved son. Even the terminology she used such as *esqi bēlūtiya*[44] or "my lordly portion" directly copied the terminology in actual royal inscriptions. It may be concluded that by building the palace and leaving the accompanying inscription, Naqia became more visible as a figure of power who enacted royal prerogatives.

Also unusual were the images of Naqia that were placed in public spaces. At least one statue was placed in the Nabû temple at Kalhu, and possibly others in temples at Assur and Harran. The bronze relief of Naqia and an Assyrian king most likely was on view in a temple or on a public monument. Another document, fragmented and difficult to read, suggests that a statue of

---

[41] Melville 1999: 42.

[42] Melville 1999: 40.

[43] "This text exists in three fragmentary copies, two of which were published as a composite by Borger. It is written and organized exactly like a royal building inscription, although (and this must have been done on purpose) it is considerably shorter and less hyperbolic than royal building inscriptions" (Melville 1999: 39).

[44] Borger 1956: 116.

Naqia was placed on a street in the town of Gadisê[45] in the Harran area. Again, no other instances are known of images of Assyrian queens on public display. Instead, this type of publicity and attention was more characteristic of Assyrian kings or perhaps the crown prince; this, of course, makes it all the more intriguing.

In the double row of stelae at Assur, between the inner and outer city walls, were monuments to officials, kings and queens. In the row of monuments to the kings and queens of Assyria was a dark grey basalt stele. Enough of the inscription on this stele survived for Andrae to believe it was for a queen of Sennacherib.[46] It is thought that this queen could be Naqia and, if so, this would be one more public monument to her.

Naqia was known to have dedicated cult objects. Two inscribed beads and the copies of two dedicatory inscriptions survive. In both dedicatory inscriptions she used the term *palû*, which has elicited much attention.[47] What she was making clear was that the objects were being dedicated for her own long life and the stability of her queenship (term of office) as well as the life and kingship of her son Esarhaddon.

Two letters written by Esarhaddon's advisors reveal the considerable respect and the influential position that Naqia had managed to acquire during her son's reign. Issar-šumu-ereš, a chief scribe, wrote to Naqia and commented that her verdict was "... as final as that of the gods. What you bless, is blessed; what you curse, is cursed."[48] Since "elsewhere only kings are credited with godlike omnipotence and perfection ..."[49] his statement was extraordinary in that it gave Naqia, the queen mother, kingly attributes and abilities. A further instance of this type of remark from Esarhaddon's advisors was a letter written to him by Marduk-šakin-šumi, one of his chief exorcists. The exorcist wrote to the king telling him that his mother had recovered from an illness and commented that "...the mother of the king is as able as (the sage) Adapa!"[50] This compliment, found in other Sargonid texts, was reserved for kings alone and it always indicated that they had acted very wisely. For Naqia to be complimented, or flattered, in such a manner meant that she was accorded exceptional respect by the chief advisors of the Assyrian court.[51]

The correspondence of Assyrian and Babylonian officials and scholars with Naqia also reflects her considerable stature. A few of the surviving letters to Naqia convey greetings, blessings and reassurances regarding the well-being

---

[45] SAA XIII 188:17-20.

[46] Andrae 1913: 9-10.

[47] See Chapter III n. 192.

[48] SAA X 17 r. 1-5.

[49] Parpola 1983: 230.

[50] SAA X 244 r. 7-9.

[51] Yet, interestingly, in a seemingly mundane matter regarding a servant, a letter assumed to have been written by Esarhaddon to Naqia reveals that when she wanted something done, his order was necessary. Although not a particularly revealing letter, it had a succinct and abbreviated style suggesting that correspondence between the king and his mother was commonplace (Melville 1999: 76-77).

of the king. The Babylonian astrologer Ašaredu assured her that he was "keeping the king's watch,"[52] meaning he was making certain the king kept on the path decreed by the gods and thus had divine protection. Was this a mere courtesy letter or did he have other reasons for wanting to be in Naqia's good graces? In another letter the Assyrian exorcist Nabû-šumu-lišir reported on a ritual regarding an eclipse[53] which could have serious implications for the king and the Assyrian empire if it was not performed correctly. A letter from the Babylonian Na'id-Marduk, governor of the Sealand, reported on an Elamite raid. He expressed the hope that Naqia would urge the king to send troops to his aid.[54] This is the only piece of Babylonian correspondence with Naqia that included political subject matter.

Finally, the loyalty oath Naqia imposed on the royal family and the Assyrian nation after the death of her son Esarhaddon for her grandson Aššurbanipal must be mentioned. All known Assyrian loyalty oaths were imposed by the kings for themselves or for the son chosen to be the crown prince – except for this one. It should be stressed that, for Naqia to have the prestige, the influence and the power to institute such an oath, and then presumably to enforce it, made her a unique and exceptional queen.

Personal Information

Almost no personal information is known about Naqia. As an individual and private person she elusively hides in the shadows of the Assyrian courts of her husband and her son. The one possible exception was an illness she suffered in 670.

An insurrection against the Assyrian king Esarhaddon began in Harran in March 670. It seems to have taken a few months to contain and there can be no doubt that it was serious. It even warranted an entry in the Babylonian Chronicles which documented that "… the Assyrian king executed many of his magnates."[55] By May the king himself had become seriously ill and for a time it was even thought that he might die. In June he began improving, but then his mother Naqia became ill.[56] Letters from three exorcists and one physician plus queries to the god Šamaš provide some interesting clues regarding the nature of her illness.

---

[52] Transliteration of ABL 254 (= SAA XVIII 10) by Parpola, translation by Melville (Melville 1999: 68).

[53] SAA X 313.

[54] Transliteration of ABL 917 (= SAA XVIII 85) by Parpola, translation by Melville (Melville 1999: 65).

[55] Borger 1956: 124.

[56] Based on the letters concerning the insurrection, the ill health of the king and the queen mother, Parpola has worked out the dating and the chronology of these events (Parpola 1983: 151).

At least two queries to Šamaš reveal that extispicy was performed and omens were requested for the recovery of Naqia when she was ill. In one query the illness, "the 'hand' of the god Iqbi-damiq was placed in extispicy."[57] The god Iqbi-damiq (literally "He-spoke-it-is-good") was the vizier of divine Niggina, a daughter of Šamaš, and was mentioned in *Šurpu*, a collection of incantations on neuroses and psychopathic states.[58] In another query the disease "'hand' of Nanaya of Uruk was placed [in extispicy]."[59] A firm, positive answer in the liver of the ram, and favorable, propitious omens were requested from Šamaš.

There were four letters to King Esarhaddon from his servants about the illness and recovery of Naqia. Adad-šumu-uṣur, the king's exorcist, wrote to him that anti-witchcraft rituals were being performed for the benefit of his mother.[60] The ritual used was called *ušburruda*. According to Parpola, the *ušburruda* was thought appropriate to perform in order to cure illnesses ascribed to sorcery. This sorcery could, in turn, cause mental and physical disorders. A ritual involving preparation of several images of the sorcerer and sorceress, a prayer to Šamaš, and subsequent burning and burial of the images would occur. Drugs might also be prescribed for the ill person.[61] In a second letter, Adad-šumu-uṣur again discusses the rituals and incantations which had seemingly cured the queen mother. Called *mamīt pašāri* they were used to cure illnesses caused by curses.[62] Kinnier Wilson has argued that being affected by a curse or the *mamīt*-state could result in obsessive-compulsive behavior or phobias that were irrational obsessional fears.[63] Thus the inference is that Naqia, haunted by curses, suffered from psychic disorders. In this second letter, Adad-šumu-uṣur also mentioned an incantation *atti* ÍD "You River"[64] which was a component of various *namburbi* rituals used against sorcery. It therefore seems a strong possibility that the illness Naqia suffered immediately after the insurrection in Harran and the serious illness of Esarhaddon, was more psychological that physical. The exorcists and physicians called in to cure her appear to have regarded her as a victim of sorcery and/or a curse and treated her accordingly.

Not too long after these rituals were performed, the chief exorcist Marduk-šakin-šumi wrote to the king that his mother had recovered. Another letter from the exorcist Nabû-naṣir and the chief physician Urad-Nanaya also reported that the mother of the king had recovered and was doing well.[65]

---

[57] SAA IV 190:2-3.

[58] Kinnier Wilson 1965: 294.

[59] "It is possible, but not certain, that the name of Esarhaddon's mother, Niq'a, is to be restored here" (SAA IV 191 *ad* l. 2).

[60] SAA X 200.

[61] Parpola 1983: 159.

[62] SAA X 201.

[63] Kinnier Wilson 1965: 294.

[64] According to W. Heimpel, this was probably an incantation prayer to motivate a river to cleanse Naqia (private communication, July 2001).

[65] SAA X 244, 297.

This brief period of time in 670 would seem to have been traumatic for at least three reasons. An insurrection within Assyria occurred which had to be quelled; Esarhaddon became so seriously ill that it was thought he might die; and Naqia also became so ill that the king's exorcists and physicians were called in to treat and heal her. As stated above, from the anti-witchcraft rituals and incantations that were used, it seems quite likely Naqia had some sort of mental collapse. Given the extreme stress Naqia must have felt, this reaction seems quite human and natural. Thus, one piece of personal information regarding the individual personality of Naqia is hinted at in these letters and queries to the sungod.

Three Theories

Various theories have been proposed about Naqia as to who she was and how she became such an influential and respected queen in Assyria. Many scholars have assumed that she was not native to Assyria. One such theory about Naqia proposed by Johns is that she was of Israelite descent,[66] which, linguistically speaking, is possible.[67] Waterman suggested that not only was Naqia a Hebrew, but that she was one of the princesses sent to the court of Sennacherib by King Hezekiah of Judah in 701 BCE.[68] Both Lewy and Melville are convinced that this was an impossibility as it would have delayed the birth of Naqia's son Esarhaddon which, in turn, would have caused Aššurbanipal to be too young at the time he acceded to the throne.[69] At present, Naqia's origins are entirely unknown and it seems an extremely unlikely possibility that she was a Hebrew princess sent by Hezekiah.

Another theory about Naqia is that she was Babylonian and even governed Babylonia during the reign of her son Esarhaddon and perhaps during the reign of her husband Sennacherib. These ideas, although totally unsubstantiated, came about because ancient sources were misread.[70] Trying to understand and explain why Esarhaddon completely reversed the Babylonian policy of his father Sennacherib, who reportedly destroyed the city of Babylon and laid waste to the Babylonian countryside, likely influenced this interpretation of events. It has been suggested that the reason Esarhaddon 'went soft' on Babylonia was because his mother Naqia and his wife Ešarra-hammat were both Babylonians and that they pressured and influenced his Babylonian policies. However, Frame, Brinkman and Melville all concur that there is no concrete evidence to substantiate such statements.[71]

---

[66] Johns (1923: 160) even suggests that "If this be the case and Esarhaddon's mother was really of Israelite descent we obtain an interesting side-light on Jewish partiality for that monarch also possibly an explanation of his clemency to Manesseh of Judah."

[67] Melville 1999: 14.

[68] Waterman 1930-36 III: 327.

[69] Lewy 1952: 272-273, Melville 1999: 14.

[70] Frame 1992: 62.

[71] Frame 1992: 62, Brinkman 1983: 36 n. 5, Melville 1999: 62.

The only economic document connecting Naqia to Babylonia came from the town of Lahiru which is thought to be in the Diyala region not far from the Elamite-Babylonian border. In 687 the town manager sold people; the document began by identifying him: "Seal of Idu'a, town manager [of] Lahiru of the domain of the queen mother...."[72] However, it must be pointed out that owning an estate in Lahiru is very different than governing the surrounding area. Not only Naqia but other members of the royal family held land there. It is known that Šamaš-šumu-ukin resided there when he was crown prince and Libbali-šarrat, queen of Aššurbanipal, owned land in Lahiru in 668. Lewy speculates that Naqia was an Aramaean princess and, in her belief, was likely born in Lahiru. When the city was captured in 712 by Sargon II, she was taken by the king to Nineveh and married to his son Sennacherib.[73]

Another reason that is given for Naqia being a Babylonian, and even ruling there, is the fact that she received letters from Babylonia. The astrologer Aplâ from Borsippa sent her greetings. The Babylonian priest Nabû-šumu-lišir reported on the rituals performed for an eclipse that occurred there. The gold she sent for the crown of Nabû in Borsippa in 671 was mentioned in a letter to the king by his agent Mar-Issar in Babylonia.[74] Ašaredu, an astrologer in Babylonia, sent Naqia greetings.[75] Clearly she must have taken an interest in Babylonia, especially in its cultic affairs, but to stretch this interest to governance is to take a considerable leap.

One final letter to Naqia which has elicited much comment because of its political content was from Na'id-Marduk, the younger son of Merodach-baladan II of the Bit-Yakin tribe. Na'id-Marduk turned to Assyria and threw himself on the mercy of Esarhaddon after his brother, the governor of the Sealand, unsuccessfully laid siege to Ur and then fled to Elam which was unsympathetic and executed him. Esarhaddon pardoned Na'id-Marduk and appointed him the governor of the Sealand. In his letter to Naqia, the queen mother, Na'id-Marduk reported how the Elamites had seized one of the Sealand bridges and he feared they might return. He requested that Naqia have the king send troops to help the Sealanders. Lewy feels that Na'id-Marduk would only have written this type of letter to Naqia if she was his official superior and a ruler in her own right.[76] Melville feels it is just as likely that Na'id-Marduk had a good rapport with the queen mother, perhaps having "...made her acquaintance when he was at the Assyrian court in 680, and, since Esarhaddon's annals tell us that he returned to Assyria with tribute annually...."[77] Na'id-Marduk might also have reasoned that if he got Naqia's support she might be able to elicit military aid from Esarhaddon. All in all,

---

[72] SAA VI 255.

[73] Lewy 1952: 273 n. 42.

[74] SAA X 154, 313, 348.

[75] Transliteration of ABL 254 (= SAA XVIII 10) by Parpola, translation by Melville (Melville 1999: 68).

[76] Lewy 1952: 274.

[77] Melville 1999: 67.

there does not appear to be conclusive evidence that Naqia was a Babylonian or that she ruled there.

A third theory about Naqia, proposed by Melville, is that her public image was manipulated by her son Esarhaddon during his reign so that she would be powerful enough to implement his will concerning the succession when he died. Because his mother was the only person Esarhaddon could completely trust, Melville feels that from the beginning of his 11-year reign, "…Esarhaddon purposefully set out to present his mother as a figure whose status was almost as high as the king's."[78]

Esarhaddon came to the throne after the death of his father Sennacherib who was murdered by his own sons. Esarhaddon's fear of rebellion was well founded as his brothers had escaped to a neighboring country and had never been apprehended or punished in Assyria. Esarhaddon also knew that his own poor health could be used as an instrument against him and might be the cause of his own early death. To assure a smooth transfer of power to his chosen heirs, Aššurbanipal and Šamaš-šumu-ukin, Melville feels that he established his mother as their guardian.

Esarhaddon implemented a program, in short, that would give his mother the necessary prestige to fulfill his plans.

She built a palace for Esarhaddon and commemorated it with a building inscription in the royal style, she gave jewellery to temples for the adornment of the gods' statues, she had rituals enacted on her behalf and may have sponsored temple restoration. Her statue was placed in a temple and she was depicted with the king on a religious relief. In every case, Naqia's activities accompanied similar actions of the king. Thus, for example when Esarhaddon built at Nineveh, she built there; he restored the temple of Sin at Harran and she worked on a temple there. Naqia even contributed to work in Babylonia.[79]

Surviving correspondence with Assyrian and Babylonian officials shows Naqia was treated with the same respect and deference that the king was. Praises normally reserved for the king alone were also applied to her.

Melville points out that while some would like to think of Naqia as being the real power behind the throne,

> … a reassessment of Esarhaddon leads to the conclusion that he was indeed an able and intelligent king who acted decisively and competently …. We must adjust our view of Naqia's role at court accordingly. If Naqia wielded real power during the reign of her son it can only be because Esarhaddon sanctioned it.[80]

In the last analysis, however, after her son Esarhaddon's death, Naqia implemented a loyalty oath for her grandson Aššurbanipal, and a peaceful transfer of power ensued.

---

[78] Melville 1999: 59-60.

[79] Melville 1999: 92.

[80] Melville 1999: 32.

Fig. 15 Bronze relief fragment of Naqia and king with cuneiform inscription
a) Photograph (AO 20.185, courtesy Musée du Louvre)
b) Drawing (drawing by R. Hall, after Börker-Klähn 1982: 220)

Visual Image: The Bronze Relief

There is a bronze relief fragment in the Louvre (AO 20.185) which was cast in a piece-mold and embossed with a picture of a man and woman in profile (Fig. 15).[81] It has cuneiform writing on it. Upon closer examination the name "Naqia" can be seen written on the woman's shoulder. The man she follows is an Assyrian king. It is a perplexing relief as it is not entirely clear who he is, where they are and what they are doing. But a careful examination provides many clues.

Bronze-working in Assyria

Although Assyria is not often regarded as being an important bronze-working center in the Ancient Near East, accomplished bronze-working was certainly done there. Curtis believes "there was in fact a thriving industry producing large amounts of bronzework, some of it in a distinctively Assyrian style."[82] Both textual records and archaeological finds prove that Assyrian metal-workers were active and extremely adept during the Neo-Assyrian period. Both monumental and small-scale bronze objects were often illustrated in palace reliefs. Many small-scale bronze objects have also been found in archaeological excavations. These objects include maceheads, weapons and armor, horse trappings, apotropaic figurines, weights, wall plaques, furniture fittings, musical instruments, vessels and jewellery.

---

[81] The relief is 33 × 31 cm, 15 cm thick and 13.9 kg in weight (about 30 pounds) (Parrot and Nougayrol 1956: 147 n. 2).

[82] Curtis 1988: 83.

But monumental bronze work was also produced by the Assyrians.[83] The bronze sheets with embossed and chased designs decorating wooden doors must have been very popular as examples have been found at Balawat, Nimrud, Khorsabad, Assur and Tell Hadad[84] and are known to have been made from the reign of Aššurnaṣirpal in the first half of the ninth century through the reign of Aššurbanipal in the middle of the seventh century.

Possibly the most famous Neo-Assyrian inscriptions regarding bronze-casting came from the reign of Sennacherib. In inscriptions on cylinders, prisms and bulls he discussed a new technique for casting colossi. He began by stating,

> In times past, when the kings my fathers fashioned a bronze image in the likeness of their members, to set up in their temples …[85]

This statement nicely illustrates the long-standing practice of Assyrian bronze working. Sennacherib went on to describe the casting of great pillars, giant trees, 12 fierce lion colossi and 12 mighty bull colossi, boasting of specialized techniques that were used. This passage has been interpreted to mean that he made solid castings of his colossi whereas his predecessors had made hollow castings.[86]

His father Sargon is known to have visited, in person, metalworking centers in Syria to watch the men at work at their furnaces and, in an example of 'like-father-like-son,' Sennacherib clearly continued this technical interest and developed it further. On a relief from his palace at Nineveh, built around 645, Sennacherib's grandson Aššurbanipal actually showed a portico consisting of lion column-bases which match written descriptions and most certainly were made of bronze.

It is not surprising that no actual sites for metal working within Assyrian city boundaries have been discovered since most excavations have not included the outer towns where such activities would have taken place. Furthermore, a Sennacherib inscription indicates that bronze work occurred in the mountainous regions where wood for fuel would have been plentiful.[87]

More to the point, Esarhaddon mentioned that he took omens to decide in which city – Assur, Nineveh or Babylon – the cult statues and ritual apparatus for the Babylonian temples should be made. Assur was chosen, which indicates that it had an excellent reputation for metalworking.[88] Thus there is a strong likelihood that the Naqia bronze relief was made in Assyria by Assyr-

---

[83] The treasurer Ṭab-šar-Aššur wrote a letter to Sargon II reporting on the progress being made on the two *hilānu* palaces and on the temple doors. He discussed the casting of four bronze column bases, large and small lions and the bronze sheets to be put on the doorways. (SAA I 66).

[84] Curtis 1988: 87-88.

[85] Account Written After the Fifth Campaign: 391 (Luckenbill 1927 II: 168-169); Undated Bull Inscription: 412 (Luckenbill 1927 II: 176).

[86] Dalley 1988: 104.

[87] Account Written After the Fifth Campaign: 391 (Luckenbill 1927 II: 168-169); Undated Bull Inscription: 412 (Luckenbill 1927 II: 176).

[88] Dalley 1988: 98.

ian metalworkers. The knowledge of casting a solid and heavy piece such as this one would have been known for decades.

Function of the bronze relief

The Naqia bronze relief was clearly part of an official monument. Most writers mentioning this relief believe it was placed in a temple as part of an altar base or a divine throne dais.[89] The possibilities for the site of the temple, however, range from the city of Babylon to that of Assur. To understand these choices, an examination of the inscription and then the images on the relief is necessary.

Inscriptions on the bronze relief

Of the two figures, the woman on the bronze relief can be identified from the epigraph which descends from her shoulder and which, without doubt, continued to her feet. The name of the queen NAQIA can be read and Parrot and Nougayrol believe that the part of the epigraph which is missing gave her titles. They propose that the epigraph read, "Image of Naqia [mother of Esarhaddon]."[90]

The general sense of the inscription which covers the surface of the relief (except for the head and hands of the two figures) is known from other royal inscriptions. It describes a ritual which took place on the river or canal banks and in the nearby orchards and gardens. Parrot and Nougayrol have pointed out that this inscription compares nicely with four other texts which describe the occurrence of the same ritual: AsBbE and AsBbH of Esarhaddon, Tablet L 4 of Aššurbanipal and the Sippar tablet of Nabû-apla-iddin, the king of Babylon in the ninth century BCE (BM 91000).[91] By comparing these four texts with the *mīs pī* ritual texts from Nineveh and Babylon[92] it is clear that the ritual described on the bronze relief is the one which purified a cult image and enabled it to function as a deity.

This purification and animation ritual, *mīs pī*, was a major cultic ritual of considerable complexity. The ritual occurred over a two day period in different locations. It began with preparations in the temple in the city, moved out to the river bank by procession and into the gardens and orchards. Eventually the ritual was concluded back at the gate of the temple and in the temple cella.

---

[89] See Parrot and Nougayrol 1956: 147, Börker-Klähn 1982: 214, Curtis 1988: 88-89, Melville 1999: 47-52.

[90] Parrot and Nougayrol 1956: 157.

[91] Parrot and Nougayrol 1956: 151-152.

[92] The Nineveh ritual text was compiled from many fragments, the majority of which were from the multiple copies found in the library of Aššurbanipal. This would date most of the fragments to the seventh century BCE. The Babylonian text belongs to the Neo-Babylonian or Persian Period, roughly the sixth century BCE. (Walker and Dick 2001: 30, 70).

On day one, the mouth-washing, which purified the statue of the deity from any contamination (i.e., contact with the craftspeople who had constructed it), occurred. (In the Nineveh ritual text seven mouth-washings are mentioned and in the Babylonian ritual text, 14.) On day two the mouth-opening took place, which meant the statue would be able to eat bread, drink water and smell incense.[93]

The inscription on the bronze relief mentions the part of the ritual which is the focal point of the historical texts and therefore thought to constitute the heart of the ritual.[94] This would be the mouth-washings which took place in the orchards and gardens and on the river bank. The inscription, as restored by Parrot and Nougayrol, reads:

> [In the orc]hards and ga[rdens of Karzaginna], [I caused a statue? o]f E[a to enter]. Through the knowledge of the experts (I performed) mouth washing, mouth opening, washing and purifying before the stars of night. Ea, Šamaš, Asalluhi, Mah, Kusu and Ningirim, I opened his mouth in an august place ...[95]

The ritual mentioned on the bronze relief seems to have occured in the specific orchards and gardens of the Karzaginna. Parrot and Nougarol believe that it was the Ekarzaginna, the river bank temple of Ea in Babylon, that is referred to in the inscription. It was located south of the Esagila and could easily be reached by walking through the two gates named "the River God" and "the Garden of the Apsu, where the mouths of the gods are opened."[96] But they also note that the Ekarzaginna was the quay where divine statues disembarked and thus the name would have been relevant for different temples in several cities.[97] They believe that the statue in question was the god Ea.[98] The rites mentioned occurred "before the stars of night" and thus referred to the ritual events on the evening of the first day. Appropriately it was the gods and goddesses of purification, "Ea, Šamaš, Asalluhi, Mah, Kusu and Ningirim" who were addressed as the washing and purifying took place.

Images on the bronze relief

On the relief fragment Naqia follows the king in what was most likely a ceremonial procession. In regal and stately fashion, the two formal figures appear to advance toward what Parrot and Nougayrol believe would have been the representations of divinities to which they were paying homage.[99]

---

[93] Walker and Dick 2001: 4-82.

[94] Walker and Dick 2001: 58 n. 73.

[95] Melville 1999: 48.

[96] The research of A.R. George (1992) and B. Pongratz-Leisten (1994) on Babylonian temple topography shows the route priests would have followed between the two temples (BM 35046:26-27). (Walker and Dick 2001: 17 n. 45 and 52 n. 38.)

[97] Parrot and Nougayrol 1956: 154 n. 3.

[98] However, because the Ekarzaginna was the river temple of Ea, the inscription might be regarding the statue of another god which was brought to the Ea temple.

[99] Parrot and Nougayrol 1956: 147.

Both figures wear royal headgear and attire and carry symbolic objects in their hands. They are both in profile, visible on their right side. Although the name of the queen is written on her shoulder, NAQIA, there is no name accompanying the king. He is a Sargonid king but he could be Naqia's husband Sennacherib, her son Esarhaddon, or her grandson Aššurbanipal.

The king's headgear identifies him as an Assyrian monarch. The fez-like cap worn by Assyrian kings was cylindrical, broader at the brim and narrower at the top. A cone projected from the upper surface. Over a period of time, beginning with Tiglath-Pileser III, the cap became higher and more elaborately decorated. From the reign of Sargon II the cone, too, had bands of decoration and during the entire Sargonid period the bands were lavishly decorated with rosettes.[100] The headgear of this king is quite high and shows diagonal bands with rosettes (most likely of gold) and two streamers which extend down the king's back to his waist.

The Assyrians always paid special attention to dressing their hair and their beards. Over time, styles became more and more elaborate and were rendered with great detail in their art. The hair of the Sargonid kings rested on their shoulders and was given a cubic shape.[101] The hair of the king on the bronze relief is very clearly depicted in this manner. It falls to the shoulders and covers the nape of the neck. Beards were depicted with vertical locks extending in tiers which ended in curls while the length of the beard was a measure of one's rank. The beard of the king on this relief fittingly extends quite far down his chest.

The king wears a long robe with short sleeves. A shawl hangs from his shoulder over his right arm, the edges of which are depicted by two vertical parallel lines. Encircling his body, the shawl lends dignity to the occasion. Royal robes and shawls were sometimes depicted as embroidered and fringed, but in this case fine details concerning the king's attire are impossible to determine, perhaps partly due to the cuneiform signs which cover his clothing.

In his left hand the king carries a mace which was the standard Assyrian symbol of authority. In Assyrian art, maces can be seen borne by the monarch, his royal attendants and soldiers and as such could be used as a weapon or a scepter. The mace was typically carried by the king when performing acts of worship.[102] The mace in this relief appears to have been the basic type used in the Middle and Neo-Assyrian periods. The macehead is pear-shaped without a knob on the top. The king grasps it close to the head which can be seen above his hand. The lower end of the mace falls on the left side of the king and is thus out of sight.

In his right hand the king holds an unknown object to his nose. Parrot and Nougayrol admit that interpretations vary as to what the object might be but they do call this "a significant ritual gesture,"[103] but take it no further. Reade

---

[100] Madhloom 1970: 75.

[101] Madhloom 1970: 85.

[102] Madhloom 1970: 61.

[103] Parrot and Nougayrol 1956: 148.

states that this ritual gesture originated in Babylonia and was adopted by Sennacherib around the time he destroyed Babylon. He says what the king holds to his nose might be a sweet-smelling object.[104] Porter reports that on the Til Barsip stele, Esarhaddon raises this same "emblem of royal power" even though the nature of the object is unclear.[105]

Naqia is directly behind the king on the relief. She wears a mural crown on her head. In the ancient Near East, examples of the mural crown can be found from the Hittites and Syrians in the west to the Elamites and Achaemenids in the east. In most cases the mural crown was worn by royal women or goddesses. In the Neo-Assyrian period, other depictions of Assyrian queens wearing the mural crown are on a stele, a relief scene and possibly a glazed tile. There are also at least two seal impressions from the palace of Sennacherib at Nineveh showing the king and queen standing before an image of a goddess who is mounted on an animal.[106] The king wears his fez-style cap with a cone protruding from the top and the queen wears the mural crown, also with a cone. As a rule, mural crowns were made in the shape of the battlements of a city, with main walls and projecting crenellated towers. Thus they looked very similar to the models of cities which were carried by foreign tributaries in palace relief scenes.

The mural crown was very probably part of the accoutremont of queenship and may have given her a political or tutelary role. That the queen's mural crown on occasion included the cone, which otherwise was only seen on the king's headgear, might be an indication of how serious and important her role was.

Naqia's hairstyle is essentially the same as the king's. It falls behind her ears, covers the nape of her neck and rests on her shoulders in the same cubic shape. She too wears a tunic with a shawl that falls vertically from her right upper arm. The edge of the shawl is again clearly delineated by two parallel lines on her right side. A plait can be seen hanging down her back which in all likelihood is the counterweight to a heavy necklace, even though the necklace cannot be seen. Her body type is nearly identical to that of Aššur-banipal's queen on the stele and in the banquet relief. Naqia has been included in this relief scene because she had a serious function. But more to the point is the fact that her body type and royal attire and pose imitate that of the king. She has a substantial presence and helps to lend dignity to an important ceremony.

Just like the king, Naqia holds something up to her nose with her right hand, but in her left hand she holds a mirror. While this is the only known example in Neo-Assyrian art of a woman with a mirror, actual mirrors have been found at Kalhu in the Northwest Palace in a well[107] and in a royal grave,[108] at

---

[104] Reade 1987: 143.

[105] Porter 2000: 143.

[106] Reade 1987: 144-145.

[107] J. and D. Oates 2001: 101

[108] Damerji 1999: 7, Table 1 and Damerji 1991: 11, Figs. 3, 6.

Dur-Šarrukin in a private residence[109] and references to mirrors in texts are known.[110] This mirror is circular with a terminal decoration in relief on the handle. The meaning or significance or symbolism of the mirror, however, is baffling.

Mirrors are generally regarded as gendered, as an attribute connected with the feminine sphere.[111] In the ancient Near East, in both the second and first millennia BCE, mirrors were often identified with goddesses. Images of goddesses holding mirrors have been found in Syria, Anatolia and northwestern and southern Iran. Most often it was the goddess Kubaba from the west who held the mirror. Called the "queen of Carchemesh," Kubaba was portrayed as sitting on a throne which was itself on the back of an animal, usually a lion, sometimes a bull. Her feet rested on a footstool and in her left hand she held a distaff or pomegranate and in her right hand a mirror.[112] She was often paired with a god and in one inscription, very interestingly, she was paired with the god Ea.

Women holding mirrors have also been found in mortuary contexts. Funerary stelae from the Syro-Hittite world depict women holding mirrors and distaffs in their hands.[113] Mirrors are also among the grave goods of women from locations as distant as Anatolia and Egypt, and in Mesopotamia from the Uruk period in the late fourth millennium through the Late Assyrian period in the first millennium. Two examples from the latter period are a mirror found in a bronze coffin at Ur but dating to the Late Assyrian period.[114] and at Kalhu a mirror was found lying on the body of one of the queens buried below the Northwest Palace.[115]

Mirrors have also been found in other contexts. "A complete copper mirror, polished on both sides, with remains of a wooden handle"[116] was found in a well in the residential section of the Northwest Palace at Kalhu and a circular bronze mirror cast with a tang was found in a private residence in Dûr-Šarrukin.[117] Mirrors were also mentioned among dowry objects.

Mirrors were certainly connected with temples. As well as being a divine attribute held by goddesses, mirrors are mentioned in inscriptions, rituals and curses. They also were precious objects belonging to divine statues and they are known to have been votive offerings. It is perhaps in this latter context that Ṭab-ṣill-Ešarra, the governor of Assur, wrote a letter to Sargon II where he mentioned the skill of a craftsman who had provided a particularly fine finish on two bronze mirrors.[118]

---

[109] Loud and Altman 1938: 68, 99, Pl. 62.

[110] Pfeiffer 1935: No. 146.

[111] Albenda 1998: 89.

[112] Vieyra 1955: Pl. 65.

[113] Akurgal 1961: Pl. 139.

[114] Curtis 1983: 91, Fig. 1.

[115] Damerji 1999: 7, Table 1; Damerji 1991: 11, Figures 3, 6.

[116] J. and D. Oates 2001: 101.

[117] Loud and Altman 1938: 68, 99, Pl. 62.

[118] Pfeiffer 1935: No. 146.

Various possibilities have been suggested as to why Naqia holds a mirror in the bronze relief. That the mirror was a personal emblem introduced by Naqia seems highly unlikely. Throughout the ancient Near East, the tradition of goddesses and royal and aristocratic women holding mirrors was very widespread. The mirror, along with the distaff and pomegranate, obviously had complex symbolic and ritualistic significance. One suggestion held that the mirror indicated Naqia came from the west and it proved her Syrian Aramaean origins. So far, however, firm information regarding Naqia's origins is not available.

Because the function of Naqia's appearance on this bronze relief appears to duplicate, imitate, substantiate and validate the image and responsibilities of the king, it seems a strong possibility that the objects held in the left hands of the king and queen, the mirror and the mace, are related and comparable – in the feminine and masculine spheres. If this is the case, the mirror would be one of the important emblems of Assyrian queenship. Perhaps, as a Neo-Assyrian proverb claims, "… the king is the mirror of the god"[119] – and the same was true of the queen. In Naqia's case the mirror, along with the mural crown, may have symbolized her political functions and duties and also her religious responsibilities. Another possibility is that one of Naqia's important roles may have been to portray (or "mirror") the state god Aššur's consort Mullissu on earth, specifically in Assyria.

Placement of the bronze relief

Whether this relief was meant for an Assyrian or Babylonian audience is, at this point, an unanswerable question. Because the main inscription on the relief describes a ritual in which a statue of the god Ea received purification and animation rites, it has been assumed that the statue in question was one of the statues returned to Babylonia after their removal by Sennacherib when he destroyed Babylon in 689. Ea, the father of Marduk, was one of the gods mentioned in Esarhaddon's inscriptions when he referred to the return of these statues. It has been theorized that the revivifying ceremony mentioned on the relief must have taken place in Babylonia and, therefore, the bronze relief would surely have been part of the decoration of the Esagila in Babylon or one of the other important Babylonian temples. Parrot and Nougayrol feel that the bronze relief is an iconographical confirmation of the return of Ea to the temple of his son Marduk. Furthermore, they state that because Naqia was probably an Aramaean born in Babylonia, Esarhaddon would be deliberately proclaiming, before the gods and men, that his mother supported, if not inspired, the enterprise of returning Ea to Babylon.[120] Börker-Klähn also believes that the relief refers to the return of Ea to Babylon.[121]

---

[119] The entire proverb says "As people say: 'Man is the shadow of a god, and a slave is the shadow of a man'; but the king is the mirror of a god" (Lambert 1960: 281-282; cf. Nemet-Nejat 1993: 167).

[120] Parrot and Nougayrol 1956: 157.

[121] Börker-Klähn 1982: 214.

However, this may not be exactly the case. Lambert has pointed out that two texts of Esarhaddon, AsBbE and K6048+8323 (Borger's Assur C text), call attention to the revivifying ritual of the statue of Marduk and the other gods of Babylonia in the court of the Ešarra temple in Assur prior to their departure from Assyria.[122] Although this same ritual would have occurred once more when the statues had ceremoniously arrived in Babylonia, it is very possible that the bronze relief shows the ceremony that took place with the Assyrian king and Naqia in Assyria.

Porter, too, notes the complexities regarding the two ceremonies. In her discussion of the AsBbE inscription, she points out that by having the revivifying ceremonies performed in both Assyria and Babylonia, it, in fact, insured "… that the statues would be accepted as valid and living receptacles of the gods' presence in both nations."[123] Of course it helped that in text AsBbA the Babylonian gods were regarded as being "… truly born in the midst of Ešarra, the house of their father …." This meant that they were cleverly relegated to being the children of the Assyrian god Aššur.[124]

Melville has noted that stylistically the relief is Assyrian, not Babylonian, and it therefore was created to reside in an Assyrian temple, not a Babylonian one. She argues that the texts which mention the restoration and decoration of the Babylonian temples are clear that the work occurred in Babylonia although materials might have been sent from Assyria.[125] She claims that it is very unlikely that the bronze relief would have been made in Assyria and then transported to Babylonia. She also mentions that Esarhaddon took care to follow Babylonian customs when it was appropriate. An example she gives is the Sam'al stele on which Esarhaddon, the king of Assyria, wears Assyrian attire, Aššurbanipal, the crown prince of Assyria, wears Assyrian attire, but Šamaš-šumu-ukin, the crown prince of Babylon, wears Babylonian attire.[126] In the bronze relief the king and Naqia most definitely wear Assyrian attire.

Current scholarly opinion seems to be that the relief was intended for a temple in Assyria, most likely the Ešarra at Assur. But in actual fact it is not clear where the bronze relief was put on display. It is very unfortunate that the original provenance of the relief is unknown. To add one more note of uncertainty, the bronze relief may, of course, have had nothing at all to do with the return of the statues of the gods to Babylon.

---

[122] Lambert 1988: 160, 165.

[123] Porter 1993: 145 n 304.

[124] This more elaborate argument by Porter meant that Assyria under Esarhaddon made the Babylonian god Marduk a son of the Assyrian god Aššur, thereby making him a subordinate god. When the statue of Marduk was returned to Babylonia Marduk was no longer the head of a rival Babylonian pantheon but became instead a divine emblem of the unity of the two states (Porter 1993: 124).

[125] Melville 1999: 49. (In n. 84, Melville mentions the letters SAA X 348, 349, 354 and 364 from Mar-Issar, the king's official in Babylonia.)

[126] Melville 1999: 50. See also Roaf 1990: n. 189. However, in her discussion on the three stelae from Til Barsip and Sam'al, B.N. Porter (2000: 161-169) points out that the Assyrians might adapt the images on their monuments to address different political and cultural circumstances. She notes that while the Sam'al stele does show the crown prince of Babylon in Babylonian dress, on the two stelae from Til Barsip he is shown in typical Assyrian dress.

Summary

Regardless of where the bronze relief was meant to be displayed, the work appears to have been made in Assyria by Assyrian metalworkers. The inscription describes a purification and animation ritual pertaining to the statue of a god. The images show an Assyrian king with the Assyrian queen, Naqia, following behind him.

What is most striking about this scene on the bronze relief is that Naqia, the queen, was fully integrated into the religious ceremony.[127] She walks as regally as the king does, she wears a royal headdress as the king does, she carries ritual and symbolic objects just as the king does. It is particularly unfortunate that so very little is known about the role of queens in religious and state ceremonies. As a result it is impossible to determine if the actions of Naqia were unusual or commonplace ones for Assyrian queens. But in this instance she was clearly vital to the message that the king and his advisers wished to proclaim.

Loyalty Oath

An Assyrian mechanism for encouraging and enforcing loyalty to the king and also to the crown prince was to institute a loyalty oath. Those swearing allegiance were obligated to report any activities disloyal or dangerous to the sovereign and his family. Typically such a pact was imposed after civil wars or at the official appointment of the heir apparent.[128] This practice seems to have been particularly popular (or thought particularly necessary) in the seventh century when the youngest sons of kings were chosen to succeed their fathers. These irregular circumstances necessitated extraordinary state ceremonies and were, it seems, a novelty in Assyria.[129] Five such loyalty oaths from the seventh century, fragmentary to be sure, exist today.

The term used in these documents is *adê*, an Aramaic word, which Parpola defines as "a general term for any *solemn, binding agreement*." He quotes agreements between the gods or peace treaties between rulers or promises made by a god to the king.[130] They were definitely regarded as binding political agreements between the contracting parties, whether human or divine, and were to be taken extremely seriously. An illustration of this point would be Esarhaddon's letter to the god Aššur, composed shortly after the fall of Šubria in 672, where those parties who broke the *adê* oath were severely punished.[131] Tadmor sees this letter as a clear "warning that a similar fate awaits any person or community that does not respect the loyalty oath

---

[127] Reade 1987: 143.

[128] Parpola and Watanabe 1988: XXIV.

[129] Tadmor 1983: 38.

[130] Parpola 1987b: 181-182.

[131] Leichty 1991: 52-57.

CHAPTER IV – NAQIA/ZAKUTU

and openly defies the emperor."[132] Thus the multitudinous ramifications of signing such a document and the serious consequences of breaking it would have been obvious to the participants.

The five surviving loyalty oaths from seventh-century Assyria, found in Assur, Nineveh and Kalhu, reflect the controversial successions of Esarhaddon, the youngest son of Sennacherib, and Aššurbanipal, the youngest son of Esarhaddon. There are three loyalty oaths concerning the succession of Esarhaddon. According to Parpola and Watanabe, the first, although only a fragment of an oath, was likely instituted by Sennacherib in either 683 or 682. Although the name of the prince it refers to is broken, the controversy surrounding Esarhaddon's accession to the throne makes it fairly conclusive that it must concern him. Parpola and Watanabe believe that the second loyalty oath was imposed by Esarhaddon on himself in the period shortly before his accession in 681 because he is not referred to as a king but as 'my lord.'[133] In 670, most likely after the unsuccessful *coup d'état* had been put down in Harran, the third loyalty oath was imposed by and for the king Esarhaddon.[134]

The final two loyalty oaths, concerning the succession of Aššurbanipal, were imposed by his father Esarhaddon and by his grandmother Naqia. Esarhaddon, toward the end of his reign, imposed a loyalty oath on his fellow countrymen when he made his youngest son Aššurbanipal the crown prince, heir to the throne of Assyria, and his older son, Šamaš-šumu-ukin, the crown prince designate to Babylon. This loyalty oath was imposed in 672.[135] Contemporary accounts of these oath-taking ceremonies which occurred throughout the Assyrian empire exist as do Aššurbanipal's later inscriptions plus at least eight fragmentary copies of the loyalty oath.[136] All clearly indicate that Esarhaddon was determined that this radical plan of his would take place.

The proposal to place two different sons on the throne of Assyria and Babylon respectively was a big departure from tradition. One suspects that the plan was fraught with controversy in Assyria. A letter from Adad-šumu-uṣur, King Esarhaddon's exorcist, states, in wonderment:

---

[132] Tadmor 1983: 43.

[133] Parpola & Watanabe 1988: XXVIII.

[134] Parpola & Watanabe 1988: XXXI.

[135] Parpola & Watanabe 1988: XXIX.

[136] In the 1955 season at Kalhu, in a building north of the Nabû temple, over 350 fragments of baked clay tablets were found. They amount to at least eight nearly identical copies of the 672 BCE loyalty oath by Esarhaddon. Wiseman believes these were vassal treaties made with Median chiefs from the eastern periphery of the Neo-Assyrian empire (Wiseman 1958: 1-3). Liverani, however, believes "the Medes who submitted to the oath were living in the Assyrian palace(s), and performing the service of a guard corps (*hurdu*) for the Assyrian king, specifically as bodyguards of the crown prince. They had to swear the loyalty oaths on the occasion of the nomination of the crown prince, not because they were 'vassals,' but because they had been appointed as bodyguards of the prince himself" (Liverani 1995: 60). In addition to these eight copies, a small fragment, basically identical to the Kalhu texts, is known from Assur (Parpola and Watanabe 1988: XLVIII).

[137] SAA X 185.

> What has not been done in heaven, the king, my lord, has done upon earth and shown us: you have girded a son of yours with headband and entrusted to him the kingship of Assyria; your eldest son you have set to the kingship of Babylon.[137]

This statement certainly reveals a mixed reaction by one influential Assyrian priest to Esarhaddon's decision.[138]

It has been theorized that because of his own problems in ascending the throne as a younger son of the king, Esarhaddon was particularly intent that Aššurbanipal not experience the same disloyalty among his brothers and the Assyrian court. Thus he reinforced his decision with a loyalty oath.

The mother of Esarhaddon, Naqia, was also actively involved in this unusual succession plan. She too imposed a loyalty oath for her grandson Aššurbanipal before his coronation. It is thought to have been drafted and implemented in the period immediately following Esarhaddon's unexpected death on his way to Egypt and Aššurbanipal's accession to the throne.[139] True to her theory as outlined above, Melville believes Naqia's involvement was part of Esarhaddon's plan as he had been carefully legitimizing his mother in various ways during the last four years of his reign.[140] Certainly the loyalty oath of Naqia is a remarkable document as it is the only known loyalty oath imposed by someone other than the king himself. In fact, it could be said that as her son the king had just died, Naqia momentarily took his place to remind the nation of the oath they took regarding the succession of Aššurbanipal. That she had the authority and the status to do so is impressive.

The loyalty oath of Naqia, now in the collection of the British Museum, is an almost complete one-column tablet from Nineveh. There is only one small fragment missing from the lower left corner.[141] It consists of Preamble, Treaty Stipulations, Violation Clause and the Traditional Curses.

The Preamble of the loyalty oath begins with Naqia reiterating her qualifications and thus her right to impose this oath. She is "... Zakutu, the queen of Sennacherib, king of Assyria, mother of Esarhaddon, king of Assyria ..."[142] The loyalty oath is for her grandson Aššurbanipal. She imposed this loyalty oath on the royal family and court, magnates, governors and the Assyrians themselves, high and low, in other words, the whole nation. It is especially noteworthy that the first person upon whom the loyalty oath was imposed was Šamaš-šumu-ukin, the older son, who was to become the king of Babylon for seventeen years. The Treaty Stipulations require loyalty to the Assyrian king,

---

[138] Porter (1993: 135) draws attention to the fact that "In Akkadian usage, the comment that an action is something 'not done in heaven' would ordinarily imply serious criticism; in the context of the effusive praises in this letter, however, the comment appears intended instead as a compliment, but one wonders whether the ambiguity might be deliberate and whether this might not in fact be a carefully veiled expression of dismay at Esarhaddon's action. If this is the case, the comment is probably as explicit a statement of such misgivings as we will ever find in writing."

[139] Parpola 1987b: 168.

[140] Melville 1999: 79.

[141] Parpola and Watanabe 1988: XLVIII-XLIX.

[142] SAA II 8:1-2.

and an obligation to report and inform on schemes, conspiracies, rebellions and any plans to kill Aššurbanipal, first to Naqia and second to Aššurbanipal the king.[143] The Violation Clauses range from harboring evil thoughts in one's heart, to listening to evil advice, to actually carrying out evil things against Aššurbanipal. The Traditional Curse section is incomplete, only mentioning some of the gods who would witness and then become involved, as agents of punishment.[144]

Naqia's loyalty oath was certainly a re-emphasis (or reminder) of the earlier vows taken in the loyalty oath imposed by Esarhaddon with regard to his heir Aššurbanipal as king of Assyria. In fact, Naqia's loyalty oath appears to have been an abbreviated form of the 672 loyalty oath of Esarhaddon. One difference, however, is that while the 672 loyalty oath stressed the succession of Aššurbanipal, it also included an oath to aid Šamaš-šumu-ukin ascend the throne of Babylon. Naqia's loyalty oath applied only to Aššurbanipal ascending the Assyrian throne; Šamaš-šumu-ukin is only mentioned as being one of those required to swear the oath of loyalty to his brother.

A final point that needs to be mentioned is that in the period following Sennnacherib's death and Esarhaddon's accession to the throne, a loyalty oath was thought necessary for the new king. Esarhaddon, the heir, imposed this loyalty oath on himself. Yet, after the death of Esarhaddon it was Naqia, not Aššurbanipal, the heir, who imposed the loyalty oath for the new king. This reveals that at the time of her husband's death, Naqia was not yet an influential or powerful enough person to perform this task legitimately. Yet, at the time of the death of her son Esarhaddon, she certainly was such a person. She could compel the Assyrians to take the loyalty oath for Aššurbanipal and also enforce it, once sworn.[145] How much this final loyalty oath influenced Assyrian politics is certainly an unknown factor today, but what is known is that the succession of Aššurbanipal, the youngest son of Esarhaddon, went smoothly and that the period following his accession to the throne was one of stability and prosperity for Assyria. Yet after this loyalty oath, Naqia fades into historical obscurity.

Conclusion

The most interesting and meaningful questions about Naqia are those that are concerned with whether, as a 'woman of the palace' during the reign of four

---

[143] See Melville's comment that "... the fact that Naqia always names herself first as the person to whom sedition and treason should be reported ... simply reflects the fact that she is imposing the treaty. It cannot be taken to mean that she had great influence over Ashurbanipal" (Melville 1999: 89).

[144] See Parpola and Watanabe 1988. The structural elements of Neo-Assyrian treaties and loyalty oaths are discussed in the Introduction. There are eleven elements, all of which may or may not be obligatory. They are: the Preamble, Seal Impressions, Divine Witnesses, Oath/Adjuration, Historical Introduction, Treaty Stipulations, Violation Clause, Traditional Curses, Vow, Ceremonial Curses, Colophon and Date. Only the composite text of Esarhaddon's 672 BCE loyalty oath concerning the succession of Aššurbanipal contains all eleven elements. The loyalty oath of Naqia has only four of the eleven structural elements.

kings, she was an extraordinary person who did exceptional things and whether or not she fit into the traditions of Assyrian queenship. Because more information about Naqia has survived than for any of the other Neo-Assyrian queens, it is very difficult to answer these questions. Most scholars seem to have assumed that the royal women of Assyria were cloistered, practically imprisoned, and were forced to live their lives in a very confined space. But this does not appear to be true. In Naqia's case, she participated in religious and state ceremonies and activities. She was politically informed and corresponded with officials, scholars and rulers within and outside Assyria who had a high respect for her abilities and authority. She had vast resources to run households, to give valuable gifts to temples and the gods and even to build a splendid palace for her son the king. And she imposed a loyalty oath on the people of Assyria.

Yet there appears to be a tendency for writers to view Naqia as a conniving manipulator behind the scenes during the reign of her husband and her son. It is often mentioned that she was the person responsible for two different succession plans and also for the conciliatory changes in the Assyrian governmental policy toward Babylonia during the reign of her son Esarhaddon. But there is absolutely no proof that either claim is true.

Naqia was most assuredly an astute and capable member of the Assyrian royal family. She played an active public and private role in the Assyrian power structure and was recognized for it. She concerned herself with spiritual and temple matters throughout the Assyrian empire. Her image would have been familiar to citizens since statues and reliefs of her were displayed in different cities, either in temples or in the public areas of towns.

It has been remarked that she had "kingly attributes and abilities" but it could just as reasonably be said that her abilities were "queenly"; in other words, what Naqia did was what queens did. Given her own personal proclivities or the circumstances of the times, Naqia may have been particularly keen to participate or she may have felt obligated to participate when drafted by the king or officials of the court or even by persons outside Assyria. That she took these responsibilities seriously is very clear.

In the final analysis what is really most important is that Naqia made significant contributions to the Neo-Assyrian world in which she lived. She upheld the values, beliefs and traditions of the Assyrians and she was respected and appreciated for her qualities. Whoever she was, and wherever she came from, once she became a 'woman of the palace' Naqia should be given credit for her grasp of contemporary events and for her determination to maintain stable and peaceful conditions within and outside Assyria.

CONCLUSION

The intent of this present study has been to examine textual and visual materials related to Neo-Assyrian temples and palaces in order to assess the role of women who lived and functioned within each institution. Beginning in the 1840s archaeological excavations in the capital cities of Assyria as well as other areas in the Assyrian empire have revealed material evidence that can be related to the women in temples and palaces. More recently during the past thirty years, transliterations and translations as well as studies of Neo-Assyrian texts have been published under the auspices of the State Archives of Assyria. These texts include correspondence, administrative records, legal transactions, grants and decrees, divination queries, astrological reports and literary texts. Within these texts are many references to women in the temples and palaces of Assyria.

This study began by focusing on women in Neo-Assyrian temples. The existing documentation on women in religious contexts includes their positions, ritual activities, cultic and non-cultic duties and personal names. The women who filled temple positions ran the entire spectrum from being members of the upper classes, even royalty, to being slaves. Their situations, therefore, varied considerably. A temple position, such as that of *entu* (the woman in charge), might be one of noticeable wealth and prestige. If a girl was given or sold to a temple, such as the *šēlûtu* (votary), her circumstances would be entirely up to the temple personnel where she made her home. Some temple positions, such as the *ištarītu* and *qadištu* and a number of the *šēlûtu*, allowed the women holding the office to have separate homes, marry and have children.

Yet some temple positions, such as the *ištarītu* and the *qadištu* have had negative images. The *ištarītu* became associated with sorcery and witchcraft while the *qadištu* has been thought to be a temple prostitute. Because sorcery and prostitution imply aberrant behavior it is important to dispel both notions. Although it may be questioned why such accusations, in ancient and modern periods, have been brought against women in these two temple offices, it certainly seems to suggest that they were thought to have magical and sexual powers which were viewed as threatening.

The office of *qadištu* had a long history in Mesopotamia and during the Neo-Assyrian period the *qadištu* is known to have been a participant in purification and exorcistic rituals. The *qadištu*'s association with prostitution can best be explained as a case of mistaken identity, a confusion with the Hebrew *qĕdēšāh* which refers to a secular prostitute; or guilt by association, inasmuch as a Middle Assyrian Law states that the unmarried *qadištu*, the *harimtu* (prostitute) and the *amtu* (female slave) could not wear veils in public; and an imagined affiliation with the cult of Ištar, even though by the first millennium Ištar had been considerably desexualized.[1]

Collections of prophecies in the imperial archives of Assyria which were assembled during the reigns of two seventh century kings, Esarhaddon and Aššurbanipal, reveal that many of the prophets who gave prophecies to the king and the queen mother were women. These collections plus royal inscriptions, letters, loyalty oaths and other documents provide information about female prophets. In many cases their personal names were recorded along with the prophecies they communicated which were most often from Ištar. The picture that emerges from the documents is that the prophets were accorded considerable respect in the seventh century. During the reign of Esarhaddon they were apparently allowed access to his person. Although many of the prophecies appear to have been uttered in the temple precincts, female prophets also had a public persona. Not only might they appear publicly before the king, but they also participated in public rituals and fulfilled governmental responsibilities which might require them to travel. Yet documents indicate that prophets were accorded a lower social status than that of other diviners. It seems highly likely that this may have been because schooling and training were not required and because so many of the prophets were women.

The present inquiry looked at the roles of women who performed music in Assyria. References to female musicians in Assyrian documents and depictions of female musicians carved in palace reliefs or in small ivory objects show that there was a distinct tradition of women performing, not only within the palaces and temples, but also in public. While they might entertain as solo performers, female musicians often performed in groups which were either composed entirely of women but often were a combination of female and male musicians. That female musicians performed in public and with male musicians shows that they were not segregated nor were they restricted to playing only for female audiences. Female musicians performed for the private pleasure of the queen and king, at victory celebrations, at sacred and secular ceremonial processions as well as during state and temple ritual occasions.

Both textual and visual sources placed an emphasis on foreign female musicians. Tribute lists, royal inscriptions and palace lists of female personnel specifically mention them along side other objects of note and designate their ethnicity or place of origin. They were even carefully distinguished from foreign male musicians that might further indicate their significance and importance.

Visual depictions of female musicians occur on decorative ivory objects and late Neo-Assyrian palace reliefs. Of the three palace reliefs with female musicians, two show Assyrian female musicians within Assyria and a third shows Elamite female musicians outside the Elamite city of Madaktu. All six ivory objects whether carved in the Syrian, Phoenician or Assyrian style depict non-Assyrian foreign female musicians.

---

[1] Assante 2000: 294.

Given the types of occasions where female musicians performed, especially state and sacred celebrations with royalty and court present, only musicians of the highest caliber would have been acceptable. The high level of competence and musicality required could only have been provided by professional female musicians.

Palace women were the subjects of the last two chapters in this study. Their residences, real estate holdings and the personnel who held offices in their households were examined and then the royal women themselves.

The households of Neo-Assyrian queens were large, complex and well-organized establishments. The queens had residences in a number of Assyrian cities, the best documented were at Kalhu and Nineveh. The female chief administrator of these residences was called a *šakintu* and written records from the seventh century indicate that she commanded a sizable staff of women and men, transacted a large volume of business and thereby wielded considerable power and influence. Among the other members of the queens' households were female and male scribes, eunuchs and extensive military units.

The incomes of royal women derived from tribute, gifts and properties owned throughout the empire. It is known that certain of the queen mothers owned real estate in a town called Šabbu, as well as Lahiru in the Diyala region. In addition, Naqia was affiliated with Gadisê in the Harran area.

Written records and archaeological finds provide data from which a picture begins to emerge of these royal women. The personal names, titles, symbols, activities, possessions and even burials of many Neo-Assyrian queens are now known.

Chapter III concludes with an examination of four known Assyrian queens: Sammuramat, Tašmetum-šarrat, Ešarra-hammat and Libbali-šarrat. Sammuramat is unusual in that her name and life became steeped in myth and legend. A first task for any researcher, therefore, is to sort out what was fact and what was fiction. Her high profile during the reign of her son Adad-nerari and the inclusion of her name on public monuments and royal inscriptions make her quite unique. It is known that she accompanied the Assyrian king on military campaigns and that she played an active role in Assyrian politics. She was also the first queen known to have a stele erected among those of the Assyrian kings at Assur. Tašmetum-šarrat is only known (1) by a vase which has an inscription providing her name, the title MÍ.É.GAL and the distinctive symbol of a scorpion on it and (2) by a pair of doorway sphinxes which carry an inscription that expresses the personal feelings which her husband, Sennacherib, had for her. Ešarra-hammat used the title of principal queen and quite uniquely for Assyrian queens was buried at Assur, normally the burial place of Assyrian kings. Libbali-šarrat is the only Assyrian queen for which there are two depictions thought to be of her: a stele found in the row of royal stelae at Assur and in the garden scene relief from Nineveh.

Chapter IV focused on the queen Naqia. She was alive during the reigns of four kings: Sargon II, Sennacherib, Esarhaddon and Aššurbanipal and much is known about her. There is information about her considerable wealth, her ill health, her consultations with the prophets of Ištar of Arbail, her participation in religious and state ceremonies and her correspondence with Assyrian and Babylonian officials. Naqia also had unique opportunities and the ability to do exceptional things. She is the only queen known (1) to have built a palace for the king and (2) to have imposed a loyalty oath (for her grandson Aššurbanipal) on the nation of Assyria.

Naqia and Sammuramat are two examples of queens who have been subjected to imaginative conjectures and inaccurate statements. They illustrate the importance of examining the precise details that are actually available in the written and visual records.

This study has examined the women in the temples and palaces of Assyria during the Neo-Assyrian period. It has drawn together the textual evidence in royal inscriptions, administrative archives, letters and legal documents and the visual evidence in palace reliefs, monuments, ivory objects and artifacts from tombs and palaces.

It is clear that certain words with encoded meanings have hindered our understanding of women in the Neo-Assyrian world. Words such as "harem" and even "queen" can suggest images which may have little or nothing to do with the circumstances, activities, responsibilities and relationships of Assyrian palace women. Another difficulty can be that assumptions imposed upon the data, such as "temple prostitution existed in the temples of Ištar," provide a bias that makes it impossible to view the evidence objectively.

In this study, visual evidence and written material have been analyzed together to provide the truest possible picture of women in the Neo-Assyrian temples and palaces. From the beginning the evidence pointed to the fact that the lives of these women were not as circumscribed or limited as had been previously supposed. Many women were definitely in the public arena. Temple women participated in rituals which could involve processing to various parts of the city. Female prophets could be called upon to reveal messages from deities to heads of state and then might be sent to perform official tasks in different cities. Female musicians performed alone or with male musicians at public events. Royal women had their names and images displayed in public.

The evidence also reveals that positions held by women in the palaces and temples often required administrative abilities, business acumen, literacy and specific skills where long periods of training were a necessity. The households of royal women contained sizable staffs many of whom were female. Those in charge, such as the *šakintu* and her deputy the *šanītu*, transacted a large volume of business, kept extensive records and were involved in legal transactions. As a result royal women and their staff, such as the *šakintu*, could acquire great wealth.

Evidence further shows that women in the temples and palaces could generate great respect from the king, his circle of advisors and Assyrian and foreign officials. Correspondence and imperial administrative records reveal that palace and temple women were consulted on diverse issues: political, religious and personal; and that they were given important responsibilities and tasks. All of the above illustrates that temple and palace women actively and noticeably participated in the "great institutions" of Assyria.

BIBLIOGRAPHY

Abusch, Tzvi
  1974   Mesopotamian Anti-Witchcraft Literature: Texts and Studies. *JNES* 33, 251-262.
  1989a   The Demonic Image of the Witch in Standard Babylonian Literature: The Reworking of Popular Conceptions by Learned Exorcists. Pages 27-58 in *Religion, Science, and Magic: In concert and Conflict*, edited by Jacob Neusner *et al*. New York: Oxford UP.
  1989b   Maqlû. *RlA* 7, 346-351.
  1992   Ritual and Incantation: Interpretation and Textual History of Maqlû VII:58-105 and IX:52-59. Pages 367-380 in *"Sha'arei Talmon": Studies in the Bible, Qumran, and the Ancient Near East Presented to Shemaryahu Talmon*, edited by Michael Fishbane and Emmanuel Tov *et al*. Winona Lake: Eisenbrauns.
  1995   The Socio-Religious Framework of the Babylonian Witchcraft Ceremony *Maqlû*: Some Observations on the Introductory Section of the Text, Part II. Pages 467-494 in *Solving Riddles and Untying Knots: Biblical, Epigraphic, and Semitic Studies in Honor of Jonas C. Greenfield*, edited by Ziony Zevit *et al*. Winona Lake: Eisenbrauns.
  1996   Some Reflections on Mesopotamian Witchcraft. Pages 21-33 in *Religion and Politics in the Ancient Near East*, edited by Adele Berlin. Baltimore: Maryland UP.

Ahmad, Ali Yaseen
  2008   The Archive of a Palace Scribe and Other Officials in the Queen's Household from the North-West Palace at Kalhu (Nimrud). Pages 271-272 in *Nimrud Conference 2002*.

Akurgal, E.
  1961   *Kunst der Hethiter*. München: Hirmer Verlag.

Albenda, Pauline
  1974   Grapevines in Ashurbanipal's Garden. *BASOR* 215, 5-17.
  1976   Landscape Bas-Reliefs in the *Bīt-Ḫilāni* of Ashurbanipal (part 1). *BASOR* 224, 49-72.
  1977   Landscape Bas-Reliefs in the *Bīt-Ḫilāni* of Ashurbanipal (part 2). *BASOR* 225, 29-48.
  1985   Mirrors in the Ancient Near East. *Source* 4, 2-9.
  1987   Woman, Child, and Family: Their Imagery in Assyrian Art. Pages 17-21 in *FPOA*.
  1989   Images of Royalty in Assyrian Art. *CMS Bulletin* 17, 7-16.
  1998   A Royal eunuch in the garden. *NABU* 1998 no. 98.

Álvarez-Mon, Javier
  2009   Ashurbanipal's Feast: A View from Elam. *Iranica Antiqua* 44, 131-180.

Andrae, Walter

1913   *Die Stelenreihen in Assur.* WVDOG 24. Leipzig: J.C. Hinrichs Verlag (reprint Osnabrück: Otto Zeller Verlag, 1972).

1935   *Die jüngeren Ischtar-Tempel in Assur.* WVDOG 58. Leipzig: J.C. Hinrichs Verlag (reprint Osnabrück: Otto Zeller Verlag, 1967).

1938   *Das Wiedererstandene Assur.* Leipzig: J.C. Hinrichs Verlag (reprint München: C.H. Beck, 1977).

Arbeli, Shoshana

1988   The Removal of the Tawananna From Her Position. Pages 79-85 in *Society and Economy in the Eastern Mediterranean (c. 1500-1000 BC)*, edited by M. Heltzer and E. Lipiński. Leuven: Peeters.

Arnaud, Daniel

1973   La prostitution sacrée en Mésopotamie, un mythe historiographique ? *Revue de l'histoire des religions* 183, 111-115.

Arzt, Jennifer

1993   Neo-Assyrian Royal Women. *YGJA* 5, 45-56.

Asher-Greve, Julia M.

1987   The Oldest Female Oneiromancer. Pages 27-32 in *FPOA*.

1997a   Feminist Research and Ancient Mesopotamia: Problems and Prospects. Pages 218-237 in *A Feminist Companion to Reading the Bible: Approaches, Methods and Strategies*, edited by Athalya Brenner and Carole Fontaine. Sheffield: Sheffield Academic press.

1997b   The Essential Body: Mesopotamian Conceptions of the Gendered Body. *GH* 9, 432-461.

Assante, Julia

1998   The kar.kid/*harimtu*, Prostitute or Single Woman? A Reconsideration of the Evidence. *Ugarit-Forschungen* 30, 5-96.

2000   *The Erotic Reliefs of Ancient Mesopotamia.* Ph.D. dissertation, Columbia University.

Avigad, Nahman

1978   The King's Daughter and the Lyre. *IEJ* 28, 146-151.

Azarpay, Guitty

1972   Crowns and Some Royal Insignia in Early Iran. *IA* 9, 108-115.

Bachmann, W.

1927   *Felsreliefs in Assyrien: Bawian, Maltai und Gunduk.* WVDOG 52. Leipzig: J.C. Hinrichs Verlag (reprint Osnabrück: Otto Zeller Verlag, 1969).

Bahrani, Zainab.

1973   The Iconography of the Nude in Mesopotamia. *Source* 12, 12-19.

1995   Assult and Abduction: the Fate of the Royal Image in the Ancient Near East. *Art History* 18, 363-382.

2000   The Whore of Babylon: truly all women and of infinite variety. *NIN* 1, 95-106.

2001   *Women of Babylon.* London and New York: Routledge.

Baker, Hollis S.

1966   *Furniture in the Ancient World: Origins & Evolution 3100-475 B.C.* London: The Connoisseur.

Barber, E.J.W.

1991   *Prehistoric Textiles.* Princeton: Princeton UP.

Barnett, Richard D.

1935 The Nimrud Ivories and the Art of the Phoenicians. *Iraq* 2, 179-210.

1939 Phoenician and Syrian Ivory Carving. *PEQ* 71, 4-19.

1956 Phoenicia and the Ivory Trade. *Archaeology* 9, 87-97.

1957 *A Catalogue of The Nimrud Ivories.* London: Trustees of The British Museum.

1967 Layard's Nimrud Bronzes and Their Inscription. *EI* 8, 1-7.

1974 The Nimrud Bowls in the British Museum. *Rivista di Studi Fenici* 2, 11-33.

1976 *The Sculptures from the North Palace of Ashurbanipal at Nineveh 668-627 BC).* London: British Museum Publications, Ltd.

1982 *Ancient Ivories in the Middle East.* QEDEM, Monographs of the Institute of Archaeology, The Hebrew University of Jerusalem 14. Jerusalem: The Institute of Archaeology.

1985 Assurbanipal's Feast. *EI* 18, 1-6.

Barnett, R., E. Bleibtreu and G. Turner

1998 *Sculptures from the Southwest Palace of Sennacherib at Nineveh.* 2 Vols. London: British Museum Publications.

Barnett, Richard D. and M. Falkner

1962 *The Sculptures of Assur-Nasir-Apli II (883-859 B.C.), Tiglath-Pileser III (745-727 B.C.) and Esarhaddon (681-669 B.C.) from the Central and South-West Palaces at Nimrud.* London: Trustees of The British Museum.

Bayer, Bathja

1980 The Finds That Could Not Be. *BAR* 8, 20-33.

Bayliss, Miranda

1981 The Cult of Dead Kin in Assyria and Babylonia. *Iraq* 35, 115-125.

Beard, Mary and John Henderson

1997 With This Body I Thee Worship: Sacred Prostitution in Antiquity. *GH* 9: 480-503.

Beckman, Gary

1998 Ištar of Nineveh Reconsidered. *JCS* 50, 1-10.

Ben-Barak, Zafrira

1987 The Queen Consort and the Struggle for Succession to the Throne. Pages 33-40 in *FPOA*.

Ben-Yehuda, Nachman

1989 Witchcraft and the Occult as Boundary Maintenance Devices. *Religion, Science, and Magic: In Concert and Conflict*, edited by Jacob Neusner *et al.* New York: Oxford UP.

Bird, Phyllis A.

1997 *Missing Persons and Mistaken Identities: Women and Gender in Ancient Israel.* Minneapolis: Fortress Press.

Black, Jeremy and Anthony Green

1992 *Gods, Demons and Symbols of Ancient Mesopotamia.* London: British Museum Press.

Bleibtreu, Erika

1980 *Die Flora der neuassyrischen Reliefs.* Wien: Verlag des Institutes für Orientalistik der Universität Wien.

Boardman, John

1990 *Symposion* Furniture. Pages 122-131 in *Sympotica: A Symposium on the Symposion*, edited by Oswyn Murray. Oxford: Clarendon Press.

Börker-Klähn, Jutta

1982   *Altvorderasiatische Bildstelen und Vergleichbare Felsreliefs.* Baghdader Forschungen 4. Mainz am Rhein: Verlag Philipp von Zabern.

Boncquet, J.

1987   De Koningin-moeder in de Neo-Assyrische periode. Pages 183-194 in *Archéologie et philologie dans l'étude des civilisations orientales,* edited by A. Théodoridès *et al.* Acta Orientalia Belgica 4. Leuven: Peeters.

Bongenaar, A.C.V.M.

1997   *The Neo-Babylonian Ebabbar Temple at Sippar: Its Administration and Its Prosopography.* PIHANS 80. Leiden: Nederlands Instituut voor het Nabije Oosten.

Borger, Riekele

1956   *Die Inschriften Asarhaddons Königs von Assyrien.* AfOB 9. Graz: (privately published) (reprint Osnabrück: Biblio-Verlag, 1967).

1961   Review of *The Assyrian Dictionary*, Vol. 4, E. *BiOr* 18, 151-152.

1972   Review of *Brief des Bischofs von Esagila an König Asarhaddon* by B. Landsberger. *BiOr* 29, 33-37.

Bossert, Helmuth Th.

1942   *Altanatolien.* Berlin: Verlag Ernst Wasmuth G.M.B.H.

Bottéro, Jean

1992   *Mesopotamia: Writing, Reasoning, and the Gods.* Chicago: The University of Chicago Press.

Bowman, Raymond A.

1948   Arameans, Aramaic, and the Bible. *JNES* 7, 65-90.

Brinkman, John A.

1983   Through A Glass Darkly: Esarhaddon's Retrospects on the Downfall of Babylon. *JAOS* 103, 35-42.

1984   *Prelude to Empire.* OPSNKF 7. Philadelphia: University Museum / Babylonian Section

1988   Textual Evidence for Bronze in Babylonia in the Early Iron Age, 1000-539 BC. Pages 135-168 in *Bronzeworking Centres of Western Asia c. 1000-539 B.C.*, edited by John Curtis. London and New York: Kegan Paul International.

1991   Babylonia in the Shadow of Assyria. *CAH* III/2. Cambridge: Cambridge UP, 1-70.

Brooks, Beatrice A.

1941   Fertility Cult Functionaries in the Old Testament. *JBL* 60, 227-253.

Brosius, Maria

1996   *Women in Ancient Persia 539-331 BC.* Oxford: Clarendon Press.

Bunnens, Guy

1997a   Carved Ivories from Til Barsib. *AJA* 101, 435-450.

1997b   Til Barsib under Assyrian Domination. Pages 17-28 in *Assyria 1995*, edited by S. Parpola and R.M. Whiting. Helsinki: The Neo-Assyrian Text Corpus Project.

Calmeyer, P.

1999   Mauerkrone. *RlA* 7/8, 595-596.

Campbell Thompson, R.

1937   An Assyrian Parallel to an Incident in the Story of Semiramis. *Iraq* 4, 35-43.

Canby, Jeanny Vorys

1976   The *Stelenreihen* at Assur, Tell Halaf, and *Maṣṣēbôt. Iraq* 38, 113-128.

Cheng, Jack
2001   *Assyrian Music as Represented and Representations of Assyrian Music.* Ph.D. dissertation, Harvard University.

Civil, Miguel
1969   *Materials for the Sumerian Lexicon XII: The Series lú-ša and related texts.* Roma: Editrice Pontificio Istituto Biblico.

Cogan, Mordechai
1983   Omens and Ideology in the Babylon Inscription of Esarhaddon. Pages 76-87 in *History, Historiography and Interpretation*, edited by H. Tadmor and M. Weinfeld. Jerusalem: Magnes Press, Hebrew University.
1991   A Plaidoyer on Behalf of the Royal Scribes. Pages 121-128 in *Ah Assyria…*, edited by Mordechai Cogan and Israel Eph'al. Jerusalem: Magnes Press, Hebrew University.

Cohen, Mark Nathan and Sharon Bennett
1998   Skeletal Evidence for Sex Roles and Gender Hierarchies in Prehistory. Pages 297-317 in *Reader in Gender Archaeology*, edited by Kelley Hays-Gilpin and David S. Whitley. London and New York: Routledge.

Cole, Steven W.
1997   The Destruction of Orchards in Assyrian Warfare. Pages 29-40 in *Assyria 1995*, edited by S. Parpola and R.M. Whiting. Helsinki: The Neo-Assyrian Text Corpus Project.

Cole, Steven W. and Peter Machinist
1998   *Letters From Priests To The Kings Esarhaddon and Assurbanipal.* SAA XIII. Helsinki: Helsinki UP.

Collon, Dominique
1987   *First Impressions: Cylinder Seals in the Ancient Near East.* London: British Museum Press.
1999   Depictions of Priests and Priestesses in the Ancient Near East. Pages 17-46 in *Priests and Officials in the Ancient Near East*, edited by Kazuko Watanabe. Heidelberg: Universitätsverlag C. Winter.
2010   Getting It Wrong in Assyria: Some Bracelets From Nimrud. *Iraq* 72, 149-162.

Collon, Dominique (ed.)
2008   Nimrud Treasures: Panel Discussion. Pages 105-118 in *Nimrud Conference 2002.*

Collon, Dominique and Anne Draffkorn Kilmer
1980   The Lute in Ancient Mesopotamia. Pages 13-28 in *Music and Civilisation*, edited by T.C. Mitchell. British Museum Yearbook 4. London: British Museum Publications, Ltd.

Congdon, Lenore O. Keene
1985   Greek Mirrors. *Source* 4, 19-25.

Conkey, Margaret W. and Joan M. Gero
1991   Tensions, Pluralities, and Engendering Archaeology: An Introduction to Women and Prehistory. Pages 3-30 in *Engendering Archaeology: Women and Prehistory,* edited by Joan M. Gero and Margaret W. Conkey. Oxford: Basil Blackwell.

Cooper, Jerrold S.
1972-75 Heilige Hochzeit. *RlA* 4, 250-269.

Crowfoot, Elisabeth
1995   Textiles from Recent Excavations at Nimrud. *Iraq* 51, 113-118.
2008   Textiles from Recent Excavations at Nimrud. Pages 149-154 in *Nimrud Conference 2002.*

Crowfoot, J.W. and Grace M. Crowfoot
1938   *Early Ivories From Samaria*. London: Palestine Exploration Fund.

Curtis, John
1983   Late Assyrian Bronze Coffins. *AnSt* 33, 85-95, pls. XXV-XXIX.
1988   Assyria as a Bronzeworking Centre in the Late Assyrian Period. Pages 83-96 in *Bronzeworking Centres of Western Asia c. 1000-539 B.C.*, edited by John Curtis. London and New York: Kegan Paul International.
1999   Assyrian Furniture: The Archaeological Evidence. Pages 167-180 in *The Furniture of Western Asia, Ancient and Traditional*, edited by Georgina Herrmann. Mainz: Verlag Philipp von Zabern.
2008   Observations on Selected Metal Objects from the Nimrud Tombs. Pages 243-253 in *Nimrud Conference 2002*.

Curtis, J.E. and J.E. Reade
1995   *Art and Empire*. New York: The Metropolitan Museum of Art.

Çağirgan†, G. and W.G. Lambert
1991-93 The Late Babylonian Kislīmu Ritual for Esagil. *JCS* 43-45, 89-106.

Dalley, Stephanie
1988   Neo-Assyrian Textual Evidence for Bronzeworking Centres. Pages 97-110 in *Bronzeworking Centres of Western Asia c. 1000-539 B.C.*, edited by John Curtis. London and New York: Kegan Paul International.
1998   Yabâ, Atalyā and the Foreign Policy of Late Assyrian Kings. *SAAB* 12, 83-98.
2008   The Identity of the Princesses in Tomb II and a New Analysis of Events in 701 BC. Pages 171-175 in *Nimrud Conference 2002*.

Dalley, Stephanie and J.N. Postgate
1984   *The Tablets From Fort Shalmaneser*. CTN III. London: British School of Archaeology in Iraq.

Damerji, Muayad Said Basim
1991   The Second Treasure of Nimrud. Pages 9-16 in *Near Eastern Studies Dedicated to H.I.H. Takahito Mikasa on the Occasion of His Seventy-Fifth Birthday*, edited by Masao Mori *et. al.* Wiesbaden: Otto Harrassowitz.
1999   *Gräber Assyrischer Königinnen aus Nimrud*. Mainz: Verlag des Römisch-Germanischen Zentralmuseums.

Deller, Karlheinz
1987   Assurbanipal in der Gartenlaube. *BaM* 18, 229-238.

Deller, Karlheinz, Frederick Mario Fales and Liane Jakob-Rost
1995   Neo-Assyrian Texts From Assur. Private Archives in the Vorderasiatisches Museum of Berlin, part 2. *SAAB* 9

Donbaz, Veysel
1990   Two Neo-Assyrian Stelae in the Antakya and Kahramanmaraş Museums. *ARRIM* 8, 5-24.

Douglas, Mary
1970   *Witchcraft Confessions and Accusations*. London: Tavistock Publications.

Driel, G. van
1968   *The Cult of Aššur*. Studia Semitica Neerlandica 13. Assen: Van Gorcum.
1981   Wine Lists and Beyond? *BiOr* 38, 259-272.

Ebeling, E.
1951   Kultische Texte aus Assur. *Orientalia* 20, 399-405.
1953   Kultische Texte aus Assur. *Orientalia* 22, 25-46.

Ellis, Maria deJong

1989   Observations on Mesopotamian Oracles and Prophetic Texts: Literary and Historiographic Considerations. *JCS* 41, 127-186.

Eph'al, Israel

1983   On Warfare And Military Control in the Ancient Near Eastern Empires: A Research Outline. Pages 88-106 in *History, Historiography and Interpretation*, edited by H. Tadmor and M. Weinfeld. Jerusalem: Magnes Press, Hebrew University.

Fadhil, Abdulillah

1990a   Die in Nimrud/Kalhu aufgefundene Grabinschrift der Jabâ. *BaM* 21, 461-470.

1990b   Die Grabinschrift der Mullissu-mukanništat-Ninua aus Nimrud/Kalhu und andere in ihrem Grab gefundene Schriftträger. *BaM* 21, 471-482.

Fales, Frederick Mario

1979   A List of Assyrian and West Semitic Women's Names. *Iraq* 41, 55-73.

1994   A Fresh Look at the Nimrud Wine Lists. Pages 361-380 in *Drinking in Ancient Societies,* edited by Lucio Milano. History of the Ancient Near East: Studies 6. Padova: Sargon srl.

1996   Prices in Neo-Assyrian Sources. *SAAB* 10, 11-55.

2000   *bīt-bēli*: An Assyrian Institutional Concept. Pages 231-249 in *Patavina Orientalia Selecta*, edited by Elena Rova. History of the Ancient Near East: Monographs 4. Padova: Sargon srl.

Fales, Frederick Mario and G.B. Lanfranchi

1997   The Impact of Oracular Material on the Political Utterances and Political Action of the Sargonid Dynasty. Pages 99-114 in *Oracles et Prophéties dans L'Antiquité,* edited by Jean-Georges Heintz. Paris: Diffusion de Boccard.

Fales, Frederick Mario and J.N. Postgate

1992   *Imperial Administrative Records, Part I*. SAA VII. Helsinki: Helsinki UP.

1995   *Imperial Administrative Records, Part II*. SAA XI. Helsinki: Helsinki UP.

Farber, Walter

1995   Witchcraft, Magic and Divination in Ancient Mesopotamia. Pages 1895-1908 in *CANE*.

Finkel, Irving L.

1983-84 Necromancy in Ancient Mesopotamia. *AfO* 29/30, 1-17.

2000   A New Assyrian Queen. *NABU* 2000 no. 8.

Fisher, Eugene

1976   Cultic Prostitution in the Ancient Near East? A Reassessment. *Biblical Theology Bulletin* 6, 225-236.

Fleming, Daniel E.

1992   *The Installation of Baal's High Priestess at Emar: A Window on Ancient Syrian Religion*. Atlanta: Scholars Press.

Frame, Grant

1992   *Babylonia 689-627 B.C.: A Political History*. PIHANS 69. Leiden: Nederlands Instituut voor het Nabije Oosten (reprint 2007).

Frankfort, Henri

1970   *The Art and Architecture of the Ancient Orient*. The Pelican History of Art. Fourth Edition. Harmondsworth: Penguin.

Frantz-Szabó, Gabriella

1995   Hittite Witchcraft, Magic, and Divination. Pages 2007-2019 in *CANE*.

Frayne, Douglas R.
1985   Notes on the Sacred Marriage Rite. *BiOr* 42, 5-20.

Frymer-Kensky, Tikva
1987   The Ideology of Gender in the Bible and the Ancient Near East. Pages 185-191 in *DUMU-E₂-DUB-BA-A: Studies in Honor of Åke W. Sjöberg*, edited by Hermann Behrens *et al.* OPSNKF 11. Philadelphia: University Museum / Babylonian Section.

Fuchs, Andreas and Simo Parpola
2001   *The Correspondence of Sargon II, Part III: Letters from Babylonia and the Eastern Provinces.* SAA XV. Helsinki: Helsinki UP.

Gadd, C.J.
1936   *The Stones of Assyria.* London: Chatto and Windus.
1951   En-an-e-du. *Iraq* 13, 27-39, Pl. XIII, XIV.
1958   The Harran Inscriptions of Nabonidus. *AnSt* 8, 35-92.

Gallery, Maureen L.
1980   Service Obligations of the *kezertu*-Women. *Orientalia* 49, 333-338.

Galter, Hannes D.
1987   On Beads and Curses. *ARRIM* 5, 11-30.

Galter, Hannes D., Louis D. Levine and Julian Reade
1986   The Colossi of Sennacherib's Palace and their Inscriptions. *ARRIM* 4, 27-32.

Gaspa, Salvatore
2007   Vessels in Neo-Assyrian Documents: Capacity Measures and Listing Conventions. *SAAB* 16, 145-184.

George, A.R.
1990   Royal Tombs at Nimrud. *Minerva* 1, 29-31.
1992   *Babylonian Topographical Texts.* Orientalia Lovaniensia Analecta 40. Leuven: Peeters.
1993   *House Most High: The Temples of Ancient Mesopotamia.* Mesopotamian Civilizations 5. Winona Lake: Eisenbrauns.
1995   The Bricks of E-sagil. *Iraq* 57, 173-197.
2000   Four Temple Rituals from Babylon. Pages 259-299 in *Wisdom, Gods and Literature: Studies in Assyriology in Honour of W.G. Lambert,* edited by A.R. George and I.L. Finkel. Winona Lake: Eisenbrauns.

George, D. *see* Youkhanna, Donny George

Gerardi, Pamela
1988   Epigraphs and Assyrian Palace Reliefs: The Development of the Epigraphic Text. *JCS* 40, 1-35.

Grabbe, Lester L.
2000   Ancient Near Eastern Prophecy from an Anthropological Perspective. Pages 13-32 in *PANEC.*

Grayson, A. Kirk
1991a   *Assyrian Rulers of the Early First Millennium BC I (1114-859 BC).* RIMA 2. Toronto: University of Toronto Press.
1991b   Assyria: Sennacherib and Esarhaddon. *CAH* III/2. Cambridge: Cambridge UP, 103-141.
1991c   Assyria 668-635 B.C.: The Reign of Ashurbanipal. *CAH* III/2. Cambridge: Cambridge UP, 142-161.
1994   Assyrian Officials and Power in the Ninth and Eighth Centuries. *SAAB* 7, 19-52.

1996   *Assyrian Rulers of the Early First Millennium BC II (858-745 BC)*. RIMA 3. Toronto: University of Toronto Press.

1999   The Struggle for Power in Assyria. Pages 253-270 in *Priests and Officials in the Ancient Near East*, edited by Kazuko Watanabe. Heidelberg: Universitätsverlag C. Winter.

Gruber, Mayer I.

1992   *The Motherhood of God and Other Studies*. Atlanta: Scholars Press.

1999   Women in the Ancient Levant. Pages 115-152 in *Women's Roles in Ancient Civilizations: A Reference Guide*, edited by Bella Vivante. Westport: Greenwood Press.

Gubel, Eric

1996   The Influence of Egypt on Western Asiatic Furniture and Evidence from Phoenicia. Pages 139-151 in *The Furniture of Western Asia, Ancient and Traditional*, edited by Georgina Herrmann. Mainz: Verlag Philipp von Zabern.

Guinan, Ann Kessler

1997a   Auguries of Hegemony: The Sex Omens of Mesopotamia. *GH* 9, 462-479.

1997b   Left/Right Symbolism in Mesopotamian Divination. *SAAB* 10, 5-10.

Haller, Arndt

1954   *Die Gräber und Grüfte von Assur*. WVDOG 65. Berlin: Verlag Gebr. Mann.

Hamilton, R.W.

1996   A Silver Bowl in the Ashmolean Museum. *Iraq* 28, 1-17.

Harper, Prudence O., Evelyn Klengel-Brandt, Joan Aruz and Kim Benzel

1995   *Discoveries at Ashur on the Tigris, Assyrian Origins*. New York: The Metropolitan Museum of Art.

Harrak, Amir

1988   Preliminary Remarks on the Grave Recently Discovered in the North-West Palace at Nimrud. *CMS Bulletin* 16, 25-29.

1989   The Royal Tombs of Nimrud and Their Jewellery. *CMS Bulletin* 20, 5-13.

Harrington, Spencer P.M.

1990   Royal Treasures of Nimrud. *Archaeology* 43, 49-53.

Harris, Rivkah

1990   The Female "Sage" in Mesopotamian Literature (with an Appendix on Egypt). Pages 3-17 in *The Sage in Israel and the Ancient Near East*, edited by John G. Gammie and Leo G. Perdue. Winona Lake: Eisenbrauns.

1991   Gendered Old Age in Enuma Elish. Pages 111-115 in *The Tablet and The Scroll: Near Eastern Studies in Honor of William W. Hallo*, edited by Mark E. Cohen *et al*. Bethesda: CDL Press.

Hawkins, J.D.

1980a   Kubaba at Karkamiš and Elsewhere. *AnSt* 31, 147-175.

1980b   Late Hittite Funerary Monuments. Pages 213-225, Pls III-VIII in *Death in Mesopotamia*, edited by Bendt Alster. Mesopotamia: Copenhagen Studies in Assyriology 8. CRRAI 26. Copenhagen: Akademisk Forlag.

Hawkins, J.D. and K. Bittel

1980-83 Kubaba. *RlA* 6, 257-264.

Heltzer, M.

1987   The Neo-Assyrian *Šakintu* and the Biblical *Sōkenet* (I Reg. 1,4). Pages 87-90 in *FPOA*.

Henshaw, Richard A.

1967   The Office of *šaknu* in Neo-Assyrian Times. I. *JAOS* 87, 517-525.

1968   The Office of *šaknu* in Neo-Assyrian Times. II. *JAOS* 88, 461-483.

1994   *Female and Male, The Cultic Personnel*. Allison Park: Pickwick Publications.

Herbordt, Suzanne

1992   *Neuassyrische Glyptik des 8-7. Jh. v.Chr.* SAAS I. Helsinki: The Neo-Assyrian Text Corpus Project.

Herodotus

1954   *Herodotus* The Histories. Aubrey de Sélincourt (translator). Baltimore: Penguin Books.

Herrmann, Georgina

1986a   *Ivories From Room SW37 Fort Shalmaneser: Commentary and Catalogue* (Ivories from Nimrud, 1949-1963, Fasc. IV, part 1) London: The British School of Archaeology in Iraq.

1986b   *Ivories From Room SW37 Fort Shalmaneser: Plates* (Ivories from Nimrud, 1949-1963, Fasc. IV, part 2). London: The British School of Archaeology in Iraq.

1989   The Nimrud Ivories, 1: The Flame and Frond School. *Iraq* 51, 85-109, pls. VIII-XIX.

1998   Ivory Furniture Pieces From Nimrud: North Syrian Evidence for a Regional Tradition of Furniture Manufacture. Pages 153-165 in *The Furniture of Western Asia, Ancient and Traditional*, edited by Georgina Herrmann. Mainz: Verlag Philipp von Zabern.

2000   Ivory Carving of First Millennium Workshops, Traditions and Diffusion. Pages 267-282 in *Images as Media: Sources for the Cultural History of the Near East and the Eastern Mediterranean (1st Millennium BCE)*, edited by Christoph Uehlinger. Orbis Biblicus et Orientalis, vol. 175. Fribourg: University Press; Gottingen: Vandenhoeck & Ruprecht.

Hoffner, Harry A. Jr.

1998   Symbols for Masculinity and Femininity. *JBL* 85, 326-334.

Huffmon, Herbert B.

2000   A Company of Prophets: Mari, Assyria, Israel. Pages 47-70 in *PANEC*.

Hughes, J.J., J.R.S. Lang, M.N. Leese and J.E. Curtis

1988   The Evidence of Scientific Analysis: a Case Study of the Nimrud Bowls. Pages 311-316 in *Bronzeworking Centers of Western Asia c. 1000-539 B.C.*, edited by John Curtis. London and New York: Kegan Paul International.

Hunger, Hermann

1992   *Astrological Reports To Assyrian Kings*. SAA VIII. Helsinki: Helsinki UP.

Hussein, Muzahim Mahmud

2008   Recent Excavations in Numrud. Pages 83-98 in *Nimrud Conference 2002*.

Jacobsen, Thorkild

1976   *The Treasures of Darkness: A History of Mesopotamian Religion*. New Haven: Yale UP.

Johns, C.H.W.

1898   *Assyrian Deeds and Documents Recording the Transfer of Property, Including the So-Called Private Contracts, Legal Decisions and Proclamations, Preserved in the Kouyunjik Collections of the British Museum, Chiefly of the 7th Century B.C.* Volume 1. Cambridge: Deighton Bell and Co.

1901a   Volume 2.

1901b   Volume 3.

1923   Volume 4.

Kataja, Laura and Robert Whiting
  1995   *Grants, Decrees and Gifts of the Neo-Assyrian Period.* SAA XII. Helsinki: Helsinki
            UP.

Kilmer, Anne Draffkorn
  1965   The Strings of Musical Instruments: Their Names, Numbers, and Significance.
            Pages 261-268 in *Studies in Honor of Benno Landsberger on His Seventy-Fifth
            Birthday, April 21, 1965*, edited by H.G. Güterbock and Thorkild Jacobsen. Assyri-
            ological Studies 16. Chicago: The University of Chicago Press.
  1993   Music and Dance in Ancient Western Asia. Pages 2601-2613 in *CANE.*

Kilmer, Anne Draffkorn, Richard L. Crocker and Robert R. Brown
  1976   *Sounds from Silence: Recent Discoveries of Mesopotamian Music.* Bit Enki Publi-
            cations (Sound Recording).

King, Leonard William
  1915   *Bronze Reliefs From The Gates of Shalmaneser, King of Assyria, B.C. 860-825.*
            London: The British Museum Press.

Kinnier Wilson, J.V.
  1965   An Introduction to Babylonian Psychiatry. Pages 289-298 in *Studies in Honor of
            Benno Landsberger on his Seventy-fifth Birthday, April 21, 1965*, edited by H.G.
            Güterbock and Thorkild Jacobsen. Assyriological Studies 16. Chicago: The Uni-
            versity of Chicago Press.
  1972   *The Nimrud Wine Lists: A Study of Men and Administration at the Assyrian Capital
            in the Eighth Century B.C.* CTN I. London: The British School of Archaeology in
            Iraq.

Koitabashi, Matahisa
  1992   Significance of Ugaritic *msltm* "Cymbals" in the Anat Text. Pages 1-5 in *Cult and
            Ritual in the Ancient Near East*, edited by H.I.H. Prince Takahito Mikasa. Wies-
            baden: Otto Harrassowitz.

Koskoff, Ellen
  1987   An Introduction to Women, Music, and Culture. Pages 1-23 in *Women and Music
            in Cross-Cultural Perspective*, edited by Ellen Koskoff. New York: Greenwood
            Press.

Kozloff, Arielle P.
  1983   Mirror, Mirror. *The Bulletin of the Cleveland Museum of Art* 71, 271-276.

Kuhrt, Amélie
  1995   *The Ancient Near East c. 3000-330 B.C.* 2 Volumes. London & New York:
            Routledge.

Kwasman, Theodore
  1988   *Neo-Assyrian Legal Documents in the Kouyunjik Collection of the British Museum.*
            Studia Pohl, Series Maior 14. Roma: Editrice Pontificio Istituto Biblico.

Kwasman, Theodore and Simo Parpola
  1991   *Legal Transactions of the Royal Court of Nineveh, Part I.* SAA VI. Helsinki:
            Helsinki UP.

Læssøe, Jørgen
  1955   *Studies on the Assyrian Ritual and Series bīt rimki.* København: Ejnar Munksgaard.

Lambert, W.G.
  1960   *Babylonian Wisdom Literature.* Oxford: Oxford UP.
  1969   An Eye-Stone of Esarhaddon's Queen and Other Similar Gems. *RA* 63, 65-71.
  1983   The God Assur. *Iraq* 45, 82-86.

1987   Goddesses in the Pantheon: A Reflection of Women in Society? Pages 125-130 in *FPOA*.

1988   Esarhaddon's Attempt to return Marduk to Babylon. Pages 157-174 in *Ad bene et fideliter seminandum: Festgabe für Karlheinz Deller zum 21. Februar 1987*, edited by Gerlinde Mauer und Ursula Magen. AOAT 220. Kevelaer: Butzon & Bercker; Neukirchen-Vluyn: Neukirchener Verlag.

Lambert, W.G. and A.R. Millard

1969   Atra-hasīs: *The Babylonian Story of the Flood*. Oxford: Clarendon Press.

Landsberger, B.

1967   Akkadisch-hebräische Wortgleichungen. Pages 176-204 in *Hebräische Wortforschung: Festschrift zum 80. Geburtstag von Walter Baumgartner*. Vetus Testamentum Supplement 16. Leiden: E.J. Brill.

Lanfranchi, Giovanni B.

1998   Esarhaddon, Assyria and Media. *SAAB* 12, 99-109.

Lanfranchi, Giovanni B. and Simo Parpola

1989   *The Correspondence of Sargon II, Part II: Letters from the Northern and Northeastern Provinces*. SAA V. Helsinki: Helsinki UP.

Leichty, Erle

1991   Esarhaddon's 'Letter To The Gods.' Pages 52-57 in *Ah, Assyria...* Studies in Assyrian History and Ancient Near Eastern Historiography Presented to Hayim Tadmor, edited by Mordechai Cogan and Israel Eph'al. Scripta Hierosolymitana 33. Jerusalem: The Magnes Press.

1995   Esarhaddon, King of Assyria. Pages 949-958 in *CANE*.

1997   Divination, Magic, and Astrology in the Assyrian Royal Court. Pages 161-164 in *Assyria 1995*, edited by S. Parpola and R.M. Whiting. Helsinki: The Neo-Assyrian Text Corpus Project.

Leick, Gwendolyn

1994   *Sex and Eroticism in Mesopotamian Literature*. London and New York: Routledge.

Levine, Louis D.

1973   Review of *Semiramis, Entstehung und Nachhall einer altorientalischen Saga* by Wilhelm Eilers. *JNES* 32, 260-261.

Lewy, Hildegard

1952   Nitokris-Naqi'a. *JNES* 11, 264-286.

Liverani, Mario

1979   The Ideology of the Assyrian Empire. Pages 297-318 in *Power and Propaganda: A Symposium on Ancient Empires*, edited by M.T. Larsen. Mesopotamia: Copenhagen Studies in Assyriology 7. Copenhagen: Akademisk Forlag.

1995   The Medes at Esarhaddon's Court. *JCS* 46, 57-62.

Livingstone, Alasdair

1988   *Mystical and Mythological Explanatory Works of Assyrian and Babylonian Scholars*. Oxford: Clarendon Press.

1989   *Court Poetry and Literary Miscellanea*. SAA III. Helsinki: Helsinki UP.

2007   Ashurbanipal: literate or not? *ZA* 97, 98-118

Loud, Gordon

1939   *The Megiddo Ivories*. OIP 52. Chicago: The University of Chicago Press.

Loud, Gordon and Charles B. Altman

1938   *Khorsabad Part II: The Citadel and the Town*. OIP 40. Chicago: The University of Chicago Press.

Luckenbill, Daniel David

1924   *The Annals of Sennacherib*. OIP 2, Chicago: The University of Chicago Press (reprint, Wipf & Stock, 2005).

1927   *Ancient Records of Assyria and Babylonia*, Volumes I, II. London: Histories and Mysteries of Man Ltd.

Luukko, Mikko and Greta Van Buylaere

2002   *The Political Correspondence of Esarhaddon*. SAA XVI. Helsinki: Helsinki UP.

MacGinnis, John

1987   A Neo-Assyrian Text Describing a Royal Funeral. *SAAB* 1, 1-11.

1988   A Letter from the *Šangû* of Kurbail. *SAAB* 2, 67-72.

Madhloom, T.A.

1970   *The Chronology of Neo-Assyrian Art*. London: The Athlone Press.

Mallowan, M.E.L.

1950   The Excavations at Nimrud (Kalḫu), 1949-1950. *Iraq* 12, 147-183.

1951   The Excavations at Nimrud (Kalḫu), 1949-1950. Ivories from the N.W. Palace. *Iraq* 13, 1-20.

1953   The Excavations at Nimrud (Kalḫu), 1952. *Iraq* 15, 1-42.

1954   The Excavations at Nimrud (Kalḫu), 1953 (continued). *Iraq* 16, 115-163.

1957   The Excavations at Nimrud (Kalḫu), 1956. *Iraq* 19, 1-25.

1966   *Nimrud and Its Remains*, 3 Volumes. London: Collins.

1978   *The Nimrud Ivories*. London: British Museum Publications, Ltd.

Mallowan, M.E.L. and Leri Glynne Davies

1970   *Ivories in Assyrian Style*. Ivories from Nimrud, 1949-1963, fasc. II. London: The British School of Archaeology in Iraq.

Mallowan, M.E.L. and Georgina Herrmann

1973   *Furniture from SW. 7 Fort Shalmaneser*. Ivories from Nimrud, 1949-1963, fasc. III. London: The British School of Archaeology in Iraq.

Marcus, Michelle I.

1994   Geography as Visual Ideology: Landscape, Knowledge and Power in Neo-Assyrian Art. Pages 193-203 in *NG*.

Markoe, Glenn E.

1986   The Emergence of Phoenician Art. Pages 13-26 in *Insight Through Images: Studies in Honor of Edith Porada*, edited by Marilyn Kelly-Buccellati. Malibu: Undena Publications.

Mattila, Raija

2000   *The King's Magnates*. SAAS XI. Helsinki: The Neo-Assyrian Text Corpus Project.

2002   *Legal Transactions of the Royal Court of Nineveh, Part II: Assurbanipal through Sin-šarru-iškun*. SAA XIV. Helsinki: Helsinki UP.

Maxwell-Hyslop, K.R.

1971   *Western Asiatic Jewellery c. 3000-612 B.C.* London: Methuen & Co.

Mazar, Amihai

1990   *Archaeology of the Land of the Bible 10,000-586 B.C.E.* New York: Doubleday.

Meier, Samuel A.

1991   Women and Communication in the Ancient Near East. *JAOS* 111, 540-547.

Melville, Sarah C.

1999   *The Role of Naqia/Zakutu in Sargonid Politics*. SAAS IX. Helsinki: The Neo-Assyrian Text Corpus Project.

2004   Neo-Assyrian Royal Women and Male Identity: Status as a Social Tool. *JAOS* 124, 36-57.

Menzel, Brigitte

1981   *Assyrische Tempel* Volumes I, II. Studia Pohl, Series Maior 10. Roma: Editrice Pontificio Istituto Biblico.

Meyers, Carol L.

1991   Of Drums and Damsels. *BiAr* 53, 16-27.

Michalowski, Piotr

1995   The Drinking Gods: Alcohol in Mesopotamian Ritual and Mythology. Pages 27-44 in *Drinking in Ancient Societies*, edited by Lucio Milano. History of the Ancient Near East: Studies 6. Padova: Sargon srl.

Millard, A.R.

1983   Assyrians and Arameans. *Iraq* 45, 101-108.

Mitchell, T.C.

1980   An Assyrian Stringed Instrument. Pages 33-42 in *Music and Civilisation*, edited by T.C. Mitchell. British Museum Yearbook 4. London: British Museum Publications, Ltd.

Moorey, P.R.S.

1996   *Ancient Mesopotamian Materials and Industries: The Archaeological Evidence*. Oxford: Clarendon Press.

Moran, William L.

1971   New Evidence from Mari on the History of Prophecy. *Biblica* 50, 15-56.

1992   *The Amarna Letters*. Baltimore and London: The Johns Hopkins UP.

Müller-Karpe, M., M. Kunter and M. Schultz

2008   Results of the Palaeopathological Investigation on the Royal Skeletons from Nimrud. Pages 141-148 in *Nimrud Conference 2002*.

Nashef, Khaled

1990   Archaeology in Iraq. *AJA* 94, 259-289.

Nemet-Nejat, Karen Rhea

1993   A Mirror Belonging to the Lady-of-Uruk. Pages 163-169 in *The Tablet and the Scroll: Near Eastern Studies in Honor of William W. Hallo*, edited by Mark Cohen *et al*. Bethesda: CDL Press.

1999   Women in Ancient Mesopotamia. Pages 84-114 in *Women's Roles in Ancient Civilizations: A Reference Guide*, edited by Bella Vivante. Westport: Greenwood Press.

Nissinen, Martti

1998   *References to Prophecy in Neo-Assyrian Sources*. SAAS VII. Helsinki: The Neo-Assyrian Text Corpus Project.

2000   The Socioreligious Role of the Neo-Assyrian Prophets. Pages 89-114 in *PANEC*.

Nylander, Carl

1998   Breaking the Cup of Kingship: An Elamite Coup in Nineveh? Pages 71-83 in *Neo-Assyrian, Median, Achaemenian and other studies in honor of David Stronach*, edited by R. Boucharlat, J. E. Curtis and E. Haerinck. *IA* 33.

Oates, Joan

1985   *Babylon*. London: Thames and Hudson.

Oates, Joan and David
  2001   *Nimrud: An Assyrian Imperial City Revealed.* London: British School of Archaeology in Iraq.

Oded, Bustenay
  1979   *Mass Deportations and Deportees in the Neo-Assyrian Empire.* Wiesbaden: Dr. Ludwig Reichert Verlag.

Oden, Robert A. Jr.
  1987   Religious Identity and the Sacred Prostitution Accusation. Pages 131-153, 186-192 in *The Bible without Theology.* San Francisco: Harper & Row.

Oppenheim, A. Leo
  1949   The Golden Garments of the Gods. *JNES* 8, 173-193.
  1964   *Ancient Mesopotamia: Portrait of a Dead Civilization.* (Revised Edition by Erica Reiner 1977) Chicago: The University of Chicago Press.
  1965   On Royal Gardens in Mesopotamia. *JNES* 24, 328-333.
  1967   *Letters from Mesopotamia.* Chicago: The University of Chicago Press.

Orchard, J.J.
  1967   *Equestrian Bridle-Harness Ornaments* (Ivories from Nimrud, 1949-1963, fasc I, part 2). London: The British School of Archaeology in Iraq.

Ornan, Tallay
  2002   The Queen in Public: Royal Women in Neo-Assyrian Art. Pages 461-477 in *Sex and Gender.*

Parker, Barbara
  1954   The Nimrud Tablets, 1952 – Business Documents. *Iraq* 16, 29-58.
  1955   Excavations at Nimrud, 1949-1953: Seals and Seal Impressions. *Iraq* 17, 93-125.
  1961   Administrative Tablets from the North-West Palace, Nimrud. *Iraq* 23, 15-67, pls. IX-XXX.
  1963   Economic Tablets From the Temple of Mamu at Balawat. *Iraq* 25, 86-103.

Parpola, Simo
  1970   *Letters from Assyrian Scholars to the Kings Esarhaddon and Assurbanipal.* Part I: Texts. AOAT 5/1. Kevelaer: Butzon & Bercker; Neukirchen-Vluyn: Neukirchener Verlag.
  1976   Review of *The Nimrud Wine Lists* by J.V. Kinnier Wilson. *JSS* 21, 165-174.
  1980   The Murderer of Sennacherib. Pages 171-182 in *Death in Mesopotamia,* edited by Bendt Alster. Mesopotamia: Copenhagen Studies in Assyriology 8. CRRAI 26. Copenhagen: Akademisk Forlag.
  1983   *Letters from Assyrian Scholars to the Kings Esarhaddon and Assurbanipal.* Part II: Commentary and Appendices. AOAT 5/2. Kevelaer: Butzon & Bercker; Neukirchen-Vluyn: Neukirchener Verlag.
  1987a   *The Correspondence of Sargon II, Part I: Letters from Assyria and the West.* SAA I. Helsinki: Helsinki UP.
  1987b   Neo-Assyrian Treaties from the Royal Archives of Nineveh. *JCS* 39, 161-190.
  1988   The Neo-Assyrian Word for 'Queen.' *SAAB* 2, 73-76.
  1993   *Letters from Assyrian and Babylonian Scholars.* SAA X. Helsinki: Helsinki UP.
  1997   *Assyrian Prophecies.* SAA IX. Helsinki: Helsinki UP.

Parpola, Simo and Michael Porter
  2001   *The Helsinki Atlas of the Near East in the Neo-Assyrian Period.* Helsinki: The Casco Bay Assyriological Institute and The Neo-Assyrian Text Corpus Project.

Parpola, Simo and Kazuko Watanabe
  1988   *Neo-Assyrian Treaties and Loyalty Oaths.* SAA II. Helsinki: Helsinki UP.

Parrot, André

1961   *Nineveh and Babylon*. London: Thames and Hudson.

Parrot, André and Jean Nougayrol

1956   Asarhaddon et Naqi'a sur un Bronze du Louvre (AO 20. 185). *Syria* 33, 147-160.

Petersen, David L.

2000   Defining Prophecy and Prophetic Literature. Pages 33-46 in *PANEC*.

Pfeiffer, Robert H.

1935   *State Letters of Assyria*. New Haven: American Oriental Society.

Pinnock, Frances

1994   Considerations on the 'Banquet Theme' in the Figurative Art of Mesopotamia and Syria. Pages 15-26 in *Drinking in Ancient Societies*, edited by Lucio Milano. History of the Ancient Near East: Studies 6. Padova: Sargon srl.

1995   Erotic Art in the Ancient Near East. Pages 2521-2531 in *CANE*.

Polin, Claire C.J.

1954   *Music of the Ancient Near East*. Westport: Greenwood Press.

Pollock, Susan

1996   Women in a Men's World: Images of Sumerian Women. Pages 366-387 in *Engendering Archaeology: Women and Prehistory*, edited by Joan M. Gero and Margaret W. Conkey. Oxford: Basil Blackwell.

Pongratz-Leisten, Beate

1994   Ina šulmi īrub: *Die kulttopographische und ideologische Programmatik der akītu-Prozession in Babylonien und Assyrien im 1. Jahrtausend v. Chr*. Baghdader Forschungen 16. Mainz am Rhein: Verlag Philipp von Zabern.

1997   The Interplay of Military Strategy and Cultic Practice in Assyrian Politics. Pages 245-252 in *Assyria 1995*, edited by S. Parpola and R.M. Whiting. Helsinki: The Neo-Assyrian Text Corpus Project.

Porada, Edith

1959a   The Hasanlu Bowl. *Expedition* 1, 19-22.

1959b   Review of *A Catalogue of the Nimrud Ivories with Other Examples of Ancient Near Eastern Ivories in The British Museum*, by R.D. Barnett. *AJA* 63, 92-94.

1980   A Cylinder Seal showing a Harpist. Pages 29-31 in *Music and Civilisation*, edited by T.C. Mitchell. British Museum Yearbook 4. British Museum Publications, Ltd.

Porter, Barbara Nevling

1993   *Images, Power and Politics: Figurative Aspects of Esarhaddon's Babylonian Policy*. Philadelphia: American Philosophical Society.

1997   What the Assyrians Thought the Babylonians Thought about the Relative Status of Nabû and Marduk in the Late Assyrian Period. Pages 253-260 in *Assyria 1995*, edited by S. Parpola and R.M. Whiting. Helsinki: The Neo-Assyrian Text Corpus Project.

2000   Assyrian Propaganda for the West: Esarhaddon's Stelae for Til Barsip and Sam'al. Pages in 143-176 in *Essays on Syria in the Iron Age*, edited by Guy Bunnens. Ancient Near Eastern Studies, Supplement 7. Louvain-Paris-Sterling: Peeters.

Postgate, J.N.

1973a   Assyrian Texts and Fragments. *Iraq* 35, 13-36.

1973b   *The Governor's Palace Archive*. CTN II. London: British School of Archaeology in Iraq.

1974   *Taxation and Conscription in the Assyrian Empire*. Rome: Biblical Institute Press.

1976   *Fifty Neo-Assyrian Legal Documents*. Warminster: Aris & Phillips Ltd.

1979   On Some Assyrian Ladies. *Iraq* 41, 89-103.

1980	The Place of the *šaknu* in Assyrian Government. *AnSt* 30, 67-76.
1995	Assyria: the Home Provinces. Pages 1-17 in *NG*.
2008	The Tombs in the Light of Mesopotamian Funerary Traditions. Pages 177-180 in *Nimrud Conference 2002*.

Postgate, J.N. and Julian Reade

1977-80	Kalḫu. *RlA* 5, 303-323.

Powell, Marvin A.

1984	On the Absolute Value of the Assyrian *qa* and *emār*. *Iraq* 46, 57-61.
1987-90	Masse und Gewichte. *RlA* 7, 457-517

Pritchard, James A.

1968	*Ancient Near Eastern Texts Relating to the Old Testament*. Princeton: Princeton UP.

Radner, Karen

2008	The Delegation of Power: Neo-Assyrian Bureau Seals. Pages 481-515 in *L'archive des Fortifications de Persépolis .... Actes du colloque organisé au Collège de France ...*, edited by P. Briant, W.F.M. Henkelman, and M. Stolper. Persika 12. Paris: de Boccard.

Rassam, Hormuzd

1897	*Asshur and the Land of Nimrod*. Cincinnati: Curts & Jennings; New York: Eaton & Mains (reprint, Farnborough: Gregg International, 1971).

Rawi, Farouk N.H. al-

2008	Inscriptions from the Tombs of the Queens of Assyria. Pages 119-138 in *Nimrud Conference 2002*.

Reade, Julian

1967	Two Slabs from Sennacherib's Palace. *Iraq* 29, 42-48, Pls. XII, XIII.
1972	The Neo-Assyrian Court and Army: Evidence from the Sculptures. *Iraq* 34, 87-112.
1979a	Ideology and Propaganda in Assyrian Art. Pages 329-343 in *Power and Propaganda: A Symposium on Ancient Empires*, edited by M.T. Larsen. Mesopotamia: Copenhagen Studies in Assyriology 7. Copenhagen: Akademisk Forlag.
1979b	Narrative Composition in Assyrian Sculpture. *BaM* 10, 52-110, pls. 12-25.
1979c	Assyrian Architectural Decoration: Techniques and Subject-Matter. *BaM* 10, 17-49, pls. 1-11.
1980	The Rassam Obelisk. *Iraq* 42, 1-22, pls. I-IX.
1981	Neo-Assyrian Monuments in Their Historical Context. Pages 143-167, Pls. I-X in *ARINH*.
1984	*Assyrian Sculpture*. Cambridge: Harvard UP.
1987	Was Sennacherib a Feminist? Pages 139-145 in *FPOA*.
1995	The *Symposion* in Ancient Mesopotamia: Archaeological Evidence. Pages 35-56 in *In Vino Veritas*, edited by Oswyn Murray and Manuela Tecuşan. London: British School at Rome.
2000	Ninive. *RlA* 9, 388-433.

Reiner, Erica

1958	*Šurpu: A Collection of Sumerian and Akkadian Incantations*. AfOB 11. Graz (privately published) (reprint, Osnabrück: Biblio-Verlag, 1970).

Renger, Johannes

1967   Untersuchungen zum Priestertum in der altbabylonischen Zeit: 1. Teil. *ZA* 58, 110-188.

1972-75 Heilige Hochzeit. *RlA* 4, 250-259.

Reynolds, Frances S.

2003   *The Babylonian Correspondence of Esarhaddon and Letters to Assurbanipal and Sin-šarru-iškun from Northern and Central Babylonia.* SAA XVIII. Helsinki: Helsinki UP.

Rich, Jack C.

1947   *The Materials and Methods of Sculpture.* New York: Oxford UP (reprinted 1958).

Rimmer, Joan

1969   *Ancient Musical Instruments of Western Asia in the Department of Western Asiatic Antiquities, The British Museum.* London: The Trustees of The British Museum.

Roaf, Michael

1990   *Cultural Atlas of Mesopotamia and the Ancient Near East.* New York: Facts On File.

Rollin, Sue

1983   Women and Witchcraft in Ancient Assyria (c. 900-600 BC). Pages 34-45 in *Images of Women in Antiquity*, edited by Averil Cameron and Amélie Kuhrt. Detroit: Wayne State UP.

Roth, Martha T.

1987   Age at Marriage and the Household: A Study of Neo-Babylonian and Neo-Assyrian Forms. *Comparative Studies in Society and History* 29, 715-747.

1997   *Law Collections from Mesopotamia and Asia Minor.* Atlanta: Scholars Press, 153-209.

Russell, John Malcolm

1991   *Sennacherib's Palace Without Rival at Nineveh.* Chicago: The University of Chicago Press.

1999   *The Writing on the Wall: Studies in the Architectural Context of Late Assyrian Palace Inscriptions.* Mesopotamian Civilizations 9. Winona Lake: Eisenbrauns.

Sachs, Curt

1940   *The History of Musical Instruments.* New York: W.W. Norton and Company (reprint, Dover Publications, 2006).

Saggs, H.W.F.

1984   *The Might That Was Assyria.* London: Sidgwick & Jackson.

Saporetti, Claudio

1974   Some Considerations on the Stelae of Assur. *Assur* 1/2. Malibu: Undena Publications.

1979   *The Status of Women in the Middle Assyrian Period.* MANE 2/1. Malibu: Undena Publications.

Schmidt-Colinet, Constanze

1997   Ashurbanipal Banqueting with his Queen? Wer Throhnt bei Assurbanipal in der Weinlaube? *Mesopotamia* 32: 289-308.

Scurlock, J.A.

1987   Baby-Snatching Demons, Restless Souls and the Dangers of Childbirth: Medico-Magical Means of Dealing with Some of the Perils of Motherhood in Ancient Mesopotamia. *Incognita* 2, 135-183.

1995a   Death and the Afterlife in Ancient Mesopotamian Thought. Pages 1883-1893 in *CANE.*

1995b   Magical Uses of Ancient Mesopotamian Festivals of the Dead. Pages 93-107 in *Ancient Magic and Ritual Power*, edited by Marvin Meyer and Paul Mirecki. Leiden, New York, Köln: E.J. Brill.

Sefati, Yitschak and Jacob Klein

2002   The Role of Women in Mesopotamian Witchcraft. Pages 569-587 in *Sex and Gender*,

Seux, M.-J.

1983   Königtum. *RlA* 6, 140-173.

Spaey, J.

1990   Some Notes on KÙ.BABBAR/nēbih kezēr(t)i(m). *Akkadica* 67, 1-9.

Starr, Ivan

1983   *The Rituals of the Diviner*. Bibliotheca Mesopotamica 12. Malibu: Undena Publications.

1990   *Queries to the Sungod: Divination and Politics in Sargonid Assyria*. SAA IV. Helsinki: Helsinki UP.

Steinkeller, Piotr

1987   On the Meaning of zabar-šu. *Acta Sumerologica* 9, 347-349.

Streck, Maximilian

1916   *Assurbanipal und die Letzten Assyrischen Könige bis zum Untergange Niniveh's*. Leipzig: J.C. Hinrichs'sche Buchhandlung.

Stronach, David

1989   The Royal Garden at Pasargadae: Evolution and Legacy. Pages 475-502 in *Archaeologica Iranica et Orientalis: Miscellanea in Honorem Louis Vanden Berghe*, edited by L. De Meyer and E. Haerinck. Gent: Peeters.

1990   The Garden as a Political Statement: Some Case Studies from the Near East in the First Millennium B.C. Pages 171-180 in *Aspects of Iranian Culture: In Honor of Richard Nelson Frye*, edited by Carol Altman Bromberg *et al*. Bulletin of the Asia Institute 4. Ames: Iowa State UP.

1996   The Imagery of the Wine Bowl: Wine in Assyria in the Early First Millennium B.C. Pages 175-195 in *The Origins and Ancient History of Wine*, edited by Patrick E. McGovern *et al*. Philadelphia: Gordon and Breach Publishers.

Suter, Claudia

1992   Die Frau am Fenster in der Orientalischen Elfenbein-Schnitzkunst des fruhen 1. Jahrtausends v. Chr. *Jahrbuch der Staatlichen Kunstsammlungen in Baden-Württemberg* 29, 7-28.

Svärd, Saana (*see also* Teppo, Saana)

2010   "Maid of the King" (GÉME *ša šarri*) in the Neo-Assyrian Texts. Pages 251-260 in *Veysel Donbaz'a Sunulan Yazılar* DUB.SAR É.DUB.BA.A *Studies Presented in Honour of Veysel Donbaz*, edited by Şevket Dönmez. Istanbul: Ege Publications.

Svärd, Saana and Mikko Luukko

2009   Who Were the "Ladies of the House" in the Assyrian Empire? Pages 279-294 in *God(s), Trees, Kings and Scholars: Neo-Assyrian and Related Studies in Honour of Simo Parpola*, edited by M. Luukko, S. Svärd and R. Mattila. Studia Orientalia 106. Helsinki: Finnish Oriental Society.

Tadmor, Hayim

1973   The Historical Inscriptions of Adad-Nirari III. *Iraq* 35, 141-150.

1975   Assyria and the West: The Ninth Century and Its Aftermath. Pages 36-48 in *Unity and Diversity: Essays in the History, Literature and Religion of the Ancient Near East*, edited by Hans Goedicke and J.J.M. Roberts. Baltimore: The Johns Hopkins UP.

1981   History and Ideology in the Assyrian Royal Inscriptions. Pages 13-33 in *ARINH*.

1982a   Treaty and Oath in the Ancient Near East. Pages 127-152 in *Humanizing America's Iconic Book*, edited by Gene M. Tucher and Douglas A. Knight. Chico: Scholars Press.

1982b   The Aramaization of Assyria: Aspects of Western Impact. Pages 449-470 in *Mesopotamia und Seine Nachbarn*, edited by H.-J. Nissen and Johannes Renger. Berlin: Dietrich Reiner Verlag.

1983   Autobiographical Apology in the Royal Assyrian Literature. Pages 36-57 in *History, Historiography and Interpretation*, edited by H. Tadmor and M. Weinfeld. Jerusalem: The Magnes Press.

Tadmor, Hayim, Benno Landsberger†, and Simo Parpola

1988   The Sin of Sargon and Sennacherib's Last Will. *SAAB* 3, 8-51.

Teppo, Saana (*see also* Svärd, Saana)

2005   Women and Their Agency in The Neo-Assyrian Empire. MA thesis, University of Helsinki.

2007   The Role and the Duties of the Neo-Assyrian *šakintu* in the Light of Archival Evidence. *SAAB* 16, 257-272.

Thomsen, Marie-Louise

1980   *Zauberdiagnose und Schwarze Magie in Mesopotamien*. Copenhagen: The Carsten Niebuhr Institute of Ancient Near Eastern Studies and the Museum Tusculanum Press.

Toorn, Karel van der

1995   The Significance of the Veil in the Ancient Near East. Pages 327-339 in *Pomegranates and Golden Bells*, edited by D. Wright *et al.* Winona Lake: Eisenbrauns.

1996   *Family Religion in Babylonia, Syria and Israel: Continuity and Change in the Forms of Religious Life*. Leiden: E.J. Brill.

2000   Mesopotamian Prophecy between Immanence and Transcendence: A Comparison of Old Babylonian and Neo-Assyrian Prophecy. Pages 71-88 in *PANEC*.

Turner, Geoffrey

1970   The State Apartments of Late Assyrian Palaces. *Iraq* 32, 177-213.

Ussishkin, David

1971   On the Date of a Group of Ivories from Nimrud. *BASOR* 203, 22-27.

Van De Mieroop, Marc

1993   An Inscribed Bead of Queen Zakutu. Pages 259-261 in *The Tablet and The Scroll: Near Eastern Studies in Honor of William W. Hallo*, edited by Mark E. Cohen *et al.* Bethesda: CDL Press.

1999   *Cuneiform Texts and the Writing of History*. London: Routledge.

Vieyra, Maurice

1955   *Hittite Art 2300-750 B.C.* London: Alec Tiranti Ltd.

Wäfler, Markus

1975   *Nicht-Assyrer neuassyrischer Darstellungen*. 2 Volumes. AOAT 26. Kevelaer: Butzon & Bercker; Neukirchen-Vluyn: Neukirchener Verlag.

Walker, C.B.F.

1988   Further Notes on Assyrian Bronzeworking. Pages 111-118 in *Bronzeworking Centres of Western Asia c. 1000-539 B.C.*, edited by John Curtis. London and New York: Kegan Paul International.

Walker, Christopher and Michael Dick

1999   The Induction of the Cult Image in Ancient Mesopotamia: The Mesopotamian *mīs pî* Ritual. Pages 55-121 in *Born in Heaven, Made on Earth: The Making of the Cult Image in the Ancient Near East*, edited by Michael B. Dick. Winona Lake: Eisenbrauns.

2001   *The Induction of the Cult Image in Ancient Mesopotamia: The Mesopotamian* Mīs Pî *Ritual*. SAALT I. Helsinki: The Neo-Assyrian Text Corpus Project.

Walters, Stanley D.

1971   The Sorceress and Her Apprentice: A Case Study of an Accusation. *JCS* 23, 27-38.

Waterman, Leroy

1930-36 *Royal Correspondence of the Assyrian Empire*. 4 Volumes. Ann Arbor: University of Michigan Press.

Weadock, Penelope N.

1975   The *Giparu* at Ur. *Iraq* 37, 101-128.

Weinfeld, Moshe

1991   Semiramis: Her Name and Her Origin. Pages 99-103 in *Ah, Assyria... Studies in Assyrian History and Ancient Near Eastern Historiography Presented to Hayim Tadmor*, edited by Mordechai Cogan and Israel Eph'al. Scripta Hierosolymitana 33. Jerusalem: The Magnes Press.

Weippert, Manfred

1981   Assyrische Prophetien der Zeit Asarhaddons und Assurbanipals. Pages 71-115 in *ARINH*.

Weissert, Elnathan

1997   Royal Hunt and Royal Triumph in a Prism Fragment of Assurbanipal (82-5-22,2). Pages 339-358 in *Assyria 1995*, edited by S. Parpola and R.M. Whiting. Helsinki: The Neo-Assyrian Text Corpus Project.

Werr, Lamia al-Gailani

2008   Nimrud Seals. Pages 155-162 in *Nimrud Conference 2002*.

Westenholz, Joan Goodnick

1989a   Tamar, *Qĕdēšā*, *Qadištu*, and Sacred Prostitution in Mesopotamia. *HTR* 82, 245-266.

1989b   Enheduanna, En-Priestess, Hen of Nanna, Spouse of Nanna. Pages 539-556 in *DUMU-E₂-DUB-BA-A: Studies in Honor of Åke W. Sjöberg*, edited by Hermann Behrens *et al.* OPSNKF 11. Philadelphia: The University Museum.

1990   Towards a New Conceptualization of the Female Role in Mesopotamian Society. *JAOS* 110, 510-521.

Winter, Irene J.

1976a   Carved Ivory Furniture Panels from Nimrud: A Coherent Subgroup of the North Syrian Style. *MMJ* 11, 25-54.

1976b   Phoenician and North Syrian Ivory Carving in Historical Context: Questions of Style and Distribution. *Iraq* 38, 1-22.

1981a   Is There a South Syrian Style of Ivory Carving in the Early First Millennium B.C.? *Iraq* 43, 101-130.

1981b   Royal Rhetoric and the Development of Historical Narrative in Neo-Assyrian Reliefs. *Studies in Visual Communication* 7, 2-38.

1982   Art as Evidence for Interaction: Relations Between the Assyrian Empire and North Syria. Pages 355-382 in *Mesopotamien und Seine Nachbarn,* edited by H.-J. Nissen and Johannes Renger. CRRAI 33. Berlin: Dietrich Reimer Verlag.

1987   Women in Public: The Disk of Enheduanna, The Beginning of the Office of En-Priestess, and the Weight of Visual Evidence. Pages 189-201 in *FPOA*.

1989a   North Syria as a Bronzeworking Centre in the Early First Millennium BC: Luxury Commodities at Home and Abroad. Pages 193-226 in *Bronzeworking Centres of Western Asia c. 1000-539 B.C.,* edited by John Curtis. London and New York: Kegan Paul International.

1989b   The "Hasanlu Gold Bowl": Thirty Years Later. Pages 87-106 in *East of Assyria: The Highland Settlement of Hasanlu*, edited by Robert H. Dyson, Jr. and Mary Mathilda Voigt. *Expedition* 31/2-3. Philadelphia: University of Pennsylvania Museum

1992   'Idols of the King': Royal Images as Recipients of Ritual Action in Ancient Mesopotamia. *Journal of Ritual Studies* 6, 13-42.

1997   Art *in* Empire: The Royal Image and the Visual Dimensions of Assyrian Ideology. Pages 359-381 in *Assyria 1995*, edited by S. Parpola and R.M. Whiting. Helsinki: The Neo-Assyrian Text Corpus Project.

Wiseman, D.J.

1958   The Vassal-Treaties of Esarhaddon. *Iraq* 20, 1-99.

1983   Mesopotamian Gardens. *AnSt* 33, 137-144.

Woolley, C. Leonard

1926   The Excavations at Ur, 1925-6. *The Antiquaries Journal* 6, 365-401.

Wyke, Maria

1994   Woman in the Mirror: The Rhetoric of Adornment in the Roman World. Pages 134-151, Plate 4 in *Women in Ancient Societies: An Illusion of the Night*, edited by Leonie J. Archer *et al*. New York: Routledge.

Yamauchi, Edwin M.

1973   Cultic Prostitution: A Case Study in Cultural Diffusion. Pages 213-222 in *Orient and Occident: Essays Presented to Cyrus H. Gordon on the Occasion of his Sixty-fifth Birthday*, edited by Harry A. Hoffner, Jr. AOAT 22. Kevelaer: Butzon & Bercker.

Youkhanna, Donny George

2008   Precision Craftsmanship of the Nimrud Gold Material. Pages 103-104 in *Nimrud Conference 2002*.

Zawadzki, Stefan

1990   Oriental and Greek Tradition about the Death of Sennacherib. *SAAB* 4, 69-72.

Zagarell, Allen

1986   Trade, Women, Class, and Society in Ancient Western Asia. *Current Anthropology* 27, 415-430.

Zgoll, Annette

1997   Inana als nugig. *ZA* 87, 181-195.

INDICES

Personal Names

Strabo: 14
Subeitu: 63

Ṣalam-šarri-iqbi: 65

Šadditu: 59, 68-69, 95
Šamaš-šumu-ukin: 59, 86-87, 107-108, 117, 119-121
Šamši-Adad (III): 3, 29, 82, 84-85
Šerua-eṭerat: 68, 70-71

Tašmetum-šarrat: 3-4, 57, 71-72, 74, 85, 94, 125
Teumman: 20-21, 36-37, 39, 93
Tiglath-Pileser (III): 3, 79-81, 113
Tukulti-Ninurta (I): 14

Ṭab-ṣill-Ešarra: 115
Ṭab-šar-Aššur: 110

Ummanigash: 37, 39
Urad-Nanaya: 105
Urkittu-šarrat: 19, 22
Ušpilulume: 83

Yabâ: 3, 71, 73, 78-80

Zakutu: 4, 95-99, 101, 120; See also Naqia
Zarpi: 62
Zimri-Lim: 16

Geographical Names

Adian: 57, 62
Akkad: 24-25
Anatolia: 2, 31, 69, 115
Arbail: 2, 17, 19-23, 25-26, 32, 57, 62, 67, 95; See also Erbil
Arpad: 32, 48, 83
Arrapha: 2, 20
Assur: 2, 10-11, 13-14, 17-18, 20-21, 24-26, 32, 37, 57, 62-64, 67, 69, 72, 74, 77, 82-88, 90-91, 94, 98-103, 110-111, 115, 117, 119, 125
Assyria: 1-3, 5, 8, 11-12, 14, 18-27, 31, 33, 37, 40, 42, 46, 53, 55, 57, 59-62, 67, 69-70, 72-74, 76, 79-84, 86-88, 91-93, 95-101, 103, 106-110, 116-124, 126

Babylon: 20, 30, 72, 82, 86, 92, 106, 110-112, 114, 116-117, 119-121
Babylonia: 17, 24, 60, 86, 96-97, 101, 106-108, 114, 116-117, 122
Bahaya: 66
Balawat: 46, 110
Baruri: 59, 95
Bet-kari: 61
Bit-Adad-leʾi: 58, 62
Bit-Gusi: 48
Bit-Purutaš: 70
Borsippa: 101, 107

Carchemesh: 115

Damascus: 61
Dannaya: 96
Dara-ahuya: 25
Diyala: 59, 88, 107, 125
Dur-Šarrukin: 75, 115; See also Khorsabad

Egypt: 2, 23, 82, 91, 115, 120
Ekallate: 57, 67
Elam: 23, 36-37, 40, 90, 107
Emar: 8, 15
Erbil: 20; See also Arbail
Ešnunna: 16, 37
Ethiopia: 82
Euphrates: 8, 16, 83

Gadisê: 59, 103, 125
Gomer: 23
Gordion: 90

Harran: 9, 20, 59, 101-105, 108, 119, 125
Hatti: 32
Haurina: 62

Iran: 2, 31, 61, 115
Iščhali: 16

Judah: 30, 106

Kahat: 58, 62
Kalhu: 2, 9, 17, 20, 31, 44-46, 48, 53, 56-57, 60-63, 65-67, 69, 72-77, 79, 82-83, 87, 89, 91-92, 94, 100-102, 114-115, 119, 125; See also Nimrud
Kasappa: 57, 62
Khafaji: 37
Khorsabad: 110; See also Dur-Šarrukin
Kilizi: 20, 57, 62, 67
Kish: 13
Kunulua: 30
Kurbail: 20

Lahiru: 59, 66, 88, 107, 125

Madaktu: 36-37, 39-40, 46, 124
Mari: 16, 21
Media: 61, 82, 119
Milqiya: 20-21

Nabû-šezib: 66
Nasibina: 58, 62
Nimrud: 4, 31, 59, 78, 80, 92, 110; See also Kalhu
Nineveh: 2, 4, 9, 11, 16-26, 30, 33, 36, 41, 56-62, 64, 67, 74-75, 85, 89-90, 92, 97-102, 107-108, 110-112, 114, 119-120, 125

Palestine: 2, 31, 82
Parsua: 61
Patinu: 30
Pazarcik: 83

Sabaʾa: 84
Samʾal: 117
Sealand: 104, 107
Sinjar: 84
Sippar: 111
Sumaria: 31
Sunê: 58, 62
Susa: 37
Syria: 8, 31, 48, 51-52, 61, 110, 115

God and Temple Names

Texts Cited or Discussed

Texts are generally indexed only under the most recent
edition, with the exception of ABL and ADD.

CT 38
  38:60f: 77

Esarhaddon
  AsBbE: 111, 117
  AsBbH: 111

IM
  76882: 9

KAR
  154: 13, 32
  154:1-14: 13
  215: 100
  321: 13
  321:7: 13

Maqlû
  V 54: 13
  VI 29 and 40: 13
  VI 39-40: 8

ND
  2307: 62
  2309: 9, 62
  2316: 9
  2803: 57
  7088: 65-66, 72
  7090: 65-66
  10047: 32
  10054: 32

SAA I
  31: 70
  34: 60
  66: 110
  99: 57

SAA II
  8:1-2: 120

SAA III
  3: 22-23
  4: 32
  7: 19
  8: 32
  9: 19
  13: 23

SAA IV
  20-21: 70
  151: 68
  190:2-3: 105
  191: 105
  321-322: 65

SAA VI
  31: 65
  81: 64
  86: 64
  88: 62, 64
  89: 64
  90: 64
  93: 64
  140 r. 11-12: 67
  143: 58
  251: 59, 69, 95
  252: 59, 95
  253: 65

255: 59, 107
310: 65
325: 65
325:2: 96

SAA VII
  5: 66-67
  6: 67
  9 i 24-25: 67
  9 r. i 27-28: 67
  9: 67
  12: 67
  23: 58, 62
  24: 31, 65
  26: 31
  48: 60
  93: 75
  94: 76
  102: 75
  115: 60, 64
  175: 60
  181: 60
  183-184: 60

SAA VIII
  104: 9
  147: 9
  307: 9
  480: 9

SAA IX
  1.2: 25
  1.2:30-35: 23
  1.3: 26
  1.4: 23
  1.7: 24-25
  1.8: 25
  1.8:12-23: 95
  2.4: 19, 24
  2.5: 23
  2.5:21-25: 23
  3: 24
  5: 19
  7: 19, 23
  9: 19

SAA X
  17 r. 1-5: 103
  41: 86
  109: 18, 22
  111: 22
  154: 107
  185: 119
  188: 87
  189: 25
  200: 105
  201: 105
  223: 68
  233-234: 87
  244 r. 7-9: 103
  244: 105
  246: 13
  273: 68-69, 95
  274: 10
  284: 22
  313 r. 1-7: 101
  313: 104, 107

348: 60, 107, 117
348:15: 101
349: 117
352: 24-25
354: 117
364: 117

SAA XI
152: 32
154: 68
219 r. iv 13: 9
219 r. iv 16: 9
221: 59, 69

SAA XII
21-23: 58
23 r. 6-7: 95
76: 101
81: 68, 87

SAA XIII
37: 25
56: 68
61 r. 1-4: 101
76-77: 60

77:7-12: 101
89: 61
101: 61
108: 61
126: 9
148: 10
154: 60
188 r. 8-13: 101
188:17-20: 103

SAA XIV
1: 59, 66, 88
2: 66
3-5: 66
29: 65
175: 64

SAA XVI
28: 70
65: 67

SAA XVIII
10: 104, 107
85: 104

STATE ARCHIVES OF ASSYRIA

VOLUME XI
IMPERIAL ADMINISTRATIVE RECORDS, PART II
Provincial and Military Administration
Edited by F. M. Fales and J. N. Postgate
1995

VOLUME XII
GRANTS, DECREES AND GIFTS OF THE NEO-ASSYRIAN PERIOD
Edited by L. Kataja and R. Whiting
1995

VOLUME XIII
LETTERS FROM PRIESTS TO THE
KINGS ESARHADDON AND ASSURBANIPAL
Edited by Steven W. Cole and Peter Machinist
1998

VOLUME XIV
LEGAL TRANSACTIONS OF THE ROYAL COURT OF NINEVEH, PART II
Assurbanipal through Sin-šarru-iškun
Raija Mattila
2002

VOLUME XV
THE CORRESPONDENCE OF SARGON II, PART III
Letters from Babylonia and the Eastern Provinces
Andreas Fuchs and Simo Parpola
2002

VOLUME XVI
THE POLITICAL CORRESPONDENCE OF ESARHADDON
Mikko Luukko and Greta Van Buylaere
2002

VOLUME XVII
THE BABYLONIAN CORRESPONDENCE OF
SARGON AND SENNACHERIB
Manfried Dietrich
2003

VOLUME XVIII
THE BABYLONIAN CORRESPONDENCE OF ESARHADDON
and Letters to Assurbanipal and Sin-šarru-iškun
from Northern and Central Babylonia
Frances Reynolds
2003

STATE ARCHIVES OF ASSYRIA STUDIES

VOLUME I
Neuassyrische Glyptik des 8.-7. Jh. v. Chr.
unter besonderer Berücksichtigung der Siegelungen
auf Tafeln und Tonverschlüsse
by Suzanne Herbordt
1992

STATE ARCHIVES OF ASSYRIA CUNEIFORM TEXTS

MELAMMU SYMPOSIA

STATE ARCHIVES OF ASSYRIA LITERARY TEXTS

VOLUME I
The Induction of the Cult Image in Ancient Mesopotamia
The Mesopotamian Mīs Pî Ritual
by Christopher Walker and Michael Dick
2001

PROSOPOGRAPHY OF THE NEO-ASSYRIAN EMPIRE

VOLUME 1   A-G
edited by Karen Radner
1998/99

VOLUME 2   Ḫ-N
edited by Heather D. Baker
2000/2001

VOLUME 3   P-Z
edited by Heather D. Baker
2002/2011

OTHER TITLES

ASSYRIA 1995
Proceedings of the 10th Annivesary Symposium of
The Neo-Assyrian Text Corpus Project
Helsinki, September 7-11, 1995
edited by S. Parpola and R. M. Whiting
1997

NINEVEH, 612 BC
The Glory and Fall of the Assyrian Empire
Catalogue of the 10th Anniversary Exhibition of the
Neo-Assyrian Text Corpus Project
edited by Raija Mattila
1995

The Mechanics of Empire
The Northern Frontier of Assyria as a Case Study in Imperial Dynamics
by Bradley J. Parker
2001

Assyrian-English-Assyrian Dictionary
edited by S. Parpola and R. M. Whiting
2007

PUBLICATIONS OF THE
FOUNDATION FOR FINNISH ASSYRIOLOGICAL RESEARCH
NO. 5

STATE ARCHIVES OF ASSYRIA STUDIES

VOLUME XXI